THE SEAL OF BILITERACY IN HIGHER EDUCATION

This book brings together the work of those implementing, using, or researching the Seal of Biliteracy (SoBL) in higher education contexts. Book chapters detail how various institutions of higher education (IHEs) are leveraging their state's SoBL policy and/or the Global SoBL to promote biliteracy within and across communities.

In all 50 United States, high school graduates can earn a state SoBL, which is noted on the high school transcript to certify the ability to read, write, speak, and listen in more than one language. An increasing number of IHEs recognize the SoBL, and evidence suggests that such policies can serve as a recruitment tool, boost enrollment in modern language departments, and facilitate placement into modern language coursework. This book provides examples of how IHEs can implement the state SoBL, the Global SoBL, or their own recognition to recognize students' multilingualism, boost enrollment, enhance practice, and nurture biliteracy in their communities. The research-based examples in each chapter provide robust examples of how IHEs can leverage the SoBL to increase equity and access to higher education for multilingual students.

This book targets educators, leaders, policymakers, and researchers interested in collaborating to enhance multilingualism in their communities. Whether working in K–12 schools or IHEs, readers can learn about potential avenues to expand pipelines, partnerships, and possibilities for learners to earn and benefit from a SoBL.

Kristin J. Davin is a Professor of Education at the University of North Carolina at Charlotte, where she directs the foreign language teacher education program.

Amy J. Heineke is a Professor of Education at Loyola University Chicago, where she prepares teachers and leaders for work with multilingual learners.

'I recommend *The Seal of Biliteracy in Higher Education: Harnessing Students' Cultural and Linguistic Strengths at Colleges and Universities* to districts and universities interested in creating pathways for Seal of Biliteracy awardees to develop higher levels of biliteracy, receive university credit(s) and become teachers, addressing the shortage of bilingual teachers.'

Shelly Spiegel Coleman, *Strategic Advisor, Californians Together*

'*The Seal of Biliteracy in Higher Education* is a transformative work that validates and celebrates the Seal of Biliteracy movement in higher education. From recognizing students' biliteracy to awarding college credits to recruiting potential students, Kristin Davin and Amy Heineke provide research-based examples and help IHEs tap into students' cultural and linguistic strengths to enhance enrollment and enrich their programs.'

Arthur Chou, *SealofBiliteracy.org*

'This edited book by Davin and Heineke is the most comprehensive and up-to-date book on the Seal of Biliteracy in higher education. It is a must read for those interested in learning more about this topic but especially those educators and policymakers implementing the Seal of Biliteracy across the United States.'

Oscar Jimenez-Castellanos, *Goizueta Endowed Professor and Executive Director for the Center for Latino Achievement and Success in Education (CLASE), University of Georgia*

THE SEAL OF BILITERACY IN HIGHER EDUCATION

Harnessing Students' Cultural and Linguistic Strengths at Colleges and Universities

Edited by Kristin J. Davin and Amy J. Heineke

NEW YORK AND LONDON

Designed cover image: ©Getty Images

First published 2025
by Routledge
605 Third Avenue, New York, NY 10158

and by Routledge
4 Park Square, Milton Park, Abingdon, Oxon, OX14 4RN

Routledge is an imprint of the Taylor & Francis Group, an informa business

ISBN: 978-1-032-66716-4 (hbk)
ISBN: 978-1-032-66715-7 (pbk)
ISBN: 978-1-032-66724-9 (ebk)

DOI: 10.4324/9781032667249

Typeset in Galliard
by SPi Technologies India Pvt Ltd (Straive)

CONTENTS

CONTRIBUTORS

Cristina Alfaro, Ph.D., is Associate Vice President of International Affairs and Professor of Multilingual and Global Education at San Diego State University.

Michele Anciaux Aoki, Ph.D., is a retired State and District World Languages and International Education Program Supervisor, member of the board of advisors of the Global Seal of Biliteracy, and Affiliate Instructor for the Department of Slavic Languages and Literatures at the University of Washington.

Reka C. Barton, Ph.D., is an Assistant Professor of Literacy Education at the University of Maryland, College Park.

Resha Cardone, Ph.D., is Associate Dean of the College of Liberal and Creative Arts at San Francisco State University.

Katherine Christoffersen, Ph.D., is Associate Professor of Applied Linguistics at the University of Texas Rio Grande Valley.

Sarah L. Cohen, Ph.D., is Dual Language Network Specialist in the Chicago Public Schools, Chicago, Illinois.

Kristin J. Davin, Ph.D., is Professor of Foreign Language Education at the University of North Carolina at Charlotte.

Janet Eckerson, Ph.D., is Associate Professor of Spanish and Associate Dean for Engagement and Retention in the College of Arts and Sciences at the University of Nebraska at Kearney.

Andrew Fiegen is a Ph.D. Student in the Multilingual Education Program in the Department of Curriculum and Instruction at the University of Minnesota.

James A. Gambrell, Ed.D., is Professor of Culturally and Linguistically Diverse Education at the University of Northern Colorado.

Dania López García, Ph.D., is Associate Professor of Applied Linguistics at the University of Texas Rio Grande Valley.

Jesse Gleason, Ph.D., is Associate Professor of Spanish and Applied Linguistics at Southern Connecticut State University.

Nick Gossett, Ph.D., is a former Professor of Russian who is currently the Higher Ed Specialist at Avant Assessment.

Amy J. Heineke, Ph.D., is Professor of Multilingual Teaching and Learning in the School of Education at Loyola University Chicago.

Russell Hugo, Ph.D., is the Director of the Language Learning Center and Affiliate Assistant Professor of Linguistics at the University of Washington.

Christopher Jacobs, Ph.D., is Assistant Professor of French, Italian, Spanish, and Linguistics at the University of Nebraska at Kearney.

Kendall King, Ph.D., is Professor of Multilingual Education and Associate Dean for Graduate Education and Faculty Development at the University of Minnesota.

Sobeira Latorre, Ph.D., is Professor of Spanish at Southern Connecticut State University.

Ji Won Lee, M.Ed., is a doctoral student in counseling psychology at Loyola University Chicago.

Cecelia Monto, Ed.D., is Vice President of Academic Affairs at Warner Pacific University in Portland, Oregon.

Grant D. Moss, Ph.D., is Professor of Spanish at Pittsburg State University.

Eric Steinmiller, Ph.D., is Principal at Lincoln Park High School.

Ayumi Stockman is the World Languages Education Specialist at the Minnesota Department of Education.

Bridget Yaden, Ph.D., is Professor of Hispanic and Latino Studies and Associate Provost for Undergraduate Programs at Pacific Lutheran University.

PART I

Introduction

1

ORIGINS AND PURPOSES OF THE SEAL OF BILITERACY

Kristin J. Davin

This book focuses on ways in which institutions of higher education (IHEs) are recognizing and celebrating students' multilingualism through a recognition called the Seal of Biliteracy (SoBL).

As of January 2024, all 50 states and the District of Columbia have policies in place to recognize students who graduate from high school with proficiency in more than one language. In most states, this policy is called the SoBL, although some states have slightly different names, such as the Global Languages Endorsement (i.e., North Carolina) or the Bilingual and Multilingual Seals (i.e., Minnesota). Across contexts, the SoBL typically takes the form of an emblem on a diploma or a notation on the transcript, although many districts also provide students with a medal or sash to wear at graduation or a certificate stating the demonstrated level of proficiency (Davin & Heineke, 2022).

The SoBL represents an important step toward embracing the pluralism of U.S. society and promoting multilingualism in schools. Historically, language education in the United States has focused on English proficiency at the expense of other languages (García & Kleifgen, 2018; Johnson, 2013; Ricento & Hornberger, 1996). Fewer than 20% of states have world language graduation requirements (American Councils for International Education, 2017), and students of color are less likely to have access to world language instruction than their white peers (Baggett, 2016; Ritz & Sherf, 2021; Schoener & McKenzie, 2016). While there are bilingual programs, particularly for Spanish speakers, the overall prioritization of multilingual education is less pronounced compared to other regions of the world. For example, the European Union has a robust commitment to multilingualism, advocating for the learning of at least two foreign languages alongside the mother tongue (European Commission, 2017). Similarly, India has a *Three Language Formula* that emphasizes the learning of the regional language, Hindi, and English (Vaish, 2008). But the SoBL offers a potential lever for change. Developed in California to push back against state law prohibiting bilingual education (i.e., Proposition 227), the SoBL offers promise for promoting multilingualism for future generations.

Although stakeholders in kindergarten through 12th-grade (K–12) settings typically talk about the SoBL due to its situation in high schools, advocates designed the language

DOI: 10.4324/9781032667249-2

education policy to impact students beyond elementary and secondary schooling. Specifically, state policymakers recognized the SoBL as directly connecting to language usage and continued development in college and career (Davin et al., 2022). Nonetheless, scant research has examined the implementation or impact of the SoBL beyond high school graduation.

This book seeks to address that gap in the literature via three goals. First, the chapters in this volume provide examples of how IHEs can implement the SoBL to boost enrollment in modern language departments and nurture biliteracy in their communities. Second, the authors provide research-based examples of how IHEs can leverage the SoBL by awarding college credit to recipients, thereby increasing equity and access to higher education for multilingual students. Third and finally, they exemplify how IHE stakeholders can tap into students' cultural and linguistic strengths and use the SoBL as a recruitment tool to enhance enrollment in colleges, universities, and teacher preparation programs.

To set the context and provide the necessary background information for this book, I begin by detailing the origins and characteristics of the SoBL. I next discuss existing research on its implementation and impact, noting that most of this research has taken place with high school students. After providing a broad overview of how IHEs are leveraging the SoBL, I preview the subsequent chapters of this volume.

A note on terminology

Throughout this book, we refer to any postsecondary academic institution that offers an associate's degree or higher as an IHE, which includes both community colleges and four-year institutions. When referring to SoBL policies in general, authors use the acronym (SoBL), an umbrella term with two different versions: state Seals of Biliteracy (SSoBL) and the Global Seal of Biliteracy (GSoBL). We use the acronym SSoBL to refer to state-specific legislated policies that recognize high school graduates. We use the acronym GSoBL to refer to the Global Seal of Biliteracy, a distinct recognition created by Avant Assessment. The GSoBL (a) is not part of state legislation, (b) is operated worldwide, and (c) does not have to be linked to high school graduation. Table 1.1 displays the similarities and differences between the SSoBLs and the GSoBL.

To date, the research that Amy Heineke and I have done has focused on the SSoBL. In our various books and manuscripts, we have always used the acronym SoBL because we did not need to make a distinction from the GSoBL. This book represents a departure because several of the authors in this book implemented the GSoBL. Most states do not allow for SSoBL implementation at the postsecondary level. The only exception, to our knowledge, is Oregon (see Chapter 4). Therefore, this first chapter focuses primarily on work related to the SSoBL. However, Chapter 2, by Nick Gossett, provides in-depth information on the GSoBL.

Several chapters in this book focus on programs with characteristics similar to the SSoBL and GSoBL but that were developed for particular IHEs. The choice to design their own recognitions allowed them to determine their own characteristics and requirements. For example, in Chapter 5, Alfaro and Barton describe the *University Seal of Biliteracy and Cultural Competence* (USBCC) that they developed at San Diego State University. In Chapter 6, Christoffersen and López García describe the B3 Scholar Seal that they developed at the University of Texas Rio Grande Valley. These two chapters provide examples of how IHEs can develop their own programs attuned to their student populations.

An additional term that appears frequently throughout this book is *proficiency*. Language proficiency is the "ability to perform an action or function" and describes one's "ability to use

TABLE 1.1 Characteristics of SSoBLs and GSoBL

	SSoBL	*GSoBL*
Requirements	Varies by state. Typically requires submission of qualifying scores on approved assessments, although some states allow for grades in course sequence	Submit qualifying scores on approved assessment
Tiers	Varies by state (see Davin et al., 2022)	Functional Fluency: Intermediate Mid Working Fluency: Advanced Low Professional Fluency: Advanced High
Founders	Varies, but typically state departments of education	Avant Assessment
Eligibility	High school graduates	No age or grade-level requirement
Notation	Varies by school but typically appears as an emblem on diploma or notation on high school transcript	Certificate with unique serial number; LinkedIn badge
College Credit	Legislated that most public IHEs in Illinois, Minnesota, and Rhode Island must award college credit (if requested), and IHEs in many other states do so voluntarily	Program with University of Idaho and the University of Texas at Arlington; may vary by IHE otherwise

a language for real-world purposes to accomplish real-world linguistic tasks across a wide range of topics and settings" (Language Testing International, 2024, para. 1). This is important because the SoBL was designed to represent what an individual can do with the language in communicative situations, not necessarily what they know about the language. Therefore, the assessments used to award the SoBL typically require students to engage in reading, writing, speaking, and listening tasks, not to respond to multiple-choice questions or conjugate verbs in isolation.

Origins of the SSoBL

The SSoBL movement originated in California, with the recognition conceptualized by the advocacy group *Californians Together* and passed into legislation in 2011. This coalition's mission was to champion "the educational success of California's more than 1.1 million English learners" (Californians Together, 2024, para. 1). The group formed in 1999 after California voters passed Proposition 227, which restricted districts' ability to offer bilingual education to students labeled as English learners. With the goal of reinstating bilingual education as an effective program for English learners and changing deficit-oriented perspectives on bilingualism, Californians Together sought to organize key stakeholders to work together to "overcome and transform the harms of systemic racial, language, and cultural inequality in education and to close opportunity gaps from early childhood through postsecondary education" (Californians Together, 2024, para. 1).

Californians Together modeled California's SSoBL after a program in place at Glendale Unified School District near Los Angeles, which recognized high school graduates proficient in multiple languages (Olsen, 2020). Using that program as a model, the group drafted a bill to propose a statewide SSoBL. They framed the resulting policy to prioritize the assets of multilingual students while honoring all students who demonstrated proficiency in English and another language. Their goals were to (a) overturn Proposition 227, (b) confront English-only ideologies by celebrating students proficient in more than one language, and (c) recognize biliteracy as an asset so that the demand for bilingual programming might increase. After multiple vetoes, the governor finally signed the bill into law in 2011, and the first schools began to award the California SSoBL in 2012 (Olsen, 2020).

As news about the California SSoBL spread, other states began to draft their own policies. Three states passed SSoBL policies in 2013, five in 2014, and seven more in 2015 (see Davin & Heineke, 2017). In January 2024, South Dakota adopted the SSoBL, becoming the 50th state to create a policy. States developed their policies through different procedures and pathways (Heineke et al., 2018). In the beginning, little guidance existed to guide policy creation. The first *State Guidelines for Implementing a Seal of Biliteracy*, published through a collaboration of various language organizations, including ACTFL, the National Association for Bilingual Education (NABE), the National Council of State Supervisors for Languages (NCSSFL), and TESOL International, were not published until March of 2015. States that adopted SSoBL policies after their publication had more guidance than those that did so before, but many questions still remained regarding how to develop and implement the SSoBL equitably.

Characteristics of the SSoBL

Due to the grassroots nature of the movement, SSoBL policies vary from state to state. Most states converge around requirements that (a) the SSoBL can only be awarded to high school graduates, (b) students must demonstrate proficiency in English and another language, and (c) students must demonstrate proficiency in a language other than English (LOTE) in reading, writing, listening, and speaking (when applicable), typically via an approved assessment. But some states depart from even these convergences. For example, Hawai'i allows the anchor language of the SSoBL to be 'Ōlelo Hawai'i, meaning that a student proficient in Hawaiian and Spanish, for example, could earn an SSoBL. Oregon also allows postsecondary institutions to award the SSoBL (see Chapter 4). And finally, some states do not require students to pass an approved assessment to demonstrate their LOTE proficiency but instead accept world language course grades as evidence (Davin et al., 2022).

Beyond those typical convergences, the divergences are vast. Variation exists regarding the minimum level of proficiency that students must demonstrate in the LOTE to earn an SSoBL. The ACTFL Proficiency Guidelines (ACTFL, 2024) describe five major levels of proficiency that include Novice (low, mid, high), Intermediate (low, mid, high), Advanced (low, mid, high), Superior, and Distinguished. Most states require that students reach a minimum level of proficiency equivalent to Intermediate Mid on all four domains (i.e., reading, writing, listening, and speaking) to earn an SSoBL. An Intermediate Mid speaker, for example, can engage in uncomplicated communication tasks, express meaning by creating with the language in concrete situations, and ask a variety of questions (ACTFL, 2024). Other states instead require students to reach a minimum equivalent to Intermediate High in the LOTE. An Intermediate High speaker, for example, has a greater breadth of vocabulary and language control than an Intermediate Mid speaker and can speak in all major time frames (e.g., past, present, future) in paragraph form, although with errors (see the ACTFL

Proficiency Guidelines, 2024, for more detailed descriptions). Still, other states set the minimum at Intermediate Low or Advanced Low. For comparison purposes, Advanced Low is the level of proficiency recommended by ACTFL and the Council for the Accreditation of Educator Preparation (CAEP) for world language teachers in the United States (ACTFL, 2015).

Forms of accepted evidence of proficiency also vary. As mentioned previously, most states require students to reach a minimum level of proficiency in reading, writing, listening, and speaking on an approved assessment to demonstrate world language proficiency. Commonly used assessments include the Advanced Placement (AP) language exams, International Baccalaureate (IB) assessments, the ACTFL Assessment of Performance toward Proficiency in Languages (AAPPL), and the Standards-based Measurement of Proficiency 4 Skills (STAMP 4S). Some states make provisions for languages without a writing system or for less commonly tested languages where reading and listening assessments are prohibitively expensive or too hard to find (Davin et al., 2022). However, some states, like North Carolina and Louisiana, instead accept a minimum grade point average in a sequence of world language coursework as evidence of proficiency. Other states, like New York, have a menu of options through which students can demonstrate world language proficiency.

Variation also exists in how students must demonstrate their English proficiency (see Davin & Heineke, 2017; Davin et al., 2022). Some states accept graduation from high school as evidence of English proficiency. Others require students to earn a minimum score on an English assessment, typically the SAT or the ACT, although more and more states recognize that those assessments measure much more than language proficiency and now also accept scores on the AAPPL or STAMP 4S for English (Davin et al., 2022). As with LOTE proficiency, some states instead accept a minimum grade point average in a sequence of English Language Arts (ELA) coursework or a passing score on required ELA state assessments.

Implementation of the SSoBL across the United States

The various nuances of SSoBL policies across states have shaped local implementation, which has varied widely across states. In many cases, states that have had SSoBL policies in place for the longest amount of time graduate the highest number of students with the recognition. States that accept course grades in world language coursework as evidence of proficiency for SSoBL attainment also graduate the highest number of students with the recognition (Aguirre & Chou, 2024; Davin et al., 2022).

But even those states with the longest duration of implementation and lowest bars for attainment do not have widespread implementation. The last nationwide report provided data on SSoBL attainment during the 2021–2022 school year and included data from 39 of the 44 states with policies in place at that time (Aguirre & Chou, 2024). Based on data from those states, 147,937 students had earned an SSoBL, up from 108,199 in the 2018–2019 school year, but still far less than one percent of high school graduates. These numbers were likely heavily impacted by the COVID-19 pandemic, which made it difficult for many schools to administer the assessments required to award the SSoBL.

Regarding implementation across states, the last report suggested that California graduated the highest number of students with an SSoBL with 57,582 recipients, followed by Florida with 14,596 recipients, and North Carolina with 11,545 recipients. Not surprisingly, these states were all early adopters of the policy and states in which students have been able to earn an SSoBL through course grades rather than an assessment. Washington awarded the

SSoBL in the largest number of languages, recognizing students who used 77 different languages, with New York close behind, recognizing students who used 65 languages.

Impacts of awarding the SSoBL

Although SSoBLs are still relatively young, various research studies have shown their promising impact on students and language programming. Research suggests that the potential of earning a SoBL motivates students to continue studying languages, whether that means taking world language courses in school or developing heritage languages outside of school (Davin & Heineke, 2018; Davin et al., 2018; Liu et al., 2024). In some of our early research, students indicated that they wished they had learned about the SSoBL sooner in their schooling so that they could have started world language study earlier (Davin & Heineke, 2018). Other students who came from homes using other languages stated that had they known about the SoBL, they would have worked harder to learn to read and write in their heritage language (Davin, 2021b).

Evidence suggests that students' increased motivation to pursue a SoBL has resulted in increased enrollment in world language programming. This has been documented at both the secondary and postsecondary levels (Davin, 2021a; Davin et al., 2018). While an increased desire to study language and an increase in enrollment are perhaps two of the most obvious and most appealing potential impacts of SoBL implementation for IHEs, the benefits actually extend much deeper. Although much of the existing research has taken place with high school students, I share findings to illustrate other potential impacts of the SoBL to set the stage for the subsequent chapters of this book.

Impact on students

Perhaps one of the most profound impacts that researchers have found related to SSoBL attainment relates to strengthening heritage learners' identities, home languages, and cultures. In one of the earliest investigations into the impact of the SSoBL, Castro (2020) interviewed high school seniors in the Los Angeles Unified School District about their perceptions of the SSoBL. They reported that the SSoBL honored their family heritage and encouraged them to embrace their culture and develop proficiency in their home language. It also helped them to recognize the sacrifices that their parents made in coming to this country. As one student described, "I want to show [my mom] that coming here was all worth it, that it was good for me, not just for her" (p. 130). Marichal et al. (2021) reported similar findings with students in a rural Florida high school. They found that awarding the SSoBL made heritage learners "feel less invisible" (p. 54) and instilled a sense of pride in their heritage.

In my own research with students who earned an SSoBL in Minnesota, I found that this increased connection to their heritage sometimes helped to alleviate intergenerational tension at home, between children and their parents who felt they were assimilating into U.S. society and forgetting their heritage (Davin, 2021b). This tension was often caused by schooling that focused too narrowly on English without validating students' home languages. Several students indicated the assessment associated with the SoBL was the first time they felt their school recognized their home language (Davin, 2021b; Davin et al., 2024). One student who spoke Somali and Arabic said that the SoBL made her feel "acknowledged", explaining,

> When you have something [language skills], and first of all, no one saw it, but then finally people get to see it, and you're like, great. I had the skills this whole time, but finally you're seeing it.
>
> *(Davin et al., 2024, p. 12)*

Connected to the impact on identity formation, researchers have also found that earning an SSoBL can boost students' confidence. Several studies reported that having to pass an assessment to earn an SSoBL provided the external validation that students sought for their language skills (Davin & Heineke, 2018; Hancock & Davin, 2020; Wesely & Gao, 2024). They perceived these external assessment results as more rigorous and meaningful than classroom grades, stating that "anyone can get an A in class" (Davin & Heineke, 2018, p. 320). Teachers interviewed by Wesely and Gao (2024) reported that the SSoBL was "transformational" (p. 16) for some students, prompting self-confidence that was previously absent. This sentiment has been expressed by both students who learned an additional language in school and by heritage learners (Davin & Heineke, 2018). Heritage learners in Davin (2021b) made comments like, "Now I know I'm proficient in Somali" (p. 189) and stated that the SSoBL test was "a good indicator [of] whether you're good enough to speak your language or not" (p. 188). Similarly, a nonheritage learner who had studied Spanish in school stated that passing the SSoBL assessment was "a confidence booster. After I found the results, talking in class was just so much easier" (p. 321).

In some studies, the boost in confidence went beyond confidence in language proficiency to self-confidence more broadly. This increase, in turn, also influenced students' educational aspirations (Davin, 2021b). As a student who spoke Tamil explained, earning an SSoBL made her "more confident about applying to higher skill colleges." She explained that earning an SSoBL gave her "the confidence that [she could] actually try for higher things" (Davin et al., 2024, p. 13).

One area in need of additional research on the impact of earning a SoBL relates to college and career. An original intention of those who developed the SSoBL was to create a recognizable symbol of bilingualism for IHEs and employers (Olsen, 2020). This book seeks to respond to the former, providing various examples of how IHEs are taking up the SoBL. But additional efforts are needed related to the latter. In a small qualitative study, colleagues and I interviewed students post-high school graduation about whether earning an SSoBL had impacted their employment (Davin et al., 2024). Thirteen of the 33 students interviewed reported that having an SSoBL had helped them find employment, although most of those interviewed were still in college. One student who spoke English, Somali, and Arabic told a story about interviewing for a position as a translator in a call center. She explained that the interview had not been going well but that once she mentioned her SSoBL, the interviewer asked for a photo of it and subsequently offered her the job.

Impact on language programming

Many language programs now have access to assessment data that they can use to evaluate curricula and improve classroom language instruction (Davin et al., 2018). Most assessments used to award the SSoBL (e.g., AAPPL, STAMP) provide disaggregated scores showing how students performed in each domain (e.g., reading, writing, speaking). They focus on what students can do with the language (e.g., describe a daily routine) rather than what they know about the language (e.g., conjugating verbs). Teachers can analyze students' scores to answer questions such as, *On which mode of communication are students scoring the lowest?* Or, *Are students progressing up the proficiency scale as they progress through the language program?*

In one related study, Davin et al. (2018) surveyed world language and English-as-a-Second-Language teachers across three school districts and found that 65% reported changing their instructional practices after SSoBL implementation. Of those teachers, 46% indicated that they included more instruction focused on speaking and listening, and 42% indicated that they included more instruction on reading and writing. Moreover, 65% reported a change in their assessment practices. As language programming improves, programs may experience an increase in student enrollment in language courses, fostering a stronger culture of multilingualism within the community (Davin et al., 2018).

Challenges to SSoBL implementation

Despite these positive impacts, there have been challenges to widespread SSoBL implementation. One of the biggest relates to uneven implementation. Because there is typically no federal or state funding to support SSoBL implementation, many districts and schools across the country do not participate (Schwedhelm & King, 2020; Subtirelu et al., 2019). Anecdotal evidence from conversations with administrators across the country suggests that many districts and schools may be unaware of the policy or unaware of how to implement it.

But recent efforts have sought to address this information gap. Arthur Chou at SealofBiliteracy.org has worked tirelessly to promote and spread the word about SSoBLs since the movement originated in California. The U.S. Secretary of Education, Miguel Cardona, and his team have included the SSoBL in their *Raise the Bar: Lead the World* initiative, aiming to raise the American public's awareness of the policy and the value of multilingualism (U.S. Department of Education, 2023). Amy Heineke and I have published a framework for SSoBL implementation called *Promoting Multilingualism in Schools: A Framework for Implementing the Seal of Biliteracy* (Davin & Heineke, 2022). We provide professional development and host book clubs for educators across states to guide schools in equitable implementation. The Center for Advanced Research on Language Education (CARLA), in partnership with the Minnesota Department of Education (MDE) World Languages Division and the Multilingual Education Program in the College of Education and Human Development at the University of Minnesota, has published a national website to support educators in implementation (CARLA et al., 2024).

In other cases, stakeholders are aware of the SoBL but might lack the resources for implementation. In their analysis of which districts and schools participated in awarding the California SSoBL in the 2015–2016 school year, Subtirelu et al. (2019) found that schools with greater numbers of students of color and higher percentages of students qualifying for free meals were less likely to award the SoBL. In their study of a large urban district in Illinois, Heineke and Davin (2024) learned that of the district's 2,000 SSoBL recipients, only five were African American. These gaps in SSoBL outcomes signal equity issues emergent in voluntary and often divergent implementation in local settings.

SoBL implementation requires that districts and schools have employees with time dedicated to administration. These individuals must familiarize themselves with the requirements to award the SoBL and find the time to identify eligible students and their LOTEs to order and administer the appropriate assessments. Schools also must have systems in place to track assessment data, in many cases for both English and the LOTE, and they must establish procedures or practices for recognizing and celebrating SoBL recipients. In addition to these human resources, schools must have the resources required to administer the required assessments, such as computers, broadband internet, headsets for the speaking and listening portions of the assessment, and keyboard overlays for nonalphabetic languages (Davin & Heineke, 2022).

Equity issues often relate to assessment, which carries a per student cost. Some schools only offer the SSoBL through world language programming, what Fisk (2020) refers to as "low hanging fruit" (p. 147), meaning that students not enrolled in those programs cannot sit for a SoBL exam. Other schools make SoBL assessments available to all students in languages other than just those taught in school, but research suggests that students enrolled in language programming are more likely to know about the SSoBL (Davin & Heineke, 2018). Further complexifying implementation, an additional major barrier is that appropriate, practical, and affordable assessments are not available in many of the languages spoken by students in U.S. schools. As Valdés (2020) contends, assessments reflect the social construction of named national languages and often are not available in Indigenous or other language varieties.

The potential of the SoBL for U.S. IHEs

Although the SSoBL originated as a K–12 policy, innovators across the country have begun to explore its applications in higher education contexts. When asked what motivated them to pursue an SSoBL, students repeatedly report wanting to be more competitive when applying to college and potentially receiving college credit for the recognition (Davin, 2021b; Davin & Heineke, 2018; Hancock & Davin, 2020). As many of the chapters in this volume mention, having an SSoBL can simplify placement processes for modern language departments. For example, if a student arrives at college with a valid and reliable proficiency rating of Intermediate Mid, departments may not need to administer their own placement test.

To be sure, recognition and use of the SoBL by IHEs helps to address some of the issues of equity and access at the high school level. IHEs might offer SoBL assessments to high schoolers at a local university (see Chapter 10) or award an SSoBL at the college level for students whose high schools did not participate (see Chapter 4). One of the most common ways that IHEs are leveraging the SoBL relates to awarding college credit. The subsequent sections explain some of the ways in which IHEs are doing this.

Current landscape

As of July 2024, three states have policies in place that require most public, state-funded IHEs to award incoming students with credit for their SSoBL: Illinois, Minnesota, and Rhode Island. Although not required by the state, the University of Maine system has adopted its own similar policy. Other systems, colleges, and universities, like those presented in the subsequent chapters, also do so voluntarily. I maintain a list of these IHEs called *SSoBL and College Credit*, based solely on internet searches and self-reports (Davin, 2024). As of July 2024, there were over 80 IHEs on the list. These IHEs recognize that awarding credit to students for their SSoBL can increase the accessibility of higher education for many students by lowering the cost of tuition and decreasing time to graduation. For example, a 2019 news article reported,

> Starting this fall, students who have earned the Maine Seal of Biliteracy will be eligible to receive six or more free college credits at Maine's public universities. The credit awards can reduce college costs by more than $1,500 for students and their families.
>
> *(WGME, 2019)*

Including the SoBL in *Prior Learning Assessment* policies, in which students receive credit for learning that occurred outside of the college classroom (García & Leibrandt, 2020), is critical for equity and access. Since World War II, many states have had legislation in place requiring IHEs to award credit to students for military experience and AP scores. But many students in U.S. schools do have access to AP courses. Not all schools offer AP classes, and even in those that do, many students, especially students of color, do not have access (Kanno & Kangas, 2014). Allowing a student to pursue college credit by passing an assessment of a home or heritage language not only increases access to college but also provides validation and emphasizes that multilingualism is an asset.

Awarding credit to students with an SSoBL

The ways in which IHEs choose to award credit to incoming students with an SSoBL is consequential for questions of equity. Just as SSoBL policies vary from state to state, so too, do ways in which credit is awarded.

Number of credits

The number of credits that an IHE awards to students for an SSoBL varies. The American Council on Education (ACE) published recommendations for how many credits they recommend that IHEs offer. For example, ACE recommends that an IHE award a student who scored the equivalent of Intermediate Mid with eight credits and a student who scored the equivalent of Advanced Mid with 16 credits (ACE, 2024). However, this decision is typically left up to the discretion of the individual IHE. In Virginia, where students must reach the equivalent of Intermediate Mid to earn an SSoBL, Virginia Commonwealth University (VCU) offers six credits (VCU, 2024). In Illinois, where students must reach the equivalent of Intermediate High, the University of Illinois Urbana-Champaign (UIUC) offers eight credits (UIUC, 2024). Other universities base the amount of credit that they award on the level of proficiency the student achieved on their SSoBL assessment. For example, the University of Maine awards nine credits to students who scored the equivalent of Advanced Low on the ACTFL Proficiency scale and six credits to students who scored the equivalent of Intermediate Mid (University of Maine, 2024).

Type of credits awarded

Also critical to equity is the type of credits that IHEs award (see Table 1.2). For some IHEs, especially those in states like Illinois where offering credit is legislated, SoBL credits are

TABLE 1.2 Three approaches to awarding credit for a SoBL

	Pros	*Cons*
Transfer Credits	Can be awarded for a SoBL in any language	Can cause issues with financial aid if student exceeds number of credits required for degree
Elective Credits	Can be awarded for a SoBL in any language May count toward students' required course of study	Can cause issues with financial aid if student exceeds number of credits required for degree
Retroactive Credits	Requires students to take a language course, potentially increasing enrollment	Challenging to implement for languages not taught at the IHE or for SSoBLs from states with different requirements Can be cumbersome for students to understand and navigate

awarded as *transfer credits.* This type of credit does not count toward students' grade point average and can be awarded for a SoBL in any language, regardless of whether that language is taught at the IHE. This approach increases equity by recognizing recipients of a SoBL in any language but can cause complications with financial aid if students exceed the number of credits required for their major. Another approach taken by some IHEs is to issue *elective credits* for a SoBL. In this approach, as long as electives are required for a student's degree, SoBL credits should not interfere with financial aid. This approach also allows for recognition of a SoBL in any language, including those not taught at the IHE.

A third approach is to issue *retroactive credits.* In this approach, students must first pass a course, typically in the language department, to earn the credits for the SoBL. Once the student passes the course, they receive the credits for all coursework that would have come prior. This approach appeals to many IHEs because it addresses enrollment concerns. Faculty in some language departments fear that offering credit to a student who earned a SoBL will discourage them from taking additional language courses. But retroactive credit policies encourage SoBL recipients to take at least one course, giving faculty an opportunity to engage students and promote their majors or minors. Evidence suggests that a retroactive credit policy may increase enrollment because students realize that they have already completed a substantial number of credits toward a minor or major (see Chapters 7 and 8).

There are several challenges to be aware of with a retroactive credit approach. A negative aspect is that they can be hard to advertise. Students may not be aware that they are eligible for credits simply by taking a world language course. Moreover, IHEs must grapple with how to provide the same recognition to students who earned a SoBL in a language not offered at the IHE. At Grand View University in Iowa, students can receive up to eight Spanish credits, the language offered at the university, by completing any course in the modern language department. For students who earned the SoBL in a language not taught by the department, students can earn eight elective credits, also by taking any course in the modern language department. Therefore, if a student got the SoBL in Hmong, he or she could take Spanish I and get eight elective credits for the Hmong SoBL (Grand View University, 2024).

Processes for awarding credits

One of the biggest challenges that IHEs face in awarding credit to SoBL recipients relates to processing. Many students do not yet know whether they will earn a SoBL when they apply to college, and most IHEs do not have an automated process in place to determine whether a student earned the recognition. Even in states in which offering credit to SSoBL recipients is legislated, students must formally request those credits. In a recent investigation in Minnesota, colleagues and I found that most students did not receive college credits for their SSoBL, largely because they did not know how to request them (Davin et al., 2024). However, the Family Educational Rights and Privacy Act policies restrict what information states and schools can share. In some states, because the SSoBL is operated at the district level, state departments of education do not have data on which students earned an SSoBL. This puts the onus on the IHE registrar or someone in the language department, typically, to verify that a student earned an SSoBL. Again, there is not a standardized way to indicate that a student earned an SSoBL on a transcript, and states have different proficiency requirements for an SSoBL, making this process quite complex and cumbersome.

Overview of chapters

The chapters in this book go into much greater depth about the implementation and uses of the SoBL in IHEs across the United States. This book includes an introductory section followed by four parts. The introductory section includes this chapter as well as a chapter by Nick Gossett that provides background on the GSoBL.

Part II, "Recognizing Students' Biliteracy in Higher Education," consists of four chapters that focus on how IHEs in various states recognize and celebrate the multilingualism of their graduates. All four chapters discuss awarding a form of the SoBL in higher education contexts, and the authors of three of those four chapters discuss the creation of their own SoBLs.

In Chapter 3, Aoki, Hugo, and Yaden describe SoBL implementation in two IHEs within the state of Washington, one large public university and one small private university. They describe how the University of Washington began by offering testing for high school students in their *Less Commonly Taught Languages* summer programs to earn the SSoBL and then expanded to offer undergraduate students access to testing to earn the GSoBL. They also describe a homegrown SoBL program created at Pacific Lutheran University to recognize multilingual students. They conclude their chapter by sharing findings from a questionnaire distributed to various IHEs in the northwestern region that surveyed awareness of the SoBL, testing opportunities, perceptions of value, and implementation concerns.

Chapter 4 is somewhat unique from the other chapters in Part I because it shares how one individual advocated for the expansion of the Oregon SSoBL into postsecondary coursework. The efforts of Monto, who was the dean of education at Chemeketa Community College at the time, resulted in Oregon becoming the first state to award the SSoBL at the higher education level. In her chapter, she details both the administrative procedures required for implementation and students' perceptions of the recognition. She highlights the benefits for both students and IHEs in fostering linguistic diversity and equity.

The context of Chapters 5 and 6 shifts from the northwestern United States to states along the Mexico border, and the authors of these chapters share their efforts to create their own versions of the SoBL. In Chapter 5, Alfaro and Barton describe the design, implementation, and value of a homegrown recognition called the *USBCC*. They created this program at San Diego State University, a designated Hispanic-serving institution (HSI), to sustain students' bilingual and bicultural identities. They explain how this program sustains, promotes, and advances students' linguistic and cultural capital. Chapter 6 presents the development of another homegrown recognition in the southwest, the *B3 Scholar Seal*, developed at the University of Texas Rio Grande Valley. Christoffersen and López García describe the development of a rare dual language program at the university level and how they developed the B3 Scholar Seal to recognize students who completed a series of courses taught in Spanish, bilingually, or with culturally sustaining pedagogy.

Part III, "Awarding College Credit for Biliteracy Attainment," includes two chapters. Chapter 7, written by Moss and Gambrell, describes how the faculty at Pittsburg State University in Kansas developed a placement and credit-granting policy for incoming students with an SSoBL. Based on the success of this process, they then began to also offer the GSoBL to language majors in their department. These two initiatives not only boosted enrollment in the department but also prompted a shift in focus from course grades to proficiency outcomes. Chapter 8, written by Gleason, Latorre, and Cardone, describes a partnership between a regional public university and a neighborhood public school district to grant credit to incoming students with an SSoBL. Their chapter sheds light on some of the challenges described previously in this chapter, describing their struggle to decide how many credits to award, how to award those credits, and how to identify SoBL recipients. Their findings also illustrate how changes in administration can profoundly impact SoBL implementation.

Part IV, "Recruiting Biliterate Individuals into Higher Education," also includes two chapters. These chapters share innovative approaches to using the SoBL for recruitment. In Chapter 9, Eckerson and Jacobs, like Chapters 7 and 8, describe how they developed a strategy to award retroactive credit to SSoBL participants. However, they also share how this policy evolved into a recruitment strategy by inviting students at local school districts to sit for an SSoBL assessment on campus. Students from area schools came to campus for a day where they took a tour, had lunch, met with various departments on campus, and sat for an SSoBL assessment. Although the data are still somewhat preliminary, they suggest that these efforts incentivize language study.

In Chapter 10, Heineke, Cohen, Steinmiller, and Lee describe a partnership between Loyola University Chicago, Arrupe College, and an urban public school to develop a pipeline of bilingual teachers using the Illinois SSoBL. Distinct from other chapters that focus primarily on departments of modern language, this chapter looks at how teacher education faculty in Loyola's School of Education partnered with school and district administrators to leverage the SSoBL to recruit, prepare, and place bilingual teachers.

In Part V, "Conclusions and Future Directions," Fiegen, King, and Stockman summarize the key themes across the chapters in this volume. They outline opportunities for enhancement of SoBL implementation and use, including (a) stemming declining world language enrollments, (b) expanding SoBL equity and access, (c) fostering positive changes to language instruction and collaboration, and (d) addressing language teacher shortages. They also offer guidance related to potential risks of SoBL use by IHEs and future needs to address those risks.

Conclusion

The SoBL represents a transformative initiative with the potential to significantly impact students' academic and personal development. By recognizing and validating multilingual proficiency, the SoBL not only enhances students' self-confidence and cultural pride but may also open doors to higher education and career opportunities. Of critical importance are equity and access, so we must ensure that all students, regardless of home language or school district, benefit from this policy. The subsequent chapters in this book delve deeper into the various applications of the SoBL in higher education, offering insights and strategies for maximizing its impact. Together, these chapters illuminate the path toward a more inclusive and linguistically diverse educational landscape.

References

ACE. (2024). *Avant assessment.* https://www.acenet.edu/National-Guide/Pages/Organization.aspx?oid=f8b8b588-3876-eb11-a812-000d3a3bd56a

American Councils for International Education. (2017). *The national K-12 foreign language enrollment survey report.* https://www.americancouncils.org/sites/default/files/FLE-report-June17.pdf

ACTFL. (2024). *ACTFL proficiency guidelines.* https://www.actfl.org/uploads/files/general/Resources-Publications/ACTFL_Proficiency_Guidelines_2024.pdf

ACTFL. (2015). *ACTFL/CAEP program standards for the preparation of foreign language teachers.* https://www.actfl.org/uploads/files/general/Documents/ACTFLCAEPStandards2013_v2015.pdf

Aguirre, S., & Chou A. (2024). *The Seal of Biliteracy 2023 national report for the 2021–2022 school year.* https://sealofbiliteracy.org/doc/2023-National-Seal-of-Biliteracy-Report-Final.pdf

Baggett, H.C. (2016). Student enrollment in world languages: L'égalité des chances? *Foreign Language Annals, 49*(1), 162–179. https://doi.org/10.1111/flan.12173

Californians Together. (2024). *About us.* https://californianstogether.org/who-we-are/about-us/

CARLA, Minnesota Department of Education, University of Minnesota. (2024). *Information for educators.* https://www.statesealsofbiliteracy.com/information-for-educators

Castro, A. (2020). Validating the linguistic strengths of English learners: Los Angeles Unified School District's implementation of the seal of biliteracy. In Heineke, A.J., Davin, K.J. (Eds.), *The Seal of Biliteracy: Case studies and considerations for policy implementation* (pp. 123–140). Information Age.

Davin, K.J. (2021a). The Seal of Biliteracy: College credit and placement. *The Language Educator, 16*(2), 24–26.

Davin, K.J. (2021b). Critical language testing: Factors influencing students' decisions to (not) pursue the Seal of Biliteracy. *Harvard Educational Review, 91*(2), 179–203. https://doi.org/10.17763/1943-5045-91.2.179

Davin, K.J. (2024). *SSoBL and college credit.* https://docs.google.com/spreadsheets/d/19oZOSGoy9Maurn0RCq8C4eC1eS7e0qU6/edit?usp=sharing&ouid=106613527737379645998&rtpof=true&sd=true

Davin, K.J., Cruz, K.R., & Hancock, C.R. (2024). An examination of the postgraduation benefits of earning a seal of biliteracy. *Foreign Language Annals, 57*(3), 634–653. https://doi.org/10.1111/flan.12753

Davin, K.J., & Heineke, A.J. (2017). The Seal of Biliteracy: Variations in policy and outcomes. *Foreign Language Annals, 50*(3), 486–499.

Davin, K.J., & Heineke, A.J. (2018). The Seal of Biliteracy: Adding students' voices to the conversation. *Bilingual Research Journal, 41*(3), 312–328. https://doi.org/10.1080/15235882.2018.1481896

Davin, K.J., & Heineke, A.J. (2022). *Promoting multilingualism in schools: A framework for implementing the Seal of Biliteracy.* ACTFL Press.

Davin, K.J., Heineke, A.J., & Egnatz, L. (2018). The Seal of Biliteracy: Successes and challenges to implementation. *Foreign Language Annals, 51*(2), 275–289. https://doi.org/10.1111/flan.12336

Davin, K.J., Heineke, A.J., & Hancock, C.R. (2022). The Seal of Biliteracy: A 10-year retrospective. *Foreign Language Annals*, *55*(1), 10–34. https://doi.org/10.1111/flan.12596

European Commission. (2017). *Strengthening European identity through education and culture*. https://eur-lex.europa.eu/legal-content/EN/TXT/?uri=COM%3A2017%3A673%3AFIN

Fisk, J.K. (2020). School-level implementation of the Seal of Biliteracy: One linguistically diverse suburban Illinois high school's journey. In Heineke, A.J., Davin, K.J. (Eds.), *The Seal of Biliteracy: Case studies and considerations for policy implementation* (pp. 139–155). Information Age.

García, O., & Kleifgen, J.A. (2018). *Educating emergent bilinguals: Policies, programs, and practices for English language learners*. Teachers College Press.

García, R.M., & Leibrandt, S. (2020). *The current state of higher learning policies*. https://files.eric.ed.gov/fulltext/ED611043.pdf

Grand View University. (2024). *Iowa Seal of Biliteracy*. https://www.grandview.edu/academics/undergraduate/biliteracy

Hancock, C., & Davin, K.J. (2020). A comparative case study: Administrators' and students' perceptions of the Seal of Biliteracy. *Foreign Language Annals*, *53*(3), 458–477. https://doi.org/10.1111/flan.12479

Heineke, A.J., Davin, K.J., & Bedford, A. (2018). The Seal of Biliteracy: Considering equity and access for English Learners. *Education Policy Analysis Archives*, *26*(99), 1–8. https://doi.org/10.14507/epaa.26.3825

Johnson, D. (2013). *Language policy*. Palgrave MacMillan.

Kanno, Y., & Kangas, S.E.N. (2014). "I'm not going to be, like, for the AP": English language learners' limited access to advanced college-preparatory courses in high school. *American Educational Research Journal*, *51*(5), 848–878. https://doi.org/10.3102/000283121454471

Language Testing International. (2024). *Para. 1*. https://www.languagetesting.com/lti-information/understanding-proficiency#:~:text=Proficiency%20refers%20to%20the%20ability,range%20of%20topics%20and%20settings

Liu, Q., Cruz, K., & Davin, K.J. (2024). Leveraging the Seal of Biliteracy in community-based heritage language schools. *The Central States Conference on the Teaching of Foreign Languages Report*, 145–162.

Marichal, N., Rosario Roldán, A., & Coady, M. (2021). "My language learners seemed like ghosts": A rural teacher's transformational journey implementing the Seal of Biliteracy. *The Rural Educator*, *42*(1), 52–56.

Olsen, L. (2020). The history of the movement: Enacting the State Seal of Biliteracy in the state of California. In Heineke, A.J., & Davin, K.J. (Eds.), *The Seal of Biliteracy: Case studies and considerations for policy implementation* (pp. 17–34). Information Age.

Ricento, T., & Hornberger, N.H. (1996). Unpeeling the onion: Language planning and policy and the ELT professional. *TESOL Quarterly*, *30*(3), 401–427.

Ritz, C., & Sherf, N. (2021). World language programming and leadership in K–12 Massachusetts public schools. *Foreign Language Annals*, *54*(2), 476–504. https://doi.org/10.1111/flan.12519

Schwedhelm, M.C., & King, K.A. (2020). The neoliberal logic of state seals of biliteracy. *Foreign Language Annals*, *53*(1), 12–27. https://doi.org/10.1111/flan.12438

Schoener, H., & McKenzie, K. (2016). Equity traps redux: Inequitable access to foreign language courses for African American high-school students. *Equity and Excellence in Education*, *49*(3), 284–299. https://doi.org/10.1080/10665684.2016.1194099

Subtirelu, N.C., Borowczyk, M., Thorson Hernández, R., & Venezia, F. (2019). Recognizing whose bilingualism? A critical policy analysis of the Seal of Biliteracy. *The Modern Language Journal*, *103*(2), 371–390. https://doi.org/10.1111/modl.12556

US Department of Education. (2023). *Raise the bar: Lead the world*. https://www.ed.gov/sites/ed/files/about/inits/ed/raise-the-bar/handout-en.pdf

University of Illinois Urbana-Champaign. (2024). *Credit for state Seal of Biliteracy*. https://registrar.illinois.edu/academic-records/credit-for-state-seal-of-biliteracy/#:~:text=Students%20with%20a%20verified%20Seal,the%20language%20other%20than%20English

University of Maine. (2024). *Seal of Biliteracy credit table*. https://catalog.umaine.edu/content.php?catoid=93&navoid=4281

Vaish, V. (2008). *Biliteracy and globalization: English language education in India* (Vol. 67). Multilingual Matters.

Valdés, G. (2020). The future of the Seal of Biliteracy: Issues of equity and inclusion. In Heineke, A.J., & Davin, K.J. (Eds.), *The Seal of Biliteracy: Case studies and considerations for policy implementation* (pp. 177–204). Information Age.

Virginia Commonwealth University. (2024). *Additional sources of academic credit.* https://bulletin.vcu.edu/undergraduate/undergraduate-study/admission-university/additional-sources-of-credit/

Wesely, P.M., & Gao, B. (2024). Patterns of integrating the Seal of Biliteracy into the school context. *Foreign Language Annals.* https://doi.org/10.1111/flan.12760

WGME. (2019). *Bilingual students eligible to receive free college credits at Maine public universities.* https://wgme.com/news/local/bilingual-students-eligible-to-receive-free-college-credits-at-maine-public-universities

2

GLOBAL SEAL OF BILITERACY PROGRAMS IN HIGHER EDUCATION AND ADULT EDUCATION SETTINGS

Nick Gossett

Introduction

The term "micro-credential", as noted by Brown et al. (2021), does not have one single agreed-upon definition. Instead, the term has come to encompass a manner of different learning experiences, both formal and semiformal accredited programs, that are also stackable (Brown et al., 2021). Based on Google Trends results, the term micro-credential has grown in popularity over the last few decades (Brown et al., 2021).

Micro-credentials are not a new concept in the field of language education. As Oliver (2019) points out, options like extension courses have provided opportunities for people to continue their education in a specific field. A simple search for language extension courses will provide thousands of different programs focusing on both general and specific languages. Programs such as these fit into the general definition of a micro-credential but are not always easily accessible to young learners or those in other degrees of study. The Seal of Biliteracy (SoBL) is a micro-credential for language learners that is more accessible than other previous micro-credentials.

The SoBL can be conceptualized as a micro-credential, given that the recognition indicates a recipient's biliteracy competencies for college and career (Seal of Biliteracy, 2024). The first SoBL was launched in 2011 in California. Since that time, all 50 states plus the District of Columbia have created programs for students in high school to be recognized for their abilities in two or more languages. Until 2018, except for learners in Oregon (see Chapter 4), there was no way for learners outside of kindergarten through grade 12 (K–12) schools to earn a SoBL. It was in 2018 that the Global Seal of Biliteracy (GSoBL), or simply the Global Seal, was launched to not only recognize those learners without access to a state Seal of Biliteracy (SSoBL) but to also spread micro-credentialing in languages internationally. Since that time, thousands of individuals of all ages have been awarded the GSoBL.

This chapter provides the background context for the creation of the GSoBL. By providing an overview of GSoBL programs currently active in institutions of higher education (IHEs) and adult education programs around the globe, this chapter supports the creation of blueprints for new programs. These programs have a significant impact on language learners

DOI: 10.4324/9781032667249-3

and promote continuous language learning throughout one's life. They also provide the external validation needed to meet the demands of the 21st-century workplace.

Language and workforce readiness

Compelling evidence suggests that current models of higher education are ill-equipped to meet the increasing demand for a wide array of skills and competencies, particularly those needed for future job opportunities (Shanahan & Organ, 2022). A 2019 European Commission report found that anticipated workforce changes indicate that 50% of employees will require reskilling by 2025, with new technologies reshaping job markets (European Commission, 2020). A 2019 survey conducted by the Society for Human Resource Management found that 75% of hiring managers reported difficulty recruiting for current job openings due to the lack of skills of those in the applicant pool (Burner et al., 2019).

Employers are not just seeking individuals with hard skills; soft skills are equally important. A hard skill is a competency or ability necessary for one to complete work, while soft skills are traits and qualities that impact how one works (Laker & Powell, 2011). In a survey of over 650 employers, Wilkie (2020) found that respondents overwhelmingly agreed that soft skills were required to move into management positions in their organizations. Seventy-seven percent agreed that communication skills were important, 75% agreed listening skills were important, 74% agreed that critical thinking skills were important, and 73% agreed that interpersonal skills were important (Wilkie, 2020). At the same time, the Society for Human Resource Management (Burner et al., 2019) found that 51% of employers reported that the education system had not prepared students to meet the skills shortage. This is not to say that students are not learning the needed skills through educational programs. Rather, students may be obtaining such skills, but employers do not realize that students possess these skills. As a result, findings highlight the immediate need for micro-credentials that certify and make it clear to employers that students have both the hard and soft skills needed to succeed in the 21st-century job market.

In response to these challenges, digital badging and credentialing have emerged as a solution and witnessed enormous growth in both popularity and acceptance by many industries, including the educational and business sectors (Olcott, 2021). Alongside or possibly due to the growth in micro-credentials, many IHEs have increasingly moved to a system of allowing students to utilize prior knowledge and work or life experience to earn credit and advance place in a program of study, shortening the length of time required for a degree (Klein-Collins & Shafenberg, 2023). As part of academic programs, micro-credentials provide a context-rich representation of student achievement, offering a more evidence-based alternative to traditional measures like grade point averages and test scores. They are especially valuable in assessing 21st-century skills, such as communication and collaboration, which are difficult to gauge using standard academic metrics (Fishman et al., 2018). Both Fishman et al. (2018) and Shanahan and Organ (2022) highlight the value of micro-credentials as they can provide evidence of both the hard and soft skills that employers desire and 21st-century jobs require.

Language skills fit the needs of 21st-century jobs as they are considered both a hard and a soft skill. Employers require employees who can complete specific tasks in another language to successfully meet the requirements of the job, as well as the needs of their clients. In this instance, language is a hard skill and is an invaluable resource in the workplace. However, it is not just about the hard skills needed to complete a task but also the way task completion is undertaken. This is where soft skills come into play. The process of acquiring a language and the methods used in teaching a language not only incorporate the use of soft skills but also instruct learners in these soft skills (Kic-Drgas, 2018). For example, it is typical in language classes for students to be put into role-playing situations or split into groups so they can create a presentation on a topic to present to their classmates. These exercises are done to complete tasks in the language, with the main goal being production in the language. But when students are asked to role-play or work in teams, they are practicing both hard and soft skills. Because of how languages are taught and learned, employees who have acquired a second language, especially those with some formal instruction in a language, are found to have obtained soft skills specifically through their language instruction (Lavrysh, 2016).

Despite the obvious connection between jobs and language, the learning of a second language is not necessarily a priority for many parts of the world. When we compare the two parts of the world with the highest gross domestic product, the United States and the European Union (EU), we observe a very different situation in regard to language education. Language instruction in the United States lags in comparison to the EU. Eurostat (2019), the EU's official statistical office, found that more than 80% of working-age adults in the EU with a college education know at least one foreign language. More than 88% of students in secondary education are taking a second language and nearly 50% of students are taking two or more languages (Eurostat, 2023). In contrast, according to a report by the American Councils for International Education (2017), only 20% of K–12 students in the United States are enrolled in a language class. The situation for higher education is not any better, as enrollments in foreign language courses have been on a steady decline for decades, according to reports published by the Modern Language Association (MLA; Looney & Lusin, 2019; Lusin et al., 2023). The American Academy of Arts and Sciences (2017) landmark report highlighted the significant impact of K–12 language education on university-level language study. The report revealed that K–12 language programs are frequently canceled due to a shortage of qualified teachers. This cancellation can lead to a reduced interest in studying languages at the university level when students miss out on language education in high school (Morgan & Thompson, 2023).

Despite the increasingly alarming statistics on language enrollments in both K–12 and higher education, there has been a glimmer of hope. In K–12, micro-credentials recognizing proficiency in two or more languages have been shown to act as a driver of increasing language course enrollments (Mihaly et al., 2022). The SSoBL has highlighted the importance of language education in K–12 settings; however, it is primarily reserved for students in high schools, thereby leaving out students enrolled in IHEs or those in other adult education programs. The GSoBL has emerged as a viable micro-credential to provide learners in higher education and adult education programs with an external, validated recognition of their multilingualism that translates to the workplace.

An overview of the GSoBL

The origins of the GSoBL

The GSoBL is an international certification program established to celebrate and validate individuals' proficiency in two or more languages. Its historical evolution is deeply intertwined with the broader societal impetus to promote multilingualism and linguistic diversity within an increasingly interconnected global context. This narrative traces the origins of the GSoBL and its current standing as an internationally recognized certification of language proficiency while also addressing its implications for employers to validate not only linguistic skills but also vital soft skills.

The GSoBL was inspired by the state Seals of Biliteracy (SSoBol) that initially emerged in the United States starting in the 2010s. The SoBL campaign emerged in response to California's ban on bilingual programs amid increasing linguistic diversity and immigration. Californians Together, a coalition of organizations focused on the education of English learners, initiated the campaign to shift perceptions of language diversity from a problem to an asset, advocating for the benefits of bilingualism in fostering skills for a globally interconnected and diverse century. The SoBL was conceived to honor students' home and heritage language skills, promote bilingualism, and contribute to creating a generation capable of bridging cultures and languages for more cohesive and connected communities (Olsen, 2020).

The developmental trajectory of the SoBL in the United States gained momentum in tandem with a growing awareness of the significance of multilingualism in an increasingly globalized world. In 2011, California became the pioneer state to officially institute the SoBL, serving as a blueprint for other states to emulate. Under this program, students were eligible to receive a unique seal on their high school diplomas and transcripts, thereby attesting to their proficiency in English and at least one additional language. This recognition not only underscored the societal value of linguistic diversity but also furnished practical advantages to students by augmenting their prospects in education and careers (Davin & Heineke, 2017).

Simultaneously, the triumph of the SoBL in the United States began to attract international attention. Educators and language advocates in various countries acknowledged the merits of such a program in promoting language proficiency, cross-cultural understanding, and academic achievement. This international recognition ignited the conceptualization of the GSoBL, intended to serve as a standardized, internationally accepted credential for bilingual and multilingual individuals. In 2018, the GSoBL was officially launched, representing a collaborative endeavor between organizations, educators, and language advocates from diverse backgrounds. The overarching objective was to establish a global framework for evaluating and certifying language proficiency, irrespective of the specific languages in question.

The SSoBLs and the GSoBL

Although its origins trace back to the SoBL movement that started in California in 2011, the GSoBL was also created to fill in the gaps left by the state-level SoBL programs. The GSoBL sought to transcend national boundaries and cultural disparities by providing a shared standard to recognize language learners on a global scale. And while the SSoBL programs have provided noteworthy opportunities to many high school students, several scholars have pointed out the gaps and inequities in some programs (e.g., Davin & Heineke, 2017; Subtirelu et al., 2019).

Since education is more locally controlled at the state and district level in the United States, there are few regulations and standards that are set at a national level. This has created a situation with SSoBL programs in which nearly every state has different stipulations for students to earn the SoBL (Davin et al., 2022). In some states, students are only required to complete certain courses to be eligible, while in other states, students must fulfill testing requirements or grade requirements in both English and another language. The minimum level of proficiency also varies across states. Some states set the minimum at Intermediate Mid on the ACTFL proficiency scale, others at Intermediate High, and still others as low as Intermediate Low. A few states, such as Missouri and South Carolina, have multiple levels to recognize students at different stages of language proficiency, as well as to entice students to continue studying languages throughout their high school careers.

In addition to requirements for demonstrating language proficiency, SSoBLs vary in implementational logistics. Some states have very controlled processes where local stakeholders must go through an office connected to the state board of education to recognize students, whereas others allow for more local control. Some states provide pathways for students in private schools or those in homeschool programs, while others only allow students enrolled in public schools to take part in the program. Some states allow students to receive the SoBL in any language spoken in the home, while others limit it to certain languages, typically those taught in traditional schools (Davin & Heineke, 2017; Davin et al., 2022). And, most applicable to IHEs, only one state, Oregon, currently allows for students in higher education programs to receive a SSoBL (see Monto, Chapter 4).

It was within this general context of the SoBL initiative that Avant Assessment created the GSoBL in 2018 as an open and free platform to complement and further support SSoBL. The goal of the GSoBL is to provide certification for anyone middle school age through adult, anywhere in the world, who can demonstrate language proficiency through any tests approved by the GSoBL's independent Board of Advisors (The Global Seal, 2024a).

The GSoBL is *global* in two ways. First, there is one pathway to obtain recognition via externally validated assessments that provide evidence of language proficiency on either the ACTFL or Common European Framework of Reference for Languages (CEFR) scale. Second, the GSoBL is open to anyone, anywhere in the world. These two distinctions make the GSoBL a viable option as a micro-credential to certify language proficiency in two or more languages for home and heritage language learners, students in private schools, students in homeschool programs, students in schools awarding the SoBL who may not meet their state's requirements (either their language is not tested or their test results fall below the state minimum), students who have been awarded their SSoBL as an additional certification, adult and independent learners, and students in IHEs.

Understanding the nuances between the different SoBLs and knowing where to look for information can be overwhelming. There are several resources available to help guide research. Davin and Heineke (2022) collected information from nearly every state that currently has a SoBL program. Their publication, *Promoting Multilingualism in Schools: A Framework for Implementing the Seal of Biliteracy*, is a great resource for understanding the different steps needed to take when implementing a SoBL at the high school level. The GSoBL website has the most up-to-date information on each state's SoBL program (The Global Seal, 2024b).

The GSoBL facts and figures

The GSoBL is truly global as learners have been awarded the certification all over the world. As of December 2023, the GSoBL has been awarded in all 50 United States (including the District of Columbia), in 33 countries, and across five continents (Africa, Asia, Europe, North America, and South America). Learners in over a dozen other countries are in the process of applying for the GSoBL, including learners in Australia and Oceania. Figure 2.1 shows the geographic spread of the GSoBL.

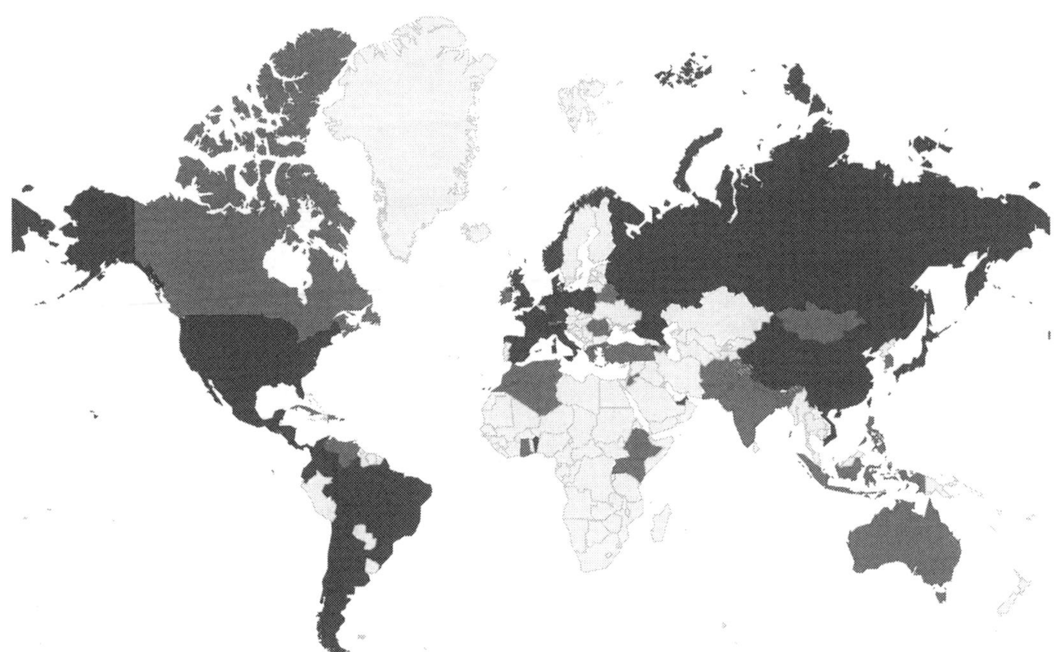

FIGURE 2.1 Countries where the GSoBL has been awarded (dark color) and where they are in process (light color) as of December 31, 2023. Copyright 2023 by Global Seal of Biliteracy.

The GSoBL employs a comprehensive methodology for assessing proficiency in multiple languages, encompassing listening, speaking, reading, and writing skills. This multifaceted approach ensures that the certification is both thorough and meaningful. It should be noted that the criteria for earning the GSoBL may exhibit regional variations, reflecting the diversity of languages and language acquisition contexts across the globe. For example, institutions in the United States may use assessments aligned to the ACTFL scale, while those in Europe or South America may use assessments aligned to the CEFR scale. This is evident through the number of languages certified and qualifying assessments aligned to either the ACTFL or CEFR scale that have been approved by the GSoBL Board of Advisors.

As of December 31, 2023, the GSoBL can certify learners in 120 languages through 46 different assessments (The Global Seal, 2024c). To be certified by the GSoBL, a learner must take a certified assessment in a proctored environment that assesses reading, writing, listening, and speaking or writing and speaking at a minimum. Learners submitting for more commonly tested languages (e.g., Spanish, French, Mandarin) that have a four-skill test available cannot submit results from a two-skill test. To allow for accessibility for the Less Commonly Tested Languages (e.g., Armenian, Marshallese, Yup'ik), the GSoBL Board of Advisors allows learners to submit the results of a two-skill test that must contain both writing and speaking sections. This decision was based on a study that showed a 92.58% correlation between receptive and productive skills across seven languages (Egnatz & Santos, 2023).

Like the SoBL in some states (e.g., Missouri, South Carolina), the GSoBL has built in a multi-level series of certifications to not only recognize learners at different stages in their

TABLE 2.1 GSoBL award levels

GSoBL Award	*Level Required to Obtain Award*	*Abilities at GSoBL Level*
Functional Fluency	Intermediate Mid (ACTFL)/B1 (CEFR)	This individual can function in the certified language when completing familiar routines and tasks in predictable situations.
Working Fluency	Advanced Low (ACTFL)/ B2 (CEFR)	This individual can handle both routine and unfamiliar situations in both formal and informal settings.
Professional Fluency	Advanced High (ACTFL)/ C1 (CEFR)	This person is able to interact with a broad range of topics with much precision and accuracy.

language development but also to promote the concept of lifelong language learning. A description of the different levels of the GSoBL that require assessment results to be submitted is outlined in Table 2.1 (The Global Seal, 2024d).

For an assessment to be accepted, the individual testing agencies submit technical reports as well as external, empirical research supporting the validity of the assessment to the GSoBL Board of Advisors who review to determine validity and reliability. As noted on their website, the assessment review process is ongoing. Should an assessment be modified in such a way that does not meet the rigorous requirements, it can be removed from the accepted list of assessments (The Global Seal, 2024e). The primary charge of the Board of Advisors is to not only confirm the validity of assessments accepted but also to ensure expanded access to credentialing. Living up to that charge has been the sole mission of the GSoBL Board of Advisors and staff.

In some instances where learners have less exposure to language education or begin acquisition at an older age, reaching that first level of the GSoBL can be challenging and require more time. Speaking from a U.S.-centric point of view where the assumption that one's dominant language is English, learners of languages similar to English (e.g., German, French) tend to reach higher levels of proficiency more quickly than learners of languages such as Russian and Mandarin, which are less similar to English (U.S. Department of State, 2024). For example, when we look at Avant STAMP test national averages for students in language programs at IHEs, learners in a Spanish program at the average IHE tend to reach higher levels of proficiency than their Chinese counterparts during the same amount of contact hours (Avant Assessment, 2023). This means that learners in a Spanish program may obtain Functional Fluency before learners in a Chinese program.

The GSoBL has also begun a pathway awards program. Pathway awards seek to better support learners who are not yet at the Intermediate Mid (ACTFL) or B1 (CEFR) level to obtain the first level of certification. Pathway awards aim to boost learners' confidence, recognize their growth, and provide a pathway to a certified award. The pathway awards, which do not require test scores to be submitted to the GSoBL for certification, are available at Novice Mid, Novice High, and Intermediate Low for learners utilizing the ACTFL scale or A1 and A2 for learners utilizing the CEFR scale.

Since its launch in 2018, the GSoBL has provided thousands of learners the opportunity to obtain official certification of their language proficiency. Table 2.2 provides the number

TABLE 2.2 Number of GSoBL recipients at the high school level as of December 31, 2023

GSoBL Level	*Number of Awards*	*Percentage of Total*
Functional Fluency *ACTFL – Intermediate Mid/CEFR – B1*	20,491	86.3%
Working Fluency *ACTFL – Advanced Low/CEFR – B2*	3,211	13.5%
Professional Fluency *ACTFL – Advanced High/CEFR – C1*	38	0.2%
Totals	23,740	100%

and percentage of certifications per level of learners at the high school level (ages 13–18). These statistics highlight the talent of learners coming out of high schools who can be a valuable source of workplace-ready multilinguals, as well as potential advanced students for language programs at the higher education level.

Table 2.3 provides the number and percentage of certifications per level of learners in programs at IHEs. These learners come from 78 institutions across Asia, Europe, and North America. What is of interest is that the percentages per level of certification of the high school learners vary little from the percentages per level of the higher education learners. One may assume that the college level would have a much higher percentage of Working Fluency recipients, assuming learners reach a certain level in high school and continue to improve their proficiency in an IHE language program. However, the difference in the percentage of learners earning the Working Fluency GSoBL (ACTFL Advanced Low/CEFR B2) is only two percent. Since learners moving into IHE programs from high school programs are not currently tracked, there is no way to know what the actual change in proficiency is from one education level to the next for a given recipient. As of the date of publication of this chapter, no research has been conducted on this topic.

As previously mentioned, 78 IHEs across the globe have implemented GSoBL programs. A list of these IHEs is available on the GSoBL website (The Global Seal, 2024g). Each institution has its own way of testing for and rewarding the GSoBL to its students. For many, it is part of a capstone course at the end of a major or minor in the language. For some, they test for the GSoBL at various points in their program, creating pathways for students. Others have created campus-wide and community-wide GSoBL programs to highlight the multilingualism of the local community. Each program is specific to the needs

TABLE 2.3 Percentage of GSoBL recipients at the higher education level as of October 01, 2023

GSoBL Level	*Number of Awards*	*Percentage of Total*
Functional Fluency *ACTFL – Intermediate Mid / CEFR – B1*	3,058	83.8%
Working Fluency *ACTFL – Advanced Low / CEFR – B2*	569	15.6%
Professional Fluency *ACTFL – Advanced High / CEFR – C1*	20	0.5%
Totals	3,647	100%

and resources available to a specific institution. Specific examples of GSoBL programs will be provided later in this chapter.

Despite the growth in universities submitting scores for the GSoBL, there is still work to be done. Tens of thousands of learners test every year, but their organizations do not go through the steps to submit their scores to the GSoBL. The next section provides a blueprint for setting up a GSoBL program at an IHE.

Setting up a GSoBL program

Setting up a GSoBL program is a straightforward process. Many of the challenges relate to internal processes at institutions. As is often the case, there is hesitation by departments or individual faculty to enact new initiatives such as the GSoBL. However, depending on how the initiative is implemented, there are little to no drawbacks to providing students with a certification of their language proficiency. The following presents the steps and considerations when setting up a GSoBL program.

Testing

Since earning a GSoBL requires qualifying test scores, the first step is to think about the assessment one will use. A department may already be testing their students with an approved test (The Global Seal, 2024f) for other purposes such as benchmarking and progress monitoring. Results used for these internal purposes can also be submitted to the GSoBL. For example, the Spanish programs at both Northwestern University and Auburn University received internal funding in the 2022–2023 academic year to assess all Spanish language students using an external assessment to monitor student progress and ensure the program was meeting its proficiency goals at each level. Since these programs had the data and the test was approved for the GSoBL, both institutions submitted scores for all qualifying students to the GSoBL.

If a program is not currently testing for other purposes, then the department must decide at what point to test students and which test works best for their purposes. Some departments test at various points during their programs, allowing programs to meet several different needs. Testing at multiple points (e.g., at the end of intermediate-level courses, at the end of the courses for a minor, and at the end of the courses for a major) can help departments set benchmark levels for their courses to better aid in proper placement, develop articulated pathways using those benchmarks, and act as a method of recruiting students to stay past those courses where there is lower retention (typically where the courses required for a major, college, or university end). The University of Texas at Arlington (UTA, 2024) has enacted such a testing regime and uses the pathways they have created to market its programs to both incoming and current students.

The next logical question is how to fund testing for the GSoBL. Accepted tests range anywhere from $20 to $310 per student. Assessments of less commonly taught and tested languages are often more expensive. Covering the cost of testing depends on the financial situation at each institution, as well as internal policies related to the use of student fees. Some programs can utilize funds collected through course fees when a student enrolls in a class. Other programs have funds within their operating budgets to cover the cost of testing for a particular group of students, such as majors and minors. Several programs have their students cover the cost of testing themselves as part of a degree requirement, a course requirement, or as an option outside of any course or degree. In the case where students pay, students access a storefront and pay the testing company directly, typically receiving an education discount.

There is no cost for the actual GSoBL, given the organization has external sponsors who fund the cost of processing certifications. The only cost to the university or student is the cost of the test required to obtain the certification.

Submitting scores to the GSoBL

Once students have tested, scores must be reported to the GSoBL organization. To ensure the validity of the results, students cannot directly submit their results. Instead, university personnel must apply for the GSoBL on behalf of the student. This can be anyone the university sees fit, including, but not limited to, departmental staff, faculty, and testing center personnel. The university representative submits all scores online through the GSoBL application. GSoBL staff validate the results submitted and reach out to the university representative if there are any questions. Once the test results have been validated, a physical certificate with a unique serial number is created and mailed to the address provided by the institution. The unique serial number allows recipients to digitally share their GSoBL certificate and add it to their LinkedIn profiles under *Licenses & Certifications*. Programs should be mindful of the time it takes to process and mail physical certificates. Those that test during final exam weeks will not receive the certificates before students have left for the break. This may create an issue with ensuring students receive the physical certificates. If a student tests individually and not as part of a university initiative, the testing entities will assist the students with submitting their results for the GSoBL.

Recognizing GSoBL recipients

Finally, language programs must consider how to celebrate the students who earn a GSoBL. The GSoBL is not just recognition of what a student has achieved, but it is also validation of the work a program puts into producing globally ready citizens. Marketing offices at institutions are often happy to publish stories about the GSoBL, as it meets the institutional strategic goals of globalizing students and connecting students to employment opportunities. Recognizing recipients also provides examples to incoming and current students in language programs of the possibilities available to them. If a department typically has an awards reception, inviting GSoBL recipients is a great opportunity to further highlight the work done in the department.

Examples of GSoBL programs

There is no single way to incorporate the GSoBL at an institution. Each program should implement the GSoBL in the way that works best in that context. The following section presents different GSoBL programs to provide ideas for implementation at IHEs.

Four-year institution programs

The University of Wisconsin System Collaborative Language Program (UW-CLP) provides online language courses to students at universities across Wisconsin and beyond (University of Wisconsin, 2024). As a final exam in any end-of-sequence course, students take a four-skill language assessment (the cost of which is currently covered by grant funding). Through end-of-semester testing, the program has also been able to collect data on student performance and effective instructional methods. The program director, Lauren Rosen, realized this was a great opportunity for students to also earn a micro-credential and decided to submit students' scores to the GSoBL. Additionally, the program used the testing data to develop its own pathway awards to keep students who are not quite at the level needed for a GSoBL motivated. Lauren has also leveraged the assessment data to apply for additional funding to expand the program to include endangered and Indigenous languages, increasing access to students throughout the region.

Unlike UW-CLP, the program at San Diego State University (SDSU) provides opportunities for students to obtain a GSoBL who are not registered in language coursework. As part of a grant from the California Department of Education's Multilingual California Initiative, faculty at SDSU launched their University Seal of Biliteracy and Cultural Competence (USBCC) in 2021. The USBCC, under the direction of its program director, Associate Vice President Cristina Alfaro, was created to value and honor the linguistic identity of students. As described in Chapter 5 of this text, the USBCC centers on language proficiency and cultural and linguistic immersion. The GSoBL and the requisite testing help SDSU students fulfill the language proficiency requirement. The cultural and linguistic immersion component can be fulfilled in several ways, including transborder courses, virtual coursework or internship in a country where the language is spoken, or by completing a department-based project focused on cultural context. The GSoBL is an ideal partner for USBCC because both seek to validate an individual's language skills no matter how those skills were acquired.

Whereas the UW-CLP and SDSU programs involve students enrolled at the institution, Metropolitan State University (MSU) has expanded GSoBL testing options to include faculty and staff. MSU is a Hispanic-serving institution in Denver, Colorado. Over the last few years, Maria Akrabova has worked to utilize the GSoBL to focus on three areas: language services, salary incentives, and continuing education. Regarding language services, various departments on campus utilize the GSoBL to understand the proficiency of their staff and determine what tasks individuals can complete in multiple languages to better support the campus community. When staff can prove their proficiency and take on more tasks, they are paid bonuses or receive a salary increase. The university also uses the GSoBL to support continuing education initiatives, providing opportunities for staff members to become official interpreters and translators, leading to salary incentives. More about this program can be found in Chapter 6 of this volume.

As described earlier in this chapter, Auburn University has also begun to award the GSoBL. Distinct from IHEs that only provide testing opportunities for students majoring or minoring in a language, Auburn provides testing opportunities to other students in their language programs. The university began by testing majors in the language department at the end of a program of study but recently expanded to include other students in language courses. As previously mentioned, Auburn tested all Spanish language students during the 2022–2023 academic year, allowing the department to gather useful data and award students not majoring in a language with a GSoBL. Since assessment is tied to the strategic goals of the institution, the department was able to secure internal grant funding to cover all testing.

Finally, the UTA hosts one of the most robust GSoBL programs. UTA originally started by offering testing for the eight languages taught in their department but recently opened testing to the entire campus community, expanding the number of languages tested to 46. Students pay for testing on their own through a store on the testing company's website. The university provides fee waivers for students with financial need, and some departments, such as International Business, pay for students to test. UTA also used the GSoBL to articulate pathways for incoming students. Students entering UTA with a GSoBL can advance place into upper-level courses, earn up to 14 credit hours for a nominal fee, and be within 3 courses of a minor upon completion of their first semester at the university. The pathways initiative provides the language department an opportunity to increase enrollment numbers in upper-level courses that can lead to an increase in the number of language minors and majors. The department did not need to make any policy or curricular changes to start the GSoBL initiative and create the pathways.

Two-year institution programs

Various two-year institutions have also implemented the GSoBL. San Diego Mesa College secured a grant to improve language instruction and focus on proficiency-based learning. As part of the grant, students taking Spanish at San Diego Mesa College are provided access to an external assessment. Several students in the Spanish program scored high enough to receive the GSoBL. San Diego Mesa College plans to expand testing for the GSoBL as part of a college-wide initiative to prepare students for the workforce.

Monica Torregrosa, professor of Spanish at Holyoke Community College in Massachusetts, began replacing her traditional final exam with an external language proficiency assessment in 2021. She did so to provide her students with the opportunity to obtain the GSoBL. Holyoke Community College has averaged around ten GSoBL recipients each year since beginning implementation. Students who have earned the GSoBL have gone on to four-year colleges or into the workforce.

Adult education and nontraditional student programs

In addition to IHEs, the GSoBL can also be awarded by other adult education and nontraditional student programs. For example, CodeDivision is a nonprofit entity based in Scotland that works to combat digital inequality by providing skills training to underserved communities. In 2023, CodeDivision ran a program called *Digital Empowerment* for displaced women from Ukraine who were living in Scotland. The purpose of the program was to provide refugees from Ukraine with the hard and soft skills and credentials to obtain gainful employment in Scotland. As part of the program, participants took an external English language assessment for the GSoBL. The tests were provided at no cost by the testing company. More than 75% of participants received the recognition, and several of the recipients were able to obtain gainful employment at the completion of the program.

Similar to CodeDivision, Amala Education uses the GSoBL to address inequity. With locations in Kenya and Jordan, Amala was launched in 2017 to address the gap in education for displaced youth aged 16 to 25. Many of these youth have their formal education interrupted due to war or other situations that cause them to have to flee their homes. To support students in their academic journeys, Amala began testing students in 2022 using tests donated by an external partner. Students in both Kenya and Jordan work to obtain the GSoBL and use the credential to continue their education after completing the Amala program.

Conclusion

In higher education, acknowledging and valuing students' multilingualism is paramount for fostering an inclusive and equitable learning environment. Recognizing the linguistic diversity within the student body not only enriches academic discourse but also promotes cultural understanding and empathy among peers (Mallinson, 2024). Embracing multilingualism at the higher ed level is essential for nurturing a global perspective and preparing students to navigate an interconnected world where linguistic versatility is an asset (Friedenberg, 2002).

The GSoBL is a tool that centers the importance of multilingualism and cultural appreciation in higher education and beyond. By encouraging individuals to maintain and celebrate their linguistic diversity, it promotes cultural awareness and understanding. The practical implications are manifold, as the recognition has the capacity to unlock doors for individuals in education and employment, presenting them as valuable assets in an increasingly globalized and interconnected world. Employers and universities have grown cognizant of the substantial advantages conferred by candidates proficient in multiple languages, recognizing their potential to foster international collaboration and cross-cultural communication.

Additionally, the GSoBL offers employers the opportunity to evaluate not only linguistic skills but also essential soft skills. Multilingual individuals often possess enhanced communication abilities, adaptability, and intercultural competence, which are highly coveted attributes in the modern workplace. Thus, the certification facilitates a more holistic assessment of a candidate's qualifications, extending beyond linguistic proficiency to encompass the broader skill set demanded in a globalized job market. Moreover, the GSoBL represents a valuable instrument for employers, enabling them to assess not only linguistic aptitude but also essential soft skills within the context of a globalized and interconnected world.

References

Commission on Language Learning. (2017, February). *America's languages: Investing in language education for the 21st century*. American Academy of Arts and Sciences. https://www.amacad.org/publication/americas-languages

American Councils for International Education. (2017). *The national K-12 foreign language enrollment survey report*. American Councils for International Education. https://www.americancouncils.org/sites/default/files/FLE-report-June17.pdf

Avant Assessment. (2023). *Avant STAMP annual averages 2022–2023*. Avant Assessment. https://cdnprodwpv2.avantassessment.com/wp-content/uploads/STAMP-2022_2023-National-Averages_FINAL.pdf

Brown, M., Nic Giolla Mhichíl, M., Beirne, E., & Mac Lochlainn, C. (2021). The global micro-credential landscape: Charting a new credential ecology for lifelong learning. *Journal of Learning for Development*, *8*(2), 228–254. https://doi.org/10.56059/jl4d.v8i2.525

Burner, T., Supinski, L., Zhu, S., Robinson, S., & Supinski, C. (2019). *The global skills shortage*. SHRM. https://www.shrm.org/content/dam/en/shrm/topics-tools/news/employee-relations/SHRM-Skills-Gap-2019.pdf

Davin, K.J., & Heineke, A.J. (2017). The Seal of Biliteracy: Variations in policy and outcomes. *Foreign Language Annals*, *50*(3), 486–499. https://doi.org/10.1111/flan.12279

Davin, K., & Heineke, A. (2022). *Promoting multilingualism in schools: A framework for implementing the Seal of Biliteracy*. ACTFL.

Davin, K.J., Heineke, A.J., & Hancock, C. (2022). The Seal of Biliteracy: A retrospective. *Foreign Language Annals*, 55(1), 10–34. http://doi.org/10.1111/flan.12596

Egnatz, L., & Santos, V. (2023). Expanding assessment options for learners and speakers of less commonly tested languages. *Journal of the National College Testing Association*, *6*(1), 1–25. https://ncta.memberclicks.net/assets/docs/JNCTA/04.14.23%20-%20NCTA%20Journal%20of%20Testing%20Vol%206%2C.pdf

European Commission. (2020). *European skills agenda for sustainable competitiveness, social fairness and resilience.* European Commission. https://ec.europa.eu/social/main.jsp?langId=en&catId=89&furtherNews=yes&newsId=9723

Eurostat. (2019). *Foreign language skills statistics.* https://ec.europa.eu/eurostat/statistics-explained/index.php?title=Foreign_language_skills_statistics

Eurostat. (2023). *Foreign language learning statistics.* https://ec.europa.eu/eurostat/statistics-explained/index.php?title=Foreign_language_learning_statistics

Fishman, B., Teasley, S., & Cederquist, S. (2018). *Micro-credentials as evidence of college readiness: Report of an NSF workshop.* https://deepblue.lib.umich.edu/handle/2027.42/143851?show=full

Friedenberg, J.E. (2002). The linguistic inaccessibility of U.S. Higher Education and the inherent inequity of U.S. IEPS: An argument for multilingual higher education. *Bilingual Research Journal, 26*(2), 309–326. https://doi.org/10.1080/15235882.2002.10668713

Kic-Drgas, J. (2018). Development of soft skills as a part of an LSP course. *E-Mentor, 2*(74), 27–36. https://doi.org/10.15219/em74.1349

Klein-Collins, R., & Shafenberg, K. (2023). When it's the learning that counts: Competency-based education and credit for prior learning for working learners. *New Directions for Adult and Continuing Education, 2023*(179), 41–52. https://doi.org/10.1002/ace.20501

Laker, D.R., & Powell, J.L. (2011). The differences between hard and soft skills and their relative impact on training transfer. *Human Resource Development Quarterly, 22*(1), 111–122. https://doi.org/10.1002/hrdq.20063

Lavrysh, Y. (2016). Soft skills acquisition through ESP classes at technical university. *The Journal of Teaching English for Specific and Academic Purposes, 4*(3), 517–525.

Looney, D., & Lusin, N. (2019). *Enrollments in languages other than English in United States institutions of higher education, summer 2016 and fall 2016: Final report.* Modern Language Association. https://www.mla.org/content/download/110154/file/2016-Enrollments-Final-Report.pdf

Lusin, N., Peterson, T., Sulewski, C., & Zafer, R. (2023). *Enrollments in languages other than English in US institutions of higher education, fall 2021.* Modern Language Association. https://www.mla.org/content/download/191324/file/Enrollments-in-Languages-Other-Than-English-in-US-Institutions-of-Higher-Education-Fall-2021.pdf

Mallinson, C. (2024). Linguistic variation and linguistic inclusion in the US educational context. *Annual Review of Linguistics, 10*(1), 37–57. https://doi.org/10.1146/annurev-linguistics-031120-121546

Mihaly, K., Arellano, B., & Prier, S. (2022). (rep.). *Biliteracy seals in a large urban district in New Mexico: Who earns them and how do they impact college outcomes?* U.S. Department of Education. https://ies.ed.gov/ncee/rel/Products/Region/southwest/Publication/100913.

Morgan, W.J., & Thompson, A.S. (2023). "My friend Travis says…": A look at enrollment trends in language classes in the United States. *Foreign Language Annals, 56*(2), 259–279. https://doi.org/10.1111/flan.12683

Olcott, D. (2021). Micro-credentials: A catalyst for strategic reset and change in U.S. higher education. *American Journal of Distance Education, 36*(1), 19–35. https://doi.org/10.1080/08923647.2021.1997537

Olsen, L. (2020). The history of the movement: Enacting the State Seal of Biliteracy in the state of California. In K. Davin & A. Heineke (eds.), *The Seal of Biliteracy: Case studies and considerations for policy implementation* (pp. 17–34). Information Age Publishing.

Seal of Biliteracy. (2024). *Steps to implement the Seal of Biliteracy.* https://sealofbiliteracy.org/steps

Shanahan, B.W., & Organ, J. (2022). Harnessing the benefits of micro credentials for Industry 4.0 and 5.0: Skills training and lifelong learning. *IFAC-PapersOnLine, 55*(39), 82–87. https://doi.org/10.1016/j.ifacol.2022.12.015

Subtirelu, N.C., Borowczyk, M., Thorson Hernandez, R., & Venezia, F. (2019). Recognizing whose bilingualism? A critical policy analysis of the Seal of Biliteracy. *The Modern Language Journal, 103*(2), 371–390. https://doi.org/10.1111/modl.12556

The Global Seal. (2024a). *Board of advisors.* https://theglobalseal.com/board-of-advisors

The Global Seal. (2024b). *State Seal of Biliteracy resources.* https://theglobalseal.com/state-resources

The Global Seal. (2024c). *Global Seal of Biliteracy test finder.* https://theglobalseal.com/qualified-tests#TestFinder

The Global Seal. (2024e). *Certifying language skills.* https://theglobalseal.com/the-global-seal

The Global Seal. (2024f). *How the Global Seal of Biliteracy tests were approved.* https://theglobalseal.com/test-selection

The Global Seal. (2024g). *Global Seal colleges and universities.* https://theglobalseal.com/higher-education

University of Texas at Arlington. (2024). *Chart your language pathway.* https://www.uta.edu/academics/schools-colleges/liberal-arts/departments/modern-languages/testing-and-student-resources/pathways

University of Wisconsin. (2024). *Collaborative language program.* https://www.wisconsin.edu/collaborative-language-program/

U.S. Department of State. (2024). *Foreign language training.* https://www.state.gov/foreign-language-training/

Wilkie, D. (2020, February 28). *Employers say students aren't learning soft skills in college.* Society for Human Resource Management. https://www.shrm.org/ResourcesAndTools/hr-topics/employee-relations/Pages/Employers-Say-Students-Arent-Learning-Soft-Skills-in-College.aspx

The Global Seal. (2024d). *ACTFL-scale levels of language proficiency.* https://theglobalseal.com/actfl-language-proficiency-levels

Oliver, B. (2019.). Micro-credentials: A learner value framework. *Journal of Teaching and Learning for Graduate Employability, 12*(1), 48–51. https://ojs.deakin.edu.au/index.php/jtlge/article/view/1456

PART II

Recognizing Students' Biliteracy in Higher Education

3

A CREATIVE AND COLLABORATIVE APPROACH TO INTRODUCING THE SEAL OF BILITERACY IN HIGHER EDUCATION

Case study and survey findings in Washington state

Michele Anciaux Aoki, Russell Hugo, and Bridget Yaden

Introduction

The state Seal of Biliteracy (SSoBL) policy passed in the state of Washington in 2014, three years after California passed the first SSoBL policy in 2011 (Davin & Heineke, 2017; Olsen, 2020). The goals of the policy in the state of Washington were to recognize public high school graduates who have satisfied graduation requirements in English and attained Intermediate-Mid proficiency in one or more world languages, including American Sign Language and Tribal languages (RCW 28A.300.575; WAC 392.410.350).

Situated in the Pacific Northwestern region of the United States, Washington is a diverse state serving approximately 130,000 kindergarten-through-grade-12 (K–12) students identified as English learners, referred to in the state and in this chapter by the more strengths-based term "multilingual learners" (Washington Office of Superintendent of Public Instruction [OSPI], 2024). The state is recognized as a leader in SoBL efforts nationwide, given their efforts to promote equity for multilingual learners and heritage language learners by committing to develop assessments in every language used by Washington students (Davin et al., 2022; Heineke & Davin, 2020).

To extend the recognition of bilingual and biliterate students beyond K–12 settings, two institutions of higher education (IHEs) in the state of Washington developed SoBL programs. The first was the Seattle campus of the University of Washington (UW), a large public institution with campuses in Bothell, Tacoma, and Seattle. The UW Language Learning Center (UW-LLC) offers the Global Seal of Biliteracy (GSoBL) through proficiency testing for languages not taught on campus. They also offer both the Washington SSoBL and the GSoBL through summer language programs for high school students and promote the implementation of the GSoBL in standard language programs at the institution. The second institution was Pacific Lutheran University (PLU), a small private college in Tacoma. In the 2021–2022 academic year, PLU piloted a homegrown SoBL program based on the Washington state high school model but expanded to recognize multiple tiers of proficiency for students. PLU also recognizes the SSoBL, as well as World Language Competency-Based Credits, for language placement purposes.

DOI: 10.4324/9781032667249-5

This chapter is divided into two parts. The first part describes how the two institutions designed and implemented the SoBL. The authors share innovations and findings based on these pilot projects at each institution. The second part presents the results of a survey administered to IHEs across the Pacific Northwest region. The goal of the survey was to study the interest in, awareness of, related needs, and possible implementations of language proficiency awards, specifically the SSoBL, GSoBL, or homegrown recognition models at their institutions. Implications from the case studies and survey results are shared, along with next steps and recommendations for any IHE that is interested in implementing a SoBL program.

SoBL implementation in Washington

Context: Language proficiency assessment

To understand SoBL implementation in Washington, one must understand the origins and characteristics of language proficiency assessment in the state, which became widespread before the SSoBL policy passed. The state of Washington has engaged in testing students' proficiency in languages other than English longer than most states. Since 2010, high school students have been able to earn from one to four high school credits for languages they use, regardless of where or how they learned them, by demonstrating their proficiency on state-recognized proficiency assessments (Washington OSPI, 2024b: competency-based credits). These credits also satisfy state college admissions requirements. Referred to as *World Language Competency-Based Credit Testing* (WAC 392.415.050), the program was a critical impetus for passing SoBL legislation in Washington state in 2014 and has provided a roadmap for advocating for a SoBL in higher education. Since 2015, following the SSoBL policy's creation, students who qualify for four competency-based credits in any language also satisfy the required level to be considered *proficient* for the SSoBL (i.e., Intermediate-Mid proficiency or higher on all test components according to the ACTFL Proficiency Guidelines (ACTFL, 2012)). Note that students can also qualify for the SSoBL using Advanced Placement (AP) and International Baccalaureate (IB) test results, but these tests are not used for competency-based credits.

Besides qualifying students for the SSoBL, competency-based credits are also useful for placing students at an appropriate level in language classes. For example, in Seattle Public Schools, students who have been participating in dual language immersion programs (e.g., learning literacy and content in Spanish, Japanese, or Mandarin Chinese alongside English) are able to complete competency-based credit testing at the end of eighth grade. With the state's competency-based credit policy, many of these young students can earn four high school credits, qualify as *proficient* for the SSoBL, and be placed into AP level 5 classes in high school.

As the demand for proficiency assessments for competency-based credit testing and the SSoBL has increased, testing companies have responded by offering lower-cost language proficiency assessments in even more languages. Washington's OSPI (2024b) provides a comprehensive list, as well as a process for adding new languages each year as new immigrant communities come to the state. In addition, Washington SSoBL policy (RCW 28A.300.575; WAC 392.410.350) has a special clause for Indigenous languages, which are also eligible for competency-based credits and the SSoBL. For these languages, tribal governments can determine the type of assessment and proficiency level for the student and language.

The process for high school students to complete language proficiency testing is well-developed. Since the launch of the competency-based credit policy over 13 years ago, thousands of students have tested and earned credits. But in addition to the high school students who are typically the target audience for this policy, the approved tests are appropriate for adults and college students, as well. Indeed, some of the most cost-effective tests (e.g., Avant Assessment's STAMP tests) are already being used at the UW and other universities for language placement and proficiency testing. In this way, the assessment results help language departments determine which level of language class is best for an incoming student.

What is lacking at Washington IHEs is a process for awarding students college credits based on competency-based credit testing or SSoBL for languages that do not have a College-Board developed AP or IB test. The GSoBL organization has recently reported that both the University of Texas in Arlington and the University of Idaho have begun offering up to 14 and 16 credit hours, respectively, based on students qualifying through proficiency assessments approved by the American Council on Education (ACE) or the GSoBL (Global Seal of Biliteracy, 2024a). In addition, several states, including Illinois, Minnesota, and Maine, have procedures in place to recognize SoBLs in areas such as admissions requirements, placements, credits, or scholarships (Davin & Heineke, 2017; Okraski et al., 2020). In Illinois, public colleges and universities must use the SSoBL for entrance requirements and establish criteria to grant course credit based on language course equivalencies (University of Illinois Office of the Registrar, n.d.).

Seal implementation at the University of Washington

The flagship university of the state, the UW, has three campuses: Seattle, Bothell, and Tacoma. In the 2023–2024 academic year, approximately 60,000 students were enrolled at the UW. More than 40 world languages are regularly taught on the Seattle campus, which is where most language testing occurs. The UW-LLC provides technological and pedagogical support for all languages taught on campus, in addition to collaborating with off-campus partners (e.g., non-governmental organizations, Indigenous language programs).

UW began supporting students to earn SoBLs in 2015 to recognize high school students in their Less Commonly Taught Languages (LCTL) summer programs. Since 2011, the UW-LLC has received federal grant funding to hold summer language programs for high school heritage language students. The primary program has been STARTALK for Russian heritage language learners and, more recently, GenCyber for Portuguese and Korean heritage language learners. Language proficiency testing has been a key part of these programs, offering an incentive for participating students to potentially earn the SSoBL and GSoBL, as well as competency-based high school credits. Pre- and post-program language proficiency testing has also served as a summative assessment and metric for program effectiveness.

In 2021, the UW-LLC also began to submit scores for the GSoBL to further recognize participants for their work and provide targets for continued language proficiency development. Most students earned the *Functional Fluency* GSoBL, but a number of them were able to attain the *Working Fluency* level (see Chapter 2). While the Washington SSoBL has a single proficiency target (i.e., Intermediate-Mid) and requires students to test for the SSoBL before high school graduation, the GSoBL has no time limit and offers proficiency pathway subawards, as well as three levels of awards. Participants in all the UW-LLC summer programs have responded very favorably to the GSoBL as an incentive and a formal recognition of their work.

Beyond these language programs for high school students, the UW-LLC also offers proficiency testing for students whose languages are not taught at the UW, also categorized as LCTLs. This testing allows students to meet the exit language requirement held by both the College of Arts and Sciences and the School of Social Work. Generally, these are students who met the UW admissions requirement for language based on having a home or heritage language other than English but had not completed competency-based credit testing during high school, so they did not have any language credits for their language posted on their high school transcript. (Note that the UW considers students with three high school credits of the same language to have met the exit language requirement without requiring further coursework or testing.)

Since 2022, when these LCTL students' test scores qualified them for the GSoBL, the UW-LLC has submitted their test results to the GSoBL, and students have received the GSoBL Certificate. To date, beyond the high school Russian and Portuguese STARTALK and Portuguese, Spanish, and Korean GenCyber participants, about 20 undergraduate students have earned the GSoBL for other languages, including Amharic, Czech, Nepali, Punjabi, Somali Maxaa, Samoan, and Tigrinya. The GSoBL is offered to further recognize and value multilingualism, particularly for heritage language users of LCTLs, which have traditionally been devalued in North America. Students have responded favorably to the additional credential and certificate.

Based on the positive response from students, the UW-LLC has been working with language departments to expand the offering of the GSoBL for proficiency testing for languages that are taught at UW. While faculty have generally been favorable to the idea, as the survey results indicate next, administrative concerns have slowed adoption.

One challenge is that most language proficiency testing coordination for languages taught at the UW are handled at the language program level, where staffing is limited and procedures vary. As of the winter quarter of 2024, the UW-LLC has begun to help with the administration of language testing for the Asian Languages and Literature Department, which includes languages such as Chinese (Mandarin), Hindi, Japanese, Korean, Vietnamese, and more, as well as the Spanish and Portuguese Department. Over time, the plan is for the UW-LLC to serve as the centralized language testing administrative unit for all language programs. One benefit of this change is that the new administrative system gives each student the option to opt-in for the GSoBL if they are taking a placement or proficiency test that is accepted by the GSoBL. While most UW language programs use the Avant STAMP 4S for placement and proficiency, some use the Avant PLACE test or a custom-built test, and the results from these latter tests would not qualify a student for the GSoBL. If students opt-in on the intake form and their results are sufficient, the UW-LLC will submit their results for the GSoBL on the student's behalf and distribute certificates and other swag, such as medals and stickers (as budgets allow), to the recipients.

The GSoBL is also a useful tool for communicating further language learning goals, as most students earn the *Functional Fluency* GSoBL and can next work toward attaining the *Working Fluency* GSoBL. Table 3.1 shows recommendations that have emerged from this initial SoBL implementation at the UW.

TABLE 3.1 Recommendations from SoBL implementation at the UW

1	Create a centralized administrative unit to facilitate language proficiency testing ordering, proctoring, and reporting. Allow students to easily opt-in to receive the GSoBL if they qualify. Make it clear to the students that there is no additional cost to them for this option.
2	Automatically send student proficiency assessment scores to GSoBL rather than showing students how to do it so that students can easily earn this additional recognition.
3	Whenever proficiency testing is occurring, use SoBLs as incentives for special language program participation (e.g., recruiting participants for summer programs).
4	Actively and regularly promote the GSoBL to students and faculty through workshops, posters, etc.
5	Work with the registrar to identify more students who are eligible for the GSoBL, particularly those who are not enrolled in language courses and who speak languages not taught at the institution.

Seal implementation at Pacific Lutheran University

Inspired by the success of the SSoBL program in Washington's K–12 schools, PLU faculty designed a pilot project for a homegrown SoBL. PLU offers four world languages for academic study: Chinese, French, Southern Lushootseed, and Spanish. The university serves just under 3,000 undergraduate students and 330 graduate students and celebrates an increasingly diverse student body that is made up of 48% students of color and 54% first-generation students. Of the overall student body, 78% of students come from Washington, and they reflect the diversity of the state (OSPI, 2024c). In terms of languages spoken at home, 8% of students speak Spanish, and 2% speak a language other than English or Spanish (including, in order of most to least number of speakers, Vietnamese, Korean, Ukrainian, and Russian). Although the registrar does not currently track information on students who arrive with an SSoBL, PLU has data and anecdotal evidence that incoming students are increasingly bilingual, providing an opportunity to celebrate linguistic assets beyond the four languages currently offered.

PLU received a small start-up grant from the Washington Association for Language Teaching (WAFLT) to help cover some costs of the pilot project, which centered on developing and implementing a SoBL program in this unique higher education setting. The pilot involved faculty from PLU's Language Resource Center who wanted to both elevate and encourage students' biliteracy development in their programs. During this pilot, the institution covered all costs of testing and the medallions. PLU recruited students by mailing invitations to all students currently enrolled in language courses, all students who live in the language residence hall, and all international students.

To promote SoBL efforts broadly across the campus, faculty hosted interest sessions for students to learn about the SoBL, explore the concept of language proficiency, and look at sample STAMP assessments. The interest sessions and flyers included an introduction to proficiency definitions and examples (ACTFL, 2017) to help students understand the proficiency levels that would subsequently determine their language proficiency and recognize their biliteracy competencies. This allowed students who had not recently or ever had academic study of the language, particularly multilingual learners and heritage language learners, to see themselves as active language learners engaged in the work of developing and maintaining biliteracy in their daily practice.

Additionally, PLU language faculty coordinated with the study abroad office. Because proficiency assessment is part of the university's predeparture and post-study processes, that office covered the costs of testing. Stakeholders recognized this as a built-in group of students from where to recruit, and they became the largest group to participate in the pilot.

A PLU student designed the seal, which resulted in a creative logo incorporating the school's rose window and themes of biliteracy (see https://www.plu.edu/lrc/). Faculty ordered medallions from a local trophy company in bulk, keeping costs low (approximately $10 each), with the expectation that the cost would continue to decrease since the cast for the medallion was kept for future reorders. Overall, PLU faculty found that a homegrown seal, which could be branded with the school logo and colors, had the added potential benefit of recruiting and retaining students, making them feel celebrated for their assets and part of the PLU multilingual community.

PLU's SoBL recognizes three tiers of proficiency, which allow for multiple entry points and encourage students to continue their path to proficiency to potentially earn a higher seal and/or seals in multiple languages. The PLU Silver SoBL requires Intermediate-Mid proficiency or higher on all test components, the Gold SoBL requires Intermediate-High, and the Platinum SoBL requires Advanced-Low or higher.

Following multiple testing sessions in the spring of 2022, PLU awarded 24 SoBLs. These included seven Silver, 14 Gold, and three Platinum in Chinese, French, and Spanish (all languages taught at PLU). Students were surveyed and generally reported that they felt prepared for the proficiency assessment and that they valued participating in the program. Sixty percent said they would or might be willing to pay a small fee ($20) to be part of a program like this in the future. Table 3.2 shows recommendations that emerged from the pilot project.

The experiences at PLU and UW of piloting the implementation of a SoBL program in two very different IHEs naturally raised questions about what other IHEs in the state might be doing to recognize students' language proficiency. This led the authors to develop a survey of other IHEs across the Pacific Northwest region.

TABLE 3.2 Recommendations from the pilot project at PLU

1 Coordinate with the study away office.
2 Provide proficiency workshops for students and faculty. This can lead to a positive washback effect on what happens in the classroom.
3 Work with the registrar to identify more students who are eligible for the SoBL, particularly those who are not enrolled in language courses and who speak languages not taught at the institution.
4 Automatically send student proficiency assessment scores to GSoBL rather than showing students how to do it so that students can earn this additional recognition.
5 Utilize the proficiency pathway subawards to recognize students who have not yet met the first level for the seal (Intermediate-Mid).

Regional survey about knowledge of SoBLs in IHEs

To better understand language educators' interest in and awareness of language proficiency awards at their institution, the authors administered the survey in the six states of the Pacific Northwest Council for Languages (PNCFL) region: Alaska, Idaho, Montana, Oregon, Washington, and Wyoming. The purpose of the survey was both to gather initial information about what people in higher education already knew about the SoBL initiative but also to educate and entice them to investigate what the SoBLs were about and engage them in the conversation about future options.

The survey, hosted by the UW and administered in spring 2023, was created using Google Forms following approval by the UW's Institutional Review Board for research. It began with a brief introduction to each state's SoBL and the GSoBL, including links to key documentation. The authors reached out to the appropriate personnel for each state's public education organizations, regional language education organizations (e.g., PNCFL, WAFLT), and other language advocacy organizations. They contacted language departments and faculty at multiple IHEs in each state about the survey. While the following sections contain the most pertinent results, more detailed data and figures can be found on the project website (Languages without Borders, 2024).

Thirty-six individuals responded to the survey. They taught a variety of languages, including Spanish (n = 9), French (n = 5), Russian (n = 4), Italian (n = 2), and German (n = 2). There was also one respondent for each of the following languages: (a) Bosnian, Croatian, Montenegrin, or Serbian; (b) Greek (ancient); (c) Hebrew (biblical); (d) Hebrew (modern); (e) Japanese; (f) Latin; (g) Persian; (h) Polish; and (i) Turkish.

Only two of the 36 respondents taught at private institutions; the other 34 taught in public institutions. The great majority of respondents were from Washington and Oregon, which are also the most populous states and have the highest number of IHEs in the PNCFL region. However, each state in the region, except Alaska, had at least one representative who participated in the survey: Washington (n = 19), Oregon (n = 13), Montana (n = 2), Wyoming (n = 2), and Idaho (n = 1).

In this section, we report survey findings. We begin by focusing on awareness of the SoBL, then move to discussing testing opportunities available to students at the institutions where respondents work. Next, we review respondents' valuation of the SoBL with respect to factors such as streamlining credentialing between institutions and incentivizing further learning. The section ends with an exploration of respondents' administrative concerns and support needs that must be addressed to optimally implement a SoBL program at their institution.

Awareness of the seals

Regarding awareness of the SoBL, results were mixed. Respondents rated their awareness on a scale of 1 (i.e., not at all familiar) to 5 (i.e., extremely familiar). Overall, awareness of SSoBL was slightly greater than that of GSoBL. About 50% of the 36 respondents were familiar with their state's SoBL, but almost 30% (n = 10) were not aware at all. The other 20% (n = 9) fell in between, reporting some familiarity with the SoBL. In contrast, when asked about the GSoBL, only around 20% (n = 9) were somewhat familiar with it, while more than 40% (n = 15) were not at all familiar with it. The other 40% (n = 10) reported some familiarity. Only one respondent was extremely familiar with GSoBL.

In addition to the SSoBL at the high school level, the GSoBL also offers pathway programs to benchmark students' proficiency levels over time (The Global Seal, 2024b). When asked about the GSoBL proficiency pathway awards (see Chapter 2), most respondents were unaware. This was not surprising because the pathway recognitions were only launched recently. Approximately 70% (n = 25) reported no awareness, and the other 30% (n = 11) reported some level of awareness.

Respondents were asked if they were aware of any students at their institution who had received a SoBL or proficiency pathway award, either before, during, or after taking their classes. Most respondents were aware of some instance of awarding, whether prior to coming to the IHE or in a class taught by the respondent. One respondent, who teaches at the high school level, shared that they mostly have "Spanish/Russian/South Pacific Island languages take the tests for Seal of Biliteracy. PRIMARILY [emphasis in original] for Competence (sic) Credit—which is a disappointing practice". Note that this concern likely refers to the perception that the awarding of competency-based credits can lead to lower enrollment in language classes.

Another respondent noted that while a SoBL has not yet been awarded in the language that they teach, they were directly involved in getting their "department/university to waive the language requirement for students who enrolled in the institution having been awarded a Seal of Biliteracy at the high school (or, less often, community college) level" and that currently, their institution only accepted their state's SoBL. Another respondent noted that their institution has had "students from Dual Language Immersion Programs ask about how their SoBL would get evaluated and if they can get college credits just for the seal". Yet, they were not certain about how many of these students enrolled in language courses at their institution, noting that sometimes students "switch to a new language in college".

Testing access

Another section of the survey asked respondents about language testing opportunities. In general, respondents reported that it was not common for students at their institutions to take formal or official proficiency tests. Of survey respondents, 27% (n = 10) reported no proficiency assessment whatsoever, 22% (n = 8) reported that proficiency assessments were rare, 30% (n = 11) reported proficiency assessment being somewhat common, 11% (n = 4) reported it was common, and another 11% (n = 4) reported it was extremely common. One respondent from the University of Oregon mentioned that they "did program-wide testing a few years ago using STAMP at U of O[regon] and over 200 students got Global Seals". However, the University of Oregon "did not have funding to continue providing STAMP tests at no cost [to students]" and thus has been unable to offer the GSoBL since.

Some institutions, such as the UW, have offered placement and proficiency testing using tests from various national testing companies (e.g., Avant STAMP 4S and STAMP WS, ALTA Language Testing, and Language Testing International OPI/OPIc and WPT) that were accepted as evidence for the GSoBL. In contexts like this, the test results are already serving another purpose, and there is no additional cost for awarding the GSoBL.

Perceived value of SoBLs

Respondents were asked to rate on a scale from 1 (i.e., no value at all) to 5 (i.e., a high degree of value) what value they saw in making pathway awards and the SoBL available in their language classrooms. Overall, the ratings skewed toward the positive, with 50% (n = 18) of respondents reporting SoBLs having a high degree of value and no one indicating it would have no value. This question was followed by an open-ended question that asked respondents to explain reasons for their value rating.

Most respondents saw SoBLs as a valuable tool for student motivation, and some reported that their students who had recently earned a SoBL were "very proud". One individual noted how their university seemed to increasingly disincentivize students from studying languages and how the SoBL could help incentivize "students to pursue language learning beyond the beginning level". Another respondent shared that their institution was "in the process of creating a credentialing program for language and intercultural competency. An existing program like Proficiency pathway awards might be an initial solution for us". Finally, others appreciated the equalizing opportunity for speakers of LCTLs and classical (i.e., dead) languages to earn the credentials.

Respondents also wrote about the value of the data associated with the assessments used for the SoBL. One noted how the SoBL could "help to make visible what functional command students are gaining in the language". Another shared that the SoBL was a means of demonstrating "language proficiency more holistically than simply by taking [just] one of the several ACTFL proficiency exams". Additionally, other comments mentioned how the credentials could streamline student progress tracking, program assessments, and even proficiency tests.

Administrative concerns

The survey also asked respondents about the challenges they foresaw, if any, for implementing language pathway awards and SoBLs in their postsecondary contexts. Themes in response to this question clustered around funding, signaling value, and enrollment.

The most reported theme was related to funding. Eight of 36 respondents expressed concerns about a lack of funding for testing, staff support hours, and even related physical artifacts (such as ribbons). The need for funding extended beyond the cost of proficiency assessments to also include human resources. One respondent reported a need for more language faculty to lay the foundation for successful testing in the future. Another wrote,

> We do NOT [emphasis in original] have the funds or the staffing to implement proficiency testing. It will never happen in public universities without the state government allocating sustainable funds for this, and I do not expect that to happen, ever.

Another individual noted that they did not rate the value of the SoBLs as a five even though they feel it has "great value" because of worries regarding "workload implications for faculty who are already overworked". This was particularly an issue for those who only have a small number of students who might potentially qualify, making the cost-benefit ratio less favorable from their perspective. In sum, as one respondent wrote, "Funding, funding, and more funding, also stop canceling language classes".

Others expressed concerns about the value of what the SoBL signals to nonlanguage specialists. For example, one person wrote that they felt that the awards were relatively redundant, stating that potential employers have other means of learning about an applicant's language proficiencies. Another explained that although they believe the SoBL is valuable for high school, they see the GSoBL and related awards as being less necessary at the college level "since we have minors, majors, and certificates already that allow for valuable qualifying certificates to graduates". Another expressed concern about the outcomes of earning an SSoBL and whether it had value outside the state of Washington, noting that it "must be useful to students".

Finally, one person described tension between colleagues in the higher education system in Oregon who preferred the official state seal. They were concerned that implementing a competing seal like the GSoBL might "muddy the waters". To sum up this theme, one respondent wrote,

> These awards, the whole "Academy Awards" phenomena permeating academe, are an attempt, doomed, sadly to say, to provide some sense of positive self-regard to youth who are finding it increasingly difficult to discover a true and genuine sense of self-worth.

They concluded by writing, "You are attempting to compete with social media and forces much larger than anything you can muster with an award. Good luck".

The last theme of these responses related to enrollment. One respondent explained that although "[i]t would be positive for students to have a credential on their record...this option might discourage students from doing a minor or major [in the target language]" and not furthering their proficiencies "...beyond what they learned as a heritage language". This individual was referring to the common fear that competency-based testing that results in credits being awarded and requirements satisfied may lead to a reduction in enrollments and the possible closing of language programs. Another noted their unease because "English is taking over the world–already has in large measure–and what it isn't dominating, AI is beginning to fill in and take over".

Requested support

Survey respondents reported that coordination and advocacy, particularly with state and IHE administrators, was important. When asked about how other organizations could best help them to promote and implement SoBLs in their programs, one individual suggested that organizations (e.g., PNCFL, WAFLT) could hold workshops to connect individuals "to those at the state level who are in charge of such programs". Another shared that "organizations could help us advocate for proficiency testing results to be documented on students' transcripts". This person explained that transcripts were "a place where that kind of information would suddenly gain real value and recognition". They expressed that "organizations could advocate for funding to conduct the testing, and we could build this into study abroad costs". Relatedly, a different respondent contributed that "[t]he higher education coordinating authority could establish a streamlined pathway for institutions and their language departments to apply for the authority to award SoB(L)". But this person also added, "With that said, I foresee that university language departments would be reluctant to deal with this if there's no clear way to differentiate from the SoBL awarded at the high school level". Another noted that they thought "it would be much better if the criteria were standardized across states, but that's unlikely".

Respondents reported a need for support related to information and promotion as well. One person indicated that simply sharing information between states in the region could be beneficial. They wrote, "It would be great to hear about how other states handle things like local coordination within districts—we are just starting out in Wyoming and don't yet have a well-established system". This person feared that they would "have a lot of kids falling through the cracks for a while, especially English Language Learners". Others wrote about the challenge of simply educating students about SoBL opportunities. They felt that organizations could also be especially helpful in developing promotional tools to inform students about these opportunities.

Discussion and implications

In this chapter, we shared the results of two separate but related research projects into SoBL implementation in IHEs in the Pacific Northwest. The first part of the chapter detailed two cases of IHEs who took unique approaches to recognizing students' biliteracy competencies via SoBL implementation. The second part of the chapter shared the results of a survey distributed to higher educators to understand their awareness and use of the SoBL in their contexts across the Pacific Northwest. Taken together, we can see both the promises of implementing the SoBL in higher education paired with the challenges that need to be tackled.

Administrative challenges pose a potential roadblock for implementing the types of programs described in this chapter. As Colomer and Chang-Bacon (2020) contend,

> Although the SoBL represents significant potential for recognizing the linguistic dexterity of multilingual students and the benefits of bilingualism writ large, the field must also be critical of the state's ability to codify biliteracy as something assessable and awardable in the first place.
>
> *(p. 387)*

The inequity of access in high school to SoBLs and proficiency testing for English language learners and heritage speakers is well-demonstrated (e.g., Davin et al., 2022; Heineke et al., 2018; Galbert & Woogen, 2021; Subtirelu et al., 2019). Without consistent and equitably distributed funding for these programs, there is a risk of increasing this problem in K–12 and duplicating it in higher education.

We can see how these challenges played out in the cases presented early in the chapter. While the UW's registrar has a rudimentary intake process to note whether a student has received an SSoBL (nothing to date for the GSoBL), the process is not well known or used beyond the initial admissions process. It appears that the UW language entrance requirement is satisfied by high school credits on the transcript, including the competency-based world language credits earned through language testing in high school, without referencing the annotation on the high school transcript that the student earned the SSoBL. Language departments and humanities advising at the UW currently have no formally approved processes for recognizing SoBLs for placement or college credit. In early 2022, a working group was formed among key language departments, advising groups, the UW-LLC, and the UW registrar to improve the systems for the intake, reporting, and recording of language proficiencies as well as for SSoBL or GSoBL attainment, but no formal changes had yet been recommended or implemented when this chapter was written in 2023. At this time, the only known UW organization that is actively engaged with the SoBL is the UW-LLC. Although the UW-LLC serves students across the entire university, it cannot dictate to specific language departments whether they participate in a SoBL program or not.

Opportunities

The SoBL movement has many implications for higher education. It is well-demonstrated in the literature that multilingual learners face considerable bias in higher education contexts (e.g., Wang et al., 2017). While more research is needed, programs like the SoBL could be a tool to provide external and institutional validation of their linguistic competencies, help promote understanding of linguistic diversity and bias across campus, and perhaps aid in identity (re)construction for students. Washington state is still in the very early stages of the SoBL, but we share several areas of opportunity drawn from the case studies and survey findings presented above.

One impact of the growth of SoBL and proficiency pathway subawards is the potential to enhance language education pathways between K–12 and higher education. While postsecondary world language programs still have a long way to go to become truly proficiency-based, SoBL programs can have a positive washback effect in that they can push programs in higher education to become more proficiency focused. These enhanced pathways could also yield clearer articulation between K–12 and higher education. The age-old question, "What do two years of high school language mean?" is easily answered if the goals are proficiency based. If students enter the university with an Intermediate-Mid proficiency level indicated by a high school SoBL, college programs that align with proficiency would have an easy placement process. Many chapters in this volume have provided examples of how IHE programs align with SoBL recognitions for placement and credit in college and university language study; readers can also learn about how PLU guides students to use the high school SoBL to articulate Spanish language coursework at the university (PLU, 2024).

Multilingual learners and heritage language learners may feel they are at a disadvantage entering college, but if they can go in with demonstrated recognition of their linguistic assets through a SoBL, that may give them the confidence and motivation to succeed academically (Davin et al., 2024; OneAmerica, 2018). Some high school students report their motivation to earn an SSoBL as being tied to their plans to continue their education at a college or university (e.g., Davin, 2021; Davin & Heineke, 2018). For people who use multiple languages, including international students, their multilingualism may be an important factor for describing who they are, as well as a valuable attribute for college and career success.

Research has also demonstrated that world language learners' efforts to learn a language and become bilingual can be validated as well (e.g., Davin et al., 2018; Subtirelu et al., 2019). Spanning multilingual, heritage language, and world language learners, these benefits must reach higher education. For example, the administrative processes for college language requirements could be streamlined if SoBLs were recognized more broadly. This would be a relatively simple administrative move to recognize students' assets to meet the kinds of university requirements that tend to be barriers to underrepresented students.

Conclusions and next steps

Although there has been more engagement in equity and inclusion in IHEs in terms of recognizing the linguistic assets within diverse student populations, considerable work remains (UW Linguistic Bias Working Group). Language educators can take small steps to get started and celebrate early accomplishments. Simply put, the benefits of SoBLs must reach higher education. With champions at state and national organizations, K–12 language educators and advocates can help expand SoBLs to IHEs. State organizations can be encouraged to offer workshops on SoBLs to language programs at their colleges and universities. Small grants could be utilized to kick-start programs by covering some assessment costs, as in the PLU model described earlier. While we recognize the important critiques of SoBLs and related programs with respect to complicated power dynamics (e.g., Subtirelu et al., 2019; Colomer & Chang-Bacon, 2020), if integrated with care and awareness, they could help to address some related inequity in higher ed contexts.

Following the lead of many of the authors and programs highlighted in this volume, institutions can begin by streamlining the administrative processes for the college language requirements by recognizing SoBLs more broadly. This would be a relatively simple administrative move to recognize students' assets to meet the kinds of university requirements that tend to be barriers to underrepresented students. An easy beginning move is to recognize and celebrate all entering students who have earned an SSoBL or GSoBL already. Another step is for institutions that currently do not have a SoBL program to shadow one that does. Educators and administrators in higher education can be inspired by the case studies described in this chapter and throughout this volume to take the next steps in recognizing the linguistic assets of all students and removing institutional barriers to student access and success.

References

ACTFL. (2017). *NCSSFL-ACTFL can-do statements*. https://www.actfl.org/educator-resources/ncssfl-actfl-can-do-statements

ACTFL. (2012). *ACTFL proficiency guidelines 2012*. https://www.actfl.org/educator-resources/actfl-proficiency-guidelines

Colomer, S.E., & Chang-Bacon, C.K. (2020). Seal of Biliteracy graduates get critical: Incorporating critical biliteracies in dual-language programs and beyond. *Journal of Adolescent & Adult Literacy*, *63*(4), 379–389. https://doi.org/10.1002/jaal.1017

Davin, K.J., Cruz, K.R., & Hancock, C.R. (2024). An examination of the postgraduation benefits of earning a Seal of Biliteracy. *Foreign Language Annals*, *57*(3), 634–653. https://doi.org/10.1111/flan.12753

Davin, K.J., Heineke, A.J., & Hancock, C. (2022). The Seal of Biliteracy: A 10-year retrospective. *Foreign Language Annals*, *55*(1), 10–34. https://doi.org/10.1111/flan.12596

Davin, K.J. (2021). Critical language testing: Factors influencing students' decisions to (not) pursue the Seal of Biliteracy. *Harvard Educational Review*, *91*(2), 179–203. https://doi.org/10.17763/1943-5045-91.2.179

Davin, K.J., & Heineke, A.J. (2018). The Seal of Biliteracy: Adding students' voices to the conversation. *Bilingual Research Journal*, *41*(3), 312–328. https://doi.org/10.1080/15235882.2018.1481896

Davin, K.J., Heineke, A.J., & Egnatz, L. (2018). The Seal of Biliteracy: Successes and challenges to implementation. *Foreign Language Annals*, *51*(2), 275–289. https://doi.org/10.1111/flan.12336

Davin, K.J., & Heineke, A.J. (2017). The Seal of Biliteracy: Variations in policy and outcomes. *Foreign Language Annals*, *50*, 486–499. https://doi.org/10.1111/flan.12279

Galbert, P.G., & Woogen, E. (2021). Barriers toward equity: Recognizing biliteracy of all students in Minnesota. *Foreign Language Annals*, *54*(3), 740–752. https://doi.org/10.1111/flan.12545
Global Seal of Biliteracy. (2024a). *College credit – Global seal of biliteracy*. https://theglobalseal.com/college-credit
Global Seal of Biliteracy. (2024b). *Global seal of biliteracy*. https://theglobalseal.com/
Heineke, A.J., & Davin, K.J. (2020). Prioritizing multilingualism in U.S. schools: States' policy journeys to enact the Seal of Biliteracy. *Educational Policy*, *34*(4), 619–643. https://doi.org/10.1177/0895904818802209
Heineke, A.J., Davin, K.J., & Bedford, A. (2018). The Seal of Biliteracy: Considering equity and access for English learners. *Education Policy Analysis Archives*, *26*, 99. https://doi.org/10.14507/epaa.26.3825
Languages without Borders. (2024). Retrieved March 10, 2024, from https://depts.washington.edu/lwbp/research/global_seal_in_higher_ed.php
Okraski, C.V., Hancock, C.R., & Davin, K.J. (2020). An innovative approach to the Seal of Biliteracy in Minnesota. In A.J. Heineke & K.J. Davin (Eds.), *The Seal of Biliteracy: Case studies and considerations for policy implementation* (pp. 67–84). Information Age Publishing.
OneAmerica. (2018, July 21). *Speak your language: Celebrating the power of bilingualism*. https://weareoneamerica.org/resource/speak-your-language-celebrating-the-power-of-bilingualism/
Olsen, L. (2020). The history of the movement: Enacting the State Seal of Biliteracy in the state of California. In A.J. Heineke & K.J. Davin (Eds.), *The Seal of Biliteracy: Case studies and considerations for policy implementation* (pp. 17–34). Information Age Publishing.
Washington Office of Superintendent of Public Instruction [OSPI]. (2024). *Competency-based credits*. https://ospi.k12.wa.us/student-success/resources-subject-area/world-languages/world-language-competency-based-credits/competency-testing-process-districts
Washington OSPI. (2024b). *World language proficiency assessment options*. https://www.k12.wa.us/student-success/resources-subject-area/world-languages/world-language-proficiency-assessment-options
Washington OSPI. (2024c). *Washington state report card*. https://washingtonstatereportcard.ospi.k12.wa.us/ReportCard/ViewSchoolOrDistrict/103300
Pacific Lutheran University. (2024). *Language placement*. https://www.plu.edu/lrc/language-placement-guide/#spanish
Subtirelu, N.C., Borowczyk, M., Hernández, R.T., & Venezia, F. (2019). Recognizing *whose* bilingualism? A critical policy analysis of the Seal of Biliteracy. *The Modern Language Journal*, *103*(2), 371–390. https://doi.org/10.1111/modl.12556
University of Illinois Office of the Registrar. (n.d.) *Credit for State Seal of Biliteracy*. https://registrar.illinois.edu/academic-records/credit-for-state-seal-of-biliteracy/
UW Linguistic Bias Working Group. (n.d.). *Linguistic bias working group*. https://depts.washington.edu/lxbias/
Wang, I.-C., Ahn, J.N., Kim, H.J., & Lin-Siegler, X. (2017). Why do international students avoid communicating with Americans? *Journal of International Students*, *7*(3), 555–582. https://doi.org/10.5281/zenodo.570023

4

INTEGRATING THE STATE SEAL OF BILITERACY INTO POSTSECONDARY STUDIES IN OREGON

A practical model

Cecelia Monto

> "I never considered my Spanish as an asset. But when I took the Spanish for Native Speakers class and...passed the test, I realized how important it could be for my future".
>
> (Leo, Chemeketa Community College student and now bilingual teacher)

Introduction

Expansion of state Seal of Biliteracy (SSoBL) programming into higher education is important because many students miss the opportunity to study and receive the credential in high school. Currently, SSoBL programs are offered almost exclusively in high schools, but the number of high school students obtaining an SSoBL remains a relatively small percentage of the secondary school population (Davin et al., 2022; Schwedhelm & King, 2020). Because SSoBLs are often awarded through Advanced Placement (AP) and International Baccalaureate (IB) programs and students of color are less likely to enroll and benefit from such programs (Kanno & Kangas, 2014), research has documented a gap in access to SSoBLs between privileged and marginalized students (Cervantes-Soon et al., 2017; Colomer & Chang-Bacon, 2020; Subtirelu et al., 2019). In existing high school programs, economically resourced, English-dominant students often have greater access to this recognition (Borowczyk, 2020; Kolluri, 2018).

Although the SSoBL remains valuable at the high school level, this chapter seeks to highlight the impact of expanding access to the credential at institutions of higher education (IHEs) to reinforce and amplify the value of SSoBLs in every educational setting. Expanding the opportunity to study languages and receive the SSoBL at IHEs could reach underserved students who lacked access in high school and therefore contribute to interrupting the cycle of advantage for privileged students (Subtirelu et al., 2019). Such expansion also has the potential to strengthen the credential's value through improved alignment and articulation between higher education and high school and may encourage participation in language study for students in both high school and IHEs (Salavert & Szalkiewicz, 2020). Therefore, many underserved students moving into higher education could benefit from expanded

DOI: 10.4324/9781032667249-6

access to the credential. In addition to expanding access and encouraging students' language development, a postsecondary SSoBL credential can have a positive effect on students' cultural identity and pride (Chang-Bacon et al., 2022).

In the paragraphs that follow, I describe how a community college SSoBL program serves linguistically diverse students who have been traditionally marginalized by the education system. Among the community college students served by this program, over 90% of those who enrolled in the coursework linked to the SSoBL were of Hispanic descent and had some level of heritage language experience. Because serving students from culturally and linguistically diverse backgrounds has been a critical focus of SSoBL programs (Heineke & Davin, 2020), culturally responsive program design and delivery was an essential aspect of program development (Gay, 2002). Topics that addressed cultural identity and pride were woven into course content in this program model and are described later in this chapter. By integrating cultural awareness and pride into language learning, the program had a broader impact on the student experience beyond language mastery. Essays written in the classes documented the important revelations students had regarding previous language shame and subsequent affirmation of both language and cultural heritage (Monto & Diaz Romero Paz, 2023). The impact provided a positive affirmation for students as they reclaimed their heritage language.

To share these findings, I begin with a description of the initial investigation taken to create a postsecondary program that integrated the existing SSoBL into college language department studies. I provide the details of the program model that we implemented at our community college in the Pacific Northwest region of the United States to provide a starting point for other colleges and universities interested in following a similar process. To provide guidance, the chapter (a) summarizes administrative procedures, (b) outlines supporting curriculum and coursework, (c) gives information about the student experience, (e) explains academic challenges presented by the model, (f) describes collaborative efforts across educational institutions, and (g) presents examples of the connections between the SSoBL credential and specific academic programs and careers. The chapter concludes with ideas for future work.

The setting and focal program

The SSoBL program model shared in this chapter was operationalized at Chemeketa Community College in Salem, Oregon, starting in the fall of 2018. Community colleges traditionally serve a large population of nontraditional and diverse students (Dougherty & Townsend, 2006), which makes them good venues for initiating SSoBL programs. In this regional setting, there was a high percentage of Spanish speakers in the community, and Chemeketa Community College was a designated Hispanic-serving institution (HSI). Therefore, we chose to develop the SSoBL program model in Spanish.

Chemeketa had an active teacher education program with faculty and leadership consistently focused on increasing the region's bilingual teaching workforce. Therefore, we designed the SSoBL to link to the academic pathway of teacher education; however, similar SSoBL projects could be linked to other academic discipline areas, such as health care, criminal justice, business, and other areas. In our case, we initiated the SSoBL program after the college dean observed that no students engaged in our Bilingual Student Teacher Leader Program had earned the SSoBL in high school despite the high level of language proficiency they demonstrated. We therefore based the program model on the potential benefits posed by the integration of an SSoBL into higher education for these bilingual students and the need for bilingual teachers in the school districts where they would be employed. The model described in this chapter also received the support of private grant funds from the Meyer Memorial Trust, which included funding for a specialized department technician, tuition supplements for students, testing costs, and the publication of a related book *Viviendo en Dos Lenguas/ Living in Two Languages* (Monto & Diaz Romero Paz, 2023).

The Chemeketa Languages Department sponsored the program model, which was founded on an existing 200-level course sequence that was designed for Spanish heritage speakers. We adapted the course curriculum to reflect the academic content aligned with the SSoBL in Spanish and ACTFL language proficiency levels (ACTFL, 2012). The college awarded a stipend to faculty teaching the courses to cover the efforts of adapting course content. As part of the curriculum redesign, we changed the course titles from Spanish for Native Speakers to Spanish for Heritage Speakers. The title and content changes moved through the regular college curriculum development process, with changes approved and reflected in subsequent course catalogs. Courses were launched in the fall of 2018.

In the five-year period between the fall term of 2018, when the program was initiated, and the summer of 2023, the program generated a total of 358 enrollments in a three-part sequence of Spanish for Heritage Speakers courses related to the SSoBL and served 342 unique students. Of the 342 unique students, 270 took courses that qualified them to take a test for the credential. The additional 72 students enrolled in the preliminary course, which did not include a testing option due to the level of instruction. Of the 270 students who enrolled and were eligible to participate in testing for the SSoBL, 147 students (54%) took and passed the exam, 10 students (4%) took but did not pass the exam, and 113 (42%) did not take the exam.

Administrative procedures supporting a postsecondary SSoBL program

To create a design for the SSoBL academic program at this community college, the first step in the process was to investigate the possibility of expansion into higher education with the Oregon Department of Education's Office of Equity, Diversity, and Inclusion, the office that administered the SSoBL in the state. Because SSoBL policy has emerged via grassroots initiatives across the United States and varies from state to state (Davin et al., 2022), each state has its own agency that issues the credential. However, linkage to the credentialing agency is an important foundational step for any institution considering implementation.

In our context, the Chemeketa department technician initially worked with the Department of Education to review state standards and assessments already approved to assess language proficiency for the SSoBL. Qualified staff from Chemeketa's Languages Department compared the academic content of their courses to the language proficiency levels outlined in the existing Oregon SSoBL framework, using ACTFL standards as a baseline. The bilingual department technician further examined language proficiency goals by reviewing the assessments used in high school SSoBL programs and took several exams himself to gain a full understanding. The technician also evaluated testing options based on how the tests were administered, their cost, and timelines. In the model created at Chemeketa, we selected the Avant STAMP 4S exam as the testing mechanism because the assessment offered online and affordable options with testing dates that could be adapted to college term dates, as well as transcribing and graduation time lines. Once the test was selected, a group of 14 college faculty, staff, and students in the Bilingual Student Teacher Leader Program took the exam as pilot testers to gain more understanding and experience with it.

Because offering the credential at an IHE was a shift in policy from the traditional focus on high school, the department technician and dean worked with the administration at the Oregon Department of Education to examine administrative rules in the state regarding the SSoBL. Chemeketa administrators presented documentation to state officials showing the alignment of coursework and academic standards. Those officials decided to adjust the Oregon Administrative Rules (OARS) to accept SSoBL program expansion beyond high school and into the postsecondary environment. The example of Oregon's ability to expand an SSoBL option into higher education could provide evidence and rationale for other states seeking postsecondary program development and implementation.

Once communication and overall alignment with the Oregon State Department of Education was established, the college undertook three key areas of project development in the implementation process of the SSoBL program. First, Chemeketa leaders collaborated to create a college-based academic infrastructure and record-keeping procedure for the SSoBL program. Second, faculty worked to academically align culturally relevant coursework and testing to complement existing SSoBL standards. Third, the SSoBL program team sought to disseminate information to students and other stakeholders, as well as initiate collaboration around these efforts with peer IHEs. I discuss each of these integral implementation steps in the following section.

Building infrastructure and procedures

Collaboration between the dean and internal departments at the college was necessary to establish academic infrastructure and methods of record-keeping to officially recognize the credential. An internal process to share information was created between the Languages Department, the College Testing Center, the Registrar's Office, and the Graduation Office. The testing center facilitated both in-person and online testing for the program. The dean worked with the Registrar's Office to record the SSoBL as a notation on student transcripts, which required sharing student names following the examination process. To embed the notation on the transcript, the college linked the notation to at least one of the Spanish for Heritage Speakers courses, which included SSoBL testing at the end of the second and third classes in the sequence. Transcript notation was a critical step that gave the student a permanent record of the SSoBL. Therefore, this program required students to enroll in at least one class related to the SSoBL and did not offer stand-alone testing. The dean also worked with the College Graduation Office to include notation of the SSoBL on student diplomas, which was an added point of pride and achievement for students.

Another administrative aspect that had to be considered was ensuring that data reporting aligned with the Family Educational Rights and Protection Act (FERPA). Because the Oregon Department of Education is considered an external organization, the college had to establish record-keeping guidelines to share student information in line with FERPA rules and state data collection procedures. To accomplish this, student grades were not shared with the state; however, test scores, ethnicity data, and student names required for state record-keeping were shared as a packet of information. Names were included because the Oregon Department of Education issued hard-copy certificates to individual students. Addresses were not shared, and certificates were mailed by the college. Because this program was initially funded through a private grant, data on student ethnicity and academic majors were shared in annual grant reports, although names were not shared with the funder. These tasks required additional attention to information-sharing procedures and FERPA regulations. Participating students had to sign FERPA documents prior to test taking, which presented a barrier in the testing process because some students did not take the time to complete the form, and the college could therefore not release their information to formalize the credential. Faculty are currently considering making the FERPA document into a formal assignment with points to improve completion.

Supporting curriculum and coursework

SSoBL implementation prompted revision of the existing curriculum. Because this SSoBL program model was directly linked to course enrollment at the college, curricular revision and adaptation of a three-part course sequence entitled Spanish for Heritage Speakers provided a foundation for initial program development. And because this program served the regional Hispanic community population, this model reflected local demographics.

Curricular redevelopment emphasized culturally responsive coursework (Gay, 2002) that centered around students' lived experiences and maintained relevance to future career pathways and functions. Course revisions highlighted real-world language and communication patterns for students. As the curriculum revisions evolved, authentic content emerged related to social issues that contextualized grammar and vocabulary, which faculty saw as consistent with best practices as recommended by researchers (Glisan & Donato, 2017; Leeman, 2005). And although enrollment was not based on ethnicity, the content and emphasis of the coursework especially welcomed linguistically diverse students with heritage language experience, encouraging enrollment of students of Hispanic descent.

The Spanish for Heritage Speakers sequence of classes also recognized that language fluency is diverse and runs along a continuum (Carreira et al., 2020; Moreno, 2021). Therefore, the course sequence allowed for various entrance points to the program, which gave students the ability to tailor course enrollment to their proficiency level. As part of the program, we created a placement test that facilitated proper placement, and students were not encouraged to take more coursework than necessary unless their financial aid allowed it. Because financial aid has been traditionally finite and language courses have not typically been part of the required general education baccalaureate core in this state, minimizing the credits needed to obtain the SSoBL was an important issue to consider (Davin et al., 2024). Reducing credit accumulation of courses not required for graduation can be an unseen equity issue for less-resourced students who depend on financial aid.

The first course in the Spanish for Heritage Speakers series prioritized written grammar and spelling needs because heritage speakers often have adequate oral experience but may lack confidence in writing depending on their experience with the language (Tallon, 2011). Although grammar has been described as inappropriate for heritage language students (Leeman, 2005), covering grammatical content in the class was important for student success in the SSoBL examination. In the course series redesign, instructors framed vocabulary and grammar within real-world course topics, such as physical and mental health, climate change, and political issues, which may have mitigated the superficiality that is sometimes part of grammar instruction. In the first class of the series, the official SSoBL exam was not offered.

The second and third courses in the series prioritized the use of language to discuss current events, such as the environment and social movements and their linkage to students' lives. Students regularly remarked that the topics felt relevant and adult, and this relevance reinforced their confidence to relate the language to their lives. To promote this linkage, the course began to require a significant personal reflective essay assignment that incorporated these topics. In this way, highly relatable instructional materials reinforced both language mastery and student confidence and identity building. As instructors developed more advanced coursework, the idea of elevating student experience and voice into a written publication emerged. To honor student voices, an anthology of student essays was compiled and published by the Chemeketa Press entitled *Viviendo en Dos Lenguas/Living in Two Languages* (Monto & Diaz Romero Paz, 2023). The book was funded by the grantor as an additional part of program development. Publication further strengthened student pride.

Both the second and third courses embedded the official SSoBL assessment into the final exam. The cost of the assessment was covered through grant funding. However, even with the embedded test and removal of the financial barrier, 42% of students elected not to take the formal examination and thus forfeited their opportunity to receive the SSoBL in the five-year period between 2018 and 2023. Future work around testing barriers is needed and will be discussed later in this chapter.

Disseminating information to students and stakeholders

Beyond the program-building at Chemeketa Community College, the project also fostered collaboration across the K–16 educational landscape to solidify the alignment of academic standards and improve cross-institutional recognition of the SSoBL. This collaborative work included sharing information regarding assessments, coursework, transferability, and implementation strategies of the SSoBL at other IHEs, with the overarching goal of greater coherence and consistency in SSoBL programs. In this case, the grant provided support for outreach and meetings, and this was part of the department technicians' role in the project.

Student experience and institutional impacts

The program impacted both students and the academic institution in mostly positive ways and held clear potential for expanded applications of the SSoBL in higher education and society in general. To analyze the impact, the college gathered institutional research related to the program and surveyed participating students to gain insight into their experience. Institutional impact was also documented via the measurement of enrollment increases and the advancement of overarching college goals. Together, these data sources provided a humanized perspective of the model described in this chapter and illuminated the various impacts the program had, including (a) positive identity building and cultural pride, (b) enrollment increases, (c) relevant linkage between language learning and majors, and (d) support for college goals related to HSI status.

Positive identity building and cultural pride

As previously discussed, a culturally responsive practice that links students' lived experience to coursework was a central element of Chemeketa's program. Students regularly commented that the course themes and content were meaningful and reinforced the importance of the language and pride in cultural heritage. In their classes, students examined oppression and inequities surrounding their language losses, and their essays revealed both sadness and pride as they reclaimed their heritage language and identity. Because heritage language students have often experienced a lack of confidence in using the language, a culturally responsive approach to the course content emerged as important. Literature in the field (Castro, 2020; Howlett & Davis, 2018) has been consistent with findings from this program that demonstrate positive identity building for heritage language speakers engaged in SSoBL programs.

In addition to these qualitative findings, survey results from the 2020 class (n = 12) indicated that students experienced a boost in pride and identity around their heritage and bilingualism. One student commented on the survey, "The class impacted my identity as a Spanish speaker in a positive way" and "made me remember where I come from and that I should be proud to speak in this beautiful language". Another wrote, "(The class) helped me look deeper into the richness of the language and made me appreciate my knowledge and share how proud I am to speak it". Another explained that the class "increased (her) ability to communicate in Spanish and my confidence to use the language". These comments suggest that acknowledging the linguistic assets of heritage language speakers built positive identity and confidence (Davin & Heineke, 2018; Hancock & Davin, 2020).

Increased enrollment

Program revisions and SSoBL implementation also corresponded to an increase in enrollment in the Spanish for Heritage Speakers classes. Enrollment data during the five years of program implementation showed a yield of 358 separate enrollments serving 342 unique students in these courses. In the two years prior to the implementation of the SSoBL and revision of the Spanish for Heritage Speakers (which was entitled Spanish for Native Speakers at that time), the courses were consistently canceled due to low enrollment. This type of enrollment boost could be very helpful in stemming recent postsecondary language enrollment declines (Lusin et al., 2023).

The instructor of the courses also reported that students who enrolled became motivated to continue their language studies when they re-engaged with their heritage language in a positive way. The professor noted that students expressed interest in continued study not only at the community college but for future transfer studies also, aligning with existing research findings (Davin et al., 2018; Howlett & Davis, 2018). The instructor's comment about motivation was also reflected in the summer 2020 survey, where 83% of students responded that they were "very likely" to continue language study. Based on these student responses and the documented enrollment increases, language courses that integrate the SSoBL may have the additional benefit of supporting enrollment in higher level language study, which could in turn reinvigorate enrollments in upper division language courses.

Relevant linkage between language learning and majors

The Chemeketa program created a meaningful connection between the SSoBL and the teacher education academic pathway. We designed the linkage to specifically address the hiring needs of future employers and the community needs of the region. In this case, the program was instrumental in recruiting bilingual students into teaching and supporting efforts to diversify the teaching workforce because the SSoBL coursework was aligned with the overall teacher education transfer degree and Bilingual Student Teacher Leader Program. The linkage created clear relevance between language study and career goals, and thus motivated students. By making this connection between career and language, the program demonstrated the potential for linkage to other career fields.

This linkage also supported efforts to gain additional recognition for the credential through the state teacher licensing agency, the Oregon Teacher Standards and Practices Commission (TSPC). In June 2022, TSPC formally recognized the SSoBL in Spanish to satisfy the Dual Language Specialization (OTSPC, 2022). This formal recognition allows SSoBL recipients a credible asset for their future careers as teachers and assists school districts in vetting future bilingual employees. Increasing the bilingual teaching workforce has been an ongoing challenge for school districts across the nation (Monto, 2021), and SSoBLs offer a promising structure to support this work.

Support of college goals related to HSI status

In addition to supporting enrollment for postsecondary language departments, the demographic profile of students engaged in courses related to the SSoBL served Chemeketa Community College goals around attaining and maintaining status as an HSI. As noted earlier, institutional data showed that over 90% of students ($n = 342$) enrolled in courses leading to the SSoBL were Hispanic. This figure can be compared with an overall college percentage of 26.8% Hispanic students. Chemeketa attained HSI status in 2017, and this program directly corresponded with college enrollment goals and practices related to that designation. As other colleges and universities consider introducing programs with SSoBLs, alignment with campus-wide initiatives such as HSI and Minority Serving Institution (MSI) status could be an important consideration.

Academic challenges in the program

In addition to the beneficial outcomes for students and the institution, program implementation also revealed challenges and areas for improvement. Despite program efforts, language proficiency assessments created barriers for students that remained persistent. Additional challenges centered around maintaining academic standards across numerous credentialing institutions and consistency issues related to the emergence of a competing private postsecondary certificate that held lower academic standards than the official SSoBL in Oregon.

Testing barriers

Data collected over the five-year period from college records revealed a testing barrier. Of the 270 students who enrolled in courses and qualified to take the assessment for the credential between 2018 and 2023, only 157 students (58%) took the test, although all but one who took the assessment passed. This meant that 42% of students ($n = 113$) elected not to take the exam, even though testing was integrated into the course and offered at no additional cost. The five-year data between 2018 and 2023 were worse than the initial data collected during the first two years (2018–2020, $n = 111$), which revealed that 83% of students took the assessment. However, the five-year data set reflected that COVID disruptions severely impacted students and complicated testing processes in general, which may have increased overall testing barriers.

Although testing challenges have emerged as an area requiring attention, the aversion to the test and subsequent forfeiture of the SSoBL credential is surprising because students consistently remarked that the credential was a motivating force in their enrollment. For example, student survey data collected from the summer 2020 survey showed that 100% of the students knew the class included the exam, and 90% noted that the assessment and credential motivated them to enroll. Additionally, data from both the five-year time period and the two-year time period demonstrated that students who took the test were well prepared and successful. The five-year data revealed a 93.6% pass rate. Only 10 of the 158 students (6%) who took the exam did not pass. In the earlier 2018–2020 data set, results showed that 92.3% of the 111 students who took the assessment passed.

Based on these data, the testing barrier seemed to originate from the assessment process or structure rather than a lack of confidence or mastery of language skills. In this program model, the testing process was a formalized exam given on the computer, which lacked personal connection and flexibility and reinforced a high-stress environment. High-stakes standardized testing often creates barriers and anxiety for students (Davin, 2021; Schwedhelm & King, 2020), and this fact appears to be reflected in the implementation model presented here. Greater programmatic support is needed for students, especially prior to the test, or alternative assessment methods could be explored. Assessment remains an essential component of SSoBL credentialing (Borowczyk, 2020), and improving testing methods would likely improve student participation and outcomes in postsecondary SSoBL programs.

Inconsistent recognition of the SSoBL in transfer and career pursuits

Inconsistent recognition of the SSoBL in higher education settings also emerged as an important concern in implementation. This inconsistency has created confusion surrounding the meaning of the state credential in relation to a newly created private certificate called the *Global Seal of Biliteracy* (GSoBL). Promotion and recognition of the SSoBL are common conundrums (Borowczyk, 2020; Davin & Heineke, 2022) and are not unique to implementation in this state. However, the disparity of recognition and acknowledgment undermines the validity of the SSoBL as a credential in postsecondary academics and in the workplace. In Oregon, where this project occurred, the SSoBL academic recognition for transfer from community colleges or high schools to universities varied from complete replacement credit for the third-year Spanish language requirement at one university to no credit replacement at another.

Additional confusion arose from cross-institutional collaborative discussions regarding the private GSoBL and its relation to the public SSoBL. The GSoBL offers three levels of distinction, with the lowest being *Functional Fluency* (see Chapter 2), which requires a minimum level of proficiency that aligns with Intermediate Mid on the ACTFL proficiency scale (ACTFL, 2012). In Oregon, the SSoBL has more rigorous standards than the GSoBL, with a minimum requirement of Intermediate High (ODE, 2014). Because the SSoBLs were the standard award to high school students while the GSoBL was more often used at universities, this discrepancy was confusing for many. Although the GSoBL has two higher tiers of distinction, the lack of alignment and differing academic standards represented in competing certificates created confusion at postsecondary institutions in this state and impeded consistent recognition of the SSoBL for transfer and use as replacement credits.

During the cross-institution collaboration process in Oregon, it also became evident that some universities adopted the GSoBL instead of the official SSoBL because they assumed the SSoBL was not available in higher education. As part of this implementation project, Chemeketa Community College facilitated conversations with other higher education peers to examine these issues and to demonstrate that the SSoBL was an option. The Oregon Department of Education also convened workgroups to address the disparities between the two seals and to discuss academic standards and content and included both higher education language departments and high school programs. These collaborations have been a promising start toward improved academic alignment and are a recommended element for the future implementation of SSoBLs into postsecondary education.

Implications

Implications from this work cluster around (a) alleviating testing barriers for students, (b) developing greater linkages between the credential and specific academic pathways, and (c) continuously improving academic alignment related to proficiency standards.

Alleviating testing barriers

The development of alternative SSoBL assessment strategies based more on authentic language mastery instead of standardized testing practices could improve rates of credential attainment for students (Siordia & Kim, 2022; Subtirelu et al., 2019). Instructors must understand the barriers and find ways to assess language proficiency in a more culturally appropriate way. Remaking assessments or creating new evaluation tools that uphold rigor and honor students' language capacity is a critical area for future work as SSoBL programs expand into higher education.

Linking credentials and academic pathways

The linkage between biliteracy credentials and specific academic and career pathways holds positive potential for developing SSoBL programs that meet community and workforce needs. These linkages affirm language relevancy in relation to career connection. The program model described in this chapter linked the SSoBL with the specific academic and career pathway of teacher education, with the intent of increasing the number of bilingual teachers in the region. Additional connections to specific pathways of study in health care, social work, law enforcement, business, and other academic areas could also provide motivation and relevance for higher level language study. Thus, SSoBL programs in higher education should build connections between the credential and specific academic programs of study.

In addition to connections made to academic subject areas, linkage and recognition that results in salary increases in these career fields would further validate the credential post-graduation. Academic institutions can highlight the SSoBL as a complement to numerous degrees and as a method of improving hireability and increasing pay rates. The Chemeketa model demonstrates that the SSoBL can be used in professional credentialing systems such as teacher licensures. This linkage would serve employers by providing credible vetting of the language proficiency of future employees. In these ways, operationalizing the SSoBL in higher education venues is a promising direction for colleges and universities with implications that underscore language relevancy in careers and honor linguistic diversity.

Enhancing alignment and collaboration

An integral part of Chemeketa's SSoBL program development was the collaboration across the secondary and postsecondary landscape to disseminate information about this SSoBL project. This collaborative outreach was done in part to fulfill requirements related to grant funding. Outreach included statewide meetings, shared materials, conference presentations, and publications. As noted, the information sharing that emerged from SSoBL program development supported important system-building that brought up the discussion about academic standards alignment and transfer credits between secondary and postsecondary institutions. The information sharing also supported program replication at other colleges and universities. As a result of this collaborative process, several IHEs in the state of Oregon have embarked on similar SSoBL academic programs, resulting in improved transfer acceptance between high schools and universities. The collaboration has also facilitated ongoing dialogue regarding academic standards and assessments related to the SSoBL. Current research suggests that greater academic consistency and recognition are needed around SSoBL academic standards (Borowczyk, 2020; Davin & Heineke, 2017). Therefore, the collaborative aspect of this program was an important aspect of the overall implementation.

Finally, if academic consistency issues are not resolved, the variety of credentials, all with similar names, will likely hamper the future use of any of these credentials in both academics and the workplace. The inconsistencies diminish the understanding and benefits that the SSoBL has for students in all levels of academia and the workplace. These inconsistencies highlight the need for unity around common academic standards and a common credential that is aligned within the state. As IHEs embark on bringing the SSoBL to college-level language study, communication and collaboration will be imperative.

Conclusion

Expansion of SSoBLs into the higher education arena holds great promise for serving linguistically diverse students and communities and advancing higher education institutional goals. Because virtually every state has an SSoBL policy in place, IHEs now have an opportunity to work with departments of education or credentialing agencies to integrate SSoBL into higher education coursework. The program model presented in this chapter demonstrates that operationalizing an SSoBL in higher education is not only possible but beneficial to students and institutions. Although the program described here focused on Spanish, the model could be tailored to the unique linguistic demographics and workplace needs of other regions. Working directly with public agencies in the states that authorize the SSoBL and adopting the academic standards already in place in each state could eliminate the confusion of multiple credentials. This would require coordination with state departments of education and peer institutions, but it would eliminate inconsistencies presented by private certification that may be out of alignment with state academic standards. Additional advocacy work is needed to unify standards and policies to present a consistent path forward for operationalizing SSoBLs in IHEs.

The opportunity to implement the SSoBL in higher education also gives IHEs across the nation the opportunity to better serve linguistically diverse students, highlight the value of bilingualism, and support efforts around HSI and MSI status designations. Implementing an SSoBL program is a promising way for postsecondary language departments to offer an asset-based approach to language instruction (Monto, 2021). Implementation of an SSoBL program can also serve to de-center language assets in an English-dominant society and demonstrate the institution's commitment to honoring non-English assets and culture. In this chapter, the shared SSoBL program underscored the college's foundational commitment to educational equity and offered a positive model for other IHEs to do so.

References

ACTFL. (2012). *ACTFL proficiency guidelines: Spanish.* https://www.actfl.org/educator-resources/actfl-proficiency-guidelines/spanish

Borowczyk, M. (2020). Credentialing heritage: The role of community heritage language schools in implementing the Seal of Biliteracy. *Foreign Language Annals, 53*(1), 28–47. https://doi.org/10.1111/flan.12439

Carreira, M., Garrett-Rucks, P., Kemp, J.A., & Randolph Jr, L.J. (2020). Introduction to heritage language learning: An interview with María Carreira. *Dimension, 55*, 6–18. https://www.scolt.org/scolt-dimensions-volumes/

Castro, A.C. (2020). Validating the linguistic strengths of English learners. In A.J. Heineke & K.J. Davin (Eds.), *The Seal of Biliteracy: Case studies and considerations for policy implementation* (pp. 121–137). Information Age.

Chang-Bacon, C.K., & Colomer, S.E. (2022). Biliteracy as property: Promises and perils of the Seal of Biliteracy. *Journal of Literacy Research, 54*(2), 182–207. https://doi.org/10.1177/1086296X221096676

Cervantes-Soon, C.G., Donner, L., Palmer, D., Helman, D., Schwerdtfeger, R., & Choi, J. (2017). Combating inequalities in two-way language immersion programs: Toward critical consciousness in bilingual education spaces. *Review of Research in Education, 41*(1), 403–427. https://doi.org/10.3102/0091732X17690120

Colomer, S.E., & Chang-Bacon, C.K. (2020). Seal of Biliteracy graduates get critical: Incorporating critical biliteracies in dual-language programs and beyond. *Journal of Adolescent & Adult Literacy, 63*(4), 379–389. https://doi.org/10.1002/jaal.1017

Davin, K.J. (2021). Critical language testing: Factors influencing students' decisions to (not) pursue the Seal of Biliteracy. *Harvard Educational Review, 91*(2), 179–203. https://doi.org/10.17763/1943-5045-91.2.179

Davin, K.J., Cruz, K.R., & Hancock, C.R. (2024). An examination of the postgraduation benefits of earning a Seal of Biliteracy. *Foreign Language Annals, 57*(3), 634–653. https://doi.org/10.1111/flan.12753

Davin, K.J., & Heineke, A.J. (2017). The Seal of Biliteracy: Variations in policy and outcomes. *Foreign Language Annals, 50*(3), 486–499. https://doi.org/10.1111/flan.12279

Davin, K.J., & Heineke, A.J. (2018). The Seal of Biliteracy: Adding students' voices to the conversation. *Bilingual Research Journal, 41*(3), 312–328. https://doi.org/10.1080/15235882.2018.1481896

Davin, K.J., Heineke, A.J., & Egnatz, L. (2018). The Seal of Biliteracy: Successes and challenges to implementation. *Foreign Language Annals, 51*(2), 275–289. https://doi.org/10.1111/flan.12336

Davin, K.J., & Heineke, A.J. (2022). *Promoting multilingualism in schools: A framework for implementing the Seal of Biliteracy.* ACTFL.

Davin, K.J., Heineke, A.J., & Hancock, C. (2022). The Seal of Biliteracy: A 10-year retrospective. *Foreign Language Annals, 55*(1), 10–34. http://doi.org/10.1111/flan.12596

Dougherty, K.J., & Townsend, B.K. (2006). Community college missions: A theoretical and historical perspective. *New Directions for Community Colleges, 2006*(136), 5–13. https://doi.org/10.1002/cc.254

Gay, G. (2002). Preparing for culturally responsive teaching. *Journal of Teacher Education, 53*(2), 106–116. https://doi.org/10.1177/0022487102053002003

Glisan, E.W., & Donato, R. (2017). *Enacting the work of language instruction: High-leverage teaching practices.* ACTFL. https://eric.ed.gov/?id=ED582346

Hancock, C.R., & Davin, K.J. (2020). A comparative case study: Administrators' and students' perceptions of the Seal of Biliteracy. *Foreign Language Annals, 53*(3), 458–477. https://doi.org/10.1111/flan.12479

Heineke, A.J., & Davin, K.J. (2020). Prioritizing multilingualism in US schools: States' policy journeys to enact the Seal of Biliteracy. *Educational Policy, 34*(4), 619–643. https://doi.org/10.1177/0895904818802099

Howlett, K.M., & Davis, W.S. (2018). Developing bilinguistic youth social capital: Voices of biliterate young adults. *Educational Borderlands: A Bilingual Journal, 2*, 3–22. https://educationalborderlands-ojs-utrgv.tdl.org/educationalborderlands/article/view/10

Kanno, Y., & Kangas, S.E.N. (2014). "I'm not going to be, like, for the AP": English language learners' limited access to advanced college-preparatory courses in high school. *American Educational Research Journal, 51*(5), 848–878. https://doi.org/10.3102/0002831214544716

Kolluri, S. (2018). Advanced placement: The dual challenge of equal access and effectiveness. *Review of Educational Research, 88*(5), 671–711. https://doi.org/10.3102/0034654318787268

Leeman, J. (2005). Engaging critical pedagogy: Spanish for native speakers. *Foreign Language Annals, 38*(1), 35–45. https://doi.org/10.1111/j.1944-9720.2005.tb02451.x

Lusin, N., Peterson, T., Sulewski, C., & Zafer, R. (2023). *Enrollments in languages other than English in US institutions of higher education: Fall 2021.* Modern Language Association of America. https://www.mla.org/content/download/191324/file/Enrollments-in-Languages-Other-Than-English-in-US-Institutions-of-Higher-Education-Fall-2021.pdf

Monto, C. (2021). Increasing diversity in teacher candidates: An Oregon model using a community college pathway into teacher education. *Community College Journal of Research and Practice, 45*(1), 54–64. https://doi.org/10.1080/10668926.2019.1640144

Monto, C., & Diaz Romero Paz (Eds.). (2023). *Viviendo en dos lenguas/Living in two languages.* Chemeketa Press.

Moreno, G. (2021). "Yo hablo el español de mi pueblo": A conscious curriculum for the heritage language learner. *Dimension, 56*, 59–71. https://files.eric.ed.gov/fulltext/EJ1294023.pdf

Oregon Department of Education (ODE). (2014). *Oregon State Seal of Biliteracy - Policy description.* https://www.oregon.gov/ode/about-us/stateboard/Documents/December2014BoardMaterials/oregon-state-seal-of-biliteracy-attachment---policy-description.pdf

Oregon Teacher Standards and Practices Commission (OTSPC). (2022). *Oregon multiple measures dual language proficiency for specializations guidance document* (June 2022). https://www.oregon.gov/tspc/EPP/Documents/Multiple%20Measures%20Dual%20Language%20Specialization%20Guidance%20Document.pdf

Salavert, R., & Szalkiewicz, D. (2020). The Seal of Biliteracy, graduates with global competence, is on the rise. *NECTFL Review, 85*, 29–49. https://files.eric.ed.gov/fulltext/EJ1251339.pdf

Schwedhelm, M.C., & King, K.A. (2020). The neoliberal logic of state seals of biliteracy. *Foreign Language Annals, 53*(1), 12–27. https://doi.org/10.1111/flan.12438

Siordia, C., & Kim, K.M. (2022). How language proficiency standardized assessments inequitably impact Latinx long-term English learners. *TESOL Journal, 13*(2), e639. https://doi.org/10.1002/tesj.639

Subtirelu, N.C., Borowczyk, M., Thorson Hernández, R., & Venezia, F. (2019). Recognizing whose bilingualism? A critical policy analysis of the Seal of Biliteracy. *The Modern Language Journal, 103*(2), 371–390. https://doi.org/10.1111/modl.12556

Tallon, M. (2011). Heritage speakers of Spanish and foreign language anxiety: A pilot study. *Texas Papers in Foreign Language Education, 15*(1), 70–87.

5

UNIVERSITY SEAL OF BILITERACY AND CULTURAL COMPETENCE AT A HISPANIC-SERVING INSTITUTION

Deepening cultural and linguistic capital

Cristina Alfaro and Reka C. Barton

Introduction

This chapter theorizes and centers the access and equity purposes of educating bilingually racialized and minoritized students in institutions of higher education (IHEs) in the United States, particularly in designated Hispanic-serving institutions (HSIs). IHEs are poised to build on Latine students' assets and assist in providing opportunities for students to enhance their heritage language to become bilingual and multilingual globally conscious leaders. One of the six considerations in Gina Ann Garcia's (2019a) text *Becoming Hispanic Serving Institutions* is to "reinforce bilingualism and the preservation of the Spanish language" (p. 118). Garcia poses the question,

> What then would it look like for an entire organization to enact an identity for serving linguistically diverse students? Even further, what would it look like for HSIs to not only embrace the language of many of their students, but simultaneously enhance it?
>
> *(Garcia, 2019b, p. 75)*

In line with this charge, U.S. Secretary of Education Miguel Cardona stated in a recent address to bilingual educators, "Bilingualism and biculturalism is a superpower, and we in the U.S. Department of Education will work to help our students become multilingual" (U.S. Department of Education, 2023, p. 1).

In this chapter, we document a case study of one university's success in enacting an identity as an HSI that embraces and enhances bilingualism, biliteracy, and biculturalism. As a southwestern university on the border of Mexico and the United States and a designated HSI, San Diego State University (SDSU) designed and implemented its own Seal of Biliteracy (SoBL) program, distinct from the state Seal of Biliteracy (SSoBL) or Global Seal of Biliteracy (GSoBL). Called the University Seal of Biliteracy and Cultural Competence (USBCC), the recognition was designed to align with the actual language and cultural experiences of diverse university students, rectifying histories of sociopolitical, linguistic, cultural, and knowledge

DOI: 10.4324/9781032667249-7

exclusions (Alfaro, 2018; Alfaro & Hernández, 2023). Based on data collected as a part of these efforts, findings suggest that specific linguistic and cultural initiatives, such as the USBCC, aid in the Latine student experiences, as they felt seen, honored, and celebrated in their bilingual and bicultural identity. Moreover, students attributed the program to expanding and deepening their own linguistic capabilities in specific Spanish language domains.

On the subsequent pages, we document our programming efforts to celebrate, sustain, and deepen the cultural and language competence of students via the USBCC. Through these efforts, faculty have designed and implemented the USBCC and examined the program's implementation of a three-year process as well as the students' perspectives as recipients. Drawing from these data, we explain how the USBCC process extends students' complex understandings of language, culture, and identity as they continue their path from college to career. This case study has implications for HSIs and other IHEs enrolling Latine students, as the USBCC can be a way to not just enroll students but to serve students and promote, sustain, and advance their linguistic and cultural capital.

Program context

SDSU is an HSI on the border of the United States and Mexico and thrives on Kumeyaay Land. SDSU enrolls about 30,000 undergraduates and 5,000 graduates each year. Thirty-three percent of enrolled students identify as Latine. SDSU has been recognized with the prestigious national *HSI Seal of Excelencia Award* by Excelencia in Education, whose mission is to accelerate Latine student success in higher education by promoting institutional practices and policies that support and enhance student academic achievement. SDSU has engaged in a *Pathway to Servingness*, an approach that is culturally and linguistically affirming (Garcia, 2019a, 2019b). This pathway focuses on three key evidence-based pillars: (1) HSI programming, (2) HSI shared governance, and (3) HSI student identity and voice. The creation of the USBCC specifically addressed the third pillar, *Identity and Voice.*

The authors of this chapter directly engaged in the design of the USBCC. The first author, Dr. Cristina Alfaro, director of the USBCC program and current International Affairs senior administrator at SDSU, is a Chicana heritage (Spanish) language speaker. She was born and raised in Southern California on the border of Mexico where her heritage Spanish language was forbidden due to an English hegemonic education. Dr. Alfaro's career and research have focused on advocating for students' linguistic rights and leading dual language-bilingual education programs from preschool to the university (P–20) level. As a researcher, she has examined and published on the role of P–20 educators' ideological and pedagogical practices that situate access and equity at the core of multilingual and global education. The second author, Dr. Reka C. Barton, has a nontraditional journey to bilingualism. As a Black female growing up in Northern Virginia, she began her pathway to bilingualism in sixth grade when she was presented with the opportunity to learn Spanish. As a doctoral student at SDSU, she served as a collaborator and coordinator of the inaugural USBCC initiative and cocreated the USBCC for the Joint Doctoral Program in Education. Her research agenda focuses on Black girl multilinguals—those young girls who, like her, added a language to their linguistic repertoires, which added to their identities and ways in which they see themselves and the world.

The USBCC

Purpose of the USBCC

The USBCC was an initiative built by bilingual advocates committed to creating a space to affirm and celebrate the bilingual and bicultural identities of university students. From a multilingual global education perspective, the overall goal is not only to improve and enhance Latine academic success but also to inspire all students to embrace multilingualism and to create sustainable pathways for a large majority of students to become bilingual and multilingual, culturally competent global leaders. The USBCC strategically aligns with SDSU's documented commitment to support the success of Latine students. The USBCC also complements SDSU's efforts and investments toward becoming a *new kind* of HSI, which acknowledges that it is not enough to enroll students who identify as Latine but to intentionally serve students by recognizing and building on their heritage assets. To truly serve students is to intentionally create and sustain space for them to show up fully (Garcia, 2019b). One essential way to do this is for students to be both seen and heard across their full cultural and linguistic repertoire. The USBCC does just that.

Now a national phenomenon in contexts across the United States, the first SoBL emerged in California in 2011 to encourage kindergarten-through-grade-12 (K–12) linguistically diverse students to learn English while maintaining their heritage language and inspiring English speakers to develop proficiency in another language (Heineke & Davin, 2020). However, although the K-12 SSoBL has garnered popularity and expansion over the last decade, there seems to be a false sense that language learning ends at the completion of high school. Language and culture are identity markers of students' intersectionality, a dynamic relationship that does not end at the 12th grade (Alfaro et al., 2022).

For these reasons, the faculty at SDSU have created the USBCC, offering a space to recognize, honor, and expand students' bilingual, biliterate, and bicultural assets. The purpose of the USBCC is to validate the continuation of biliteracy and bicultural competence and to lengthen the language learning of students beyond 12th grade (Alfaro et al., 2022). The recognition supports students in sustaining and nurturing their linguistic genius (Alfaro & Bartolomé, 2018) as they move into higher education spaces and into their careers. Whether a student's linguistic proficiency is a result of their heritage language, or from years of Spanish courses, or another alternative, this program was designed to recognize cultural competence and language learning.

From a multilingual global education perspective, the overall goal of the USBCC was not only to improve and enhance Latine academic success. With the recognition, faculty sought to inspire all students to embrace multilingualism and create sustainable pathways for a large majority of students to become bilingual and multilingual, culturally competent global leaders. By acknowledging SDSU's unique position as an HSI that serves transborder students, meaning students that live in Tijuana, Baja California (across the border) and study in the United States (in California; Falcón Orta & Orta Falcón, 2018), it was also imperative to honor the language (i.e., Spanish) of the binational region, of many of its students, faculty, and staff. To truly serve students is to intentionally create and sustain space for them to show up fully (Garcia, 2019b). One essential way to do this is for students to be both seen and heard across their full cultural and linguistic repertoire.

The objectives of the USBCC focus on four integral and intersecting facets. These facets, referred to in Figure 5.1, make up the Global Learning Outcomes for SDSU. The *Cultural*

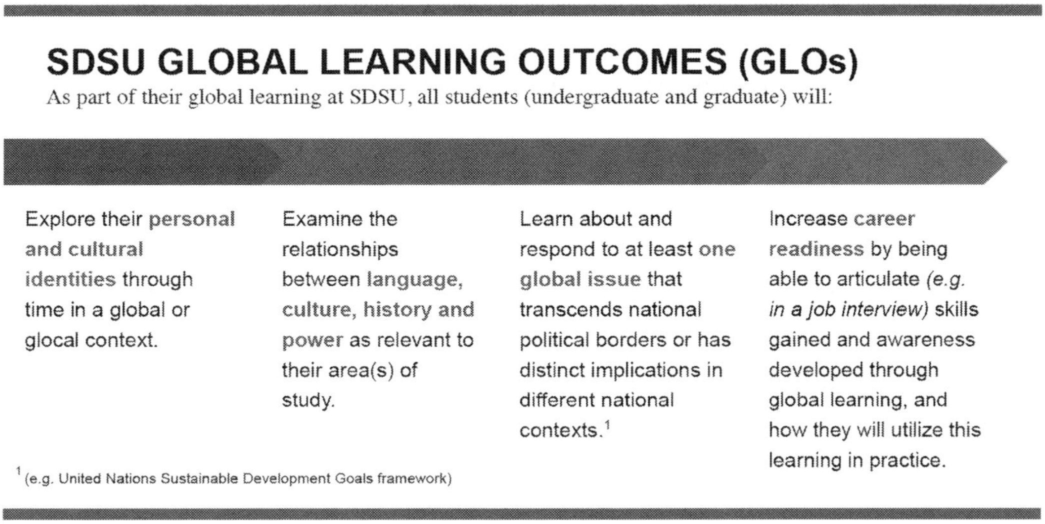

SDSU GLOBAL LEARNING OUTCOMES (GLOs)

As part of their global learning at SDSU, all students (undergraduate and graduate) will:

Explore their **personal and cultural identities** through time in a global or glocal context.	Examine the relationships between **language, culture, history and power** as relevant to their area(s) of study.	Learn about and respond to at least **one global issue** that transcends national political borders or has distinct implications in different national contexts.[1]	Increase **career readiness** by being able to articulate *(e.g. in a job interview)* skills gained and awareness developed through global learning, and how they will utilize this learning in practice.

[1] (e.g. United Nations Sustainable Development Goals framework)

FIGURE 5.1 SDSU Global learning outcomes.

Identities facet encourages students to explore their personal and cultural identities through time in a study abroad or glocal (global perspective through a local experience) context (SDSU Global Learning Outcomes, 2023). The *Language, Culture, History, and Power* facet prompts students to examine the relationships between language, culture, history, and power as relevant to their content area(s) of study. In the *Global Issues* facet, students learn about and respond to at least one global issue transcending national political borders or having distinct implications in different national contexts. Finally, the *Career Readiness* facet aims for students to increase career readiness by articulating (e.g., in a job interview) skills gained and awareness developed through university learning and how they will utilize this learning in practice.

As noted in the first objective, the USBCC program allows students to explore their personal, linguistic, and cultural identities, which directly supports the third pillar of the HSI Framework—student identity and voice. Macedo et al. (2003) have asserted, "As subjects of our language, we possess a particular identity that is always crossed along the lines of race, ethnicity, class, gender, sexual orientation, and so forth" (p. 27). The USBCC acknowledges that many of the students who participate in the program come to SDSU with bilingual and bicultural identities shaped by their unique stories and journeys. The intention behind the USBCC is to meet these students at their existing language competencies and offer a supportive and positive space to explore, strengthen, and enhance their bilingual identities with respect to language, culture, and other identity markers. The USBCC initiative also carves out a space at the university that encourages language learning that started as part of their heritage or developed during their K–12 experience, which now has a place in their higher education journey.

As we seek to preserve, honor, and enhance students' linguistic genius, this work cannot, and should not, be done without regard to their cultural identities. With respect to the interwoven nature of language and culture, it was essential that the USBCC worked in tandem to not only embrace and enhance language practices but also to embrace and enhance cultural diversity and humility (Nguyen et al., 2021; Nieto, 2001). While there are many language programs, proficiency exams, and proficiency scales in postsecondary education, the USBCC is unique for its fusion of culture and language. The authors of this chapter, even with their vastly different bilingual pathways, have both centered the sentiment that language does not exist without culture, and therefore, it was essential to continue this interwoven nature of language and culture when creating the USBCC. In this way, the program offers an authentic and holistic space, which includes deepening cultural humility, a process that requires self-reflection and self critique, which leads to cultural competence while simultaneously expanding students' linguistic repertoire and identity (Caffrey et al., 2005; Nguyen et al., 2021; Tervalon & Murray-García, 1998).

Program characteristics

Faculty designing the USBCC prioritized accessibility to all students from the beginning. While we worked strategically with some departments that wanted to embed the USBCC initiative into their own programs, all interested students could participate in the program at any level of their university studies and from any program or major. For students across the university, SDSU awards the USBCC to recipients with a digital biliteracy badge and cultural competence certificate when they meet two core requirements. First, students must demonstrate working proficiency in a language other than English in reading, writing, listening, and speaking. Second, students must participate in a cultural and linguistic immersion experience during their time as an SDSU student. To demonstrate proficiency, students must receive a score that meets the working fluency (i.e., Advanced Low) level in all four domains on the Spanish language exam.

Another priority of the USBCC recognition emerged as the cultural competence component of the program. Engaged faculty agreed that the language exam could not be the only requirement for obtaining a USBCC. While we applaud the work of the SoBL awarded at the high school level, it was important to us that the USBCC became integrated into the design of this transborder HSI and that it also acknowledged the presence and importance of culture. To do this, faculty added the cultural competence portion of the USBCC, where recipients immerse themselves in an ongoing Spanish language and culture experience. While study abroad was one option for this requirement, it was imperative to expand the possibilities for the USBCC cohorts. Acknowledging the uniqueness of a transborder HSI, the possibilities for both local and global, *glocal*, experiences were vast. Recipients have (a) served as translators for community events, (b) attended and participated in transborder conferences and events, (c) created and engaged in ongoing learning on both sides of the border, and (d) been a part of a service project or research project that had a bilingual component. This component of the program design encouraged students to think about possibilities that were meaningful to them.

In alignment with the program's objective of career readiness, the USBCC also incorporates a digital badge, which USBCC recipients can display on their LinkedIn profile, demonstrating their bilingual and biliteracy skills as well as a certificate of cultural and linguistic competence. While we understand that there is no test that can adequately demonstrate the depth and personal influence of Spanish language and culture, we do understand the importance of being able to present your skills and credentials on the job market. This program allows students to not only say they are bilingual or answer an interview question in Spanish but also have university-level documentation that provides evidence of their linguistic capacity.

USBCC design, implementation, and value

USBCC design

In honor of SDSU's identity as a *new kind* of HSI, faculty defined the inaugural language of implementation for the USBCC as Spanish. While students use additional languages on campus, we placed specific attention and focus on embracing the language and bilingualism of the large Latine population and the growing number of transborder students. Due to the geographical location of SDSU and its proximity to the US-Mexico border, there is a large population of transfronterizo students who bring a cultural and linguistic reality that is steeped in the goals and objectives of the USBCC program. By offering this opportunity to students who have the lived experience of daily border-crossing and negotiating two worlds, it provides a space where they can connect with each other, and with their university in a more profound, purposeful, and powerful manner.

Latinidad does not exist as a monolith and not all of the students who identify as Latine speak Spanish; however, when the data and demographics of the student population were taken into consideration to initiate the USBCC, we found that Latine students make up over 36% of SDSU's full-time student population. Hence, at the inception of the program, we found a large demand for Spanish as a language of interest for the USBCC. To this day, it continues to be the largest demand, followed by Chinese and Japanese languages. We have also found that students showed up with an array of language typologies and experiences (Hernández & Alfaro, 2020). Students came to this space ready to share their bilingual and multilingual journeys. Although these varied, one thing they all had in common was the desire to reclaim, embrace, and enhance their language and cultural competence, as well as to enrich their pathway from college to career as global-ready graduates.

To move forward on the *Pathway of Servingness*, it was not enough to acknowledge and embrace language and culture through the USBCC program. We also had to enhance the language and culture opportunities through language seminars focused on the four language domains: reading, speaking, listening, and writing. Students brought themselves, full of the languages and cultures that make up their identities and influence how they see and move through the world. We met students where they were, both linguistically and culturally, and created space for them to enhance their skills and deepen their experiences. Many of the USBCC cohort students self-identified as heritage speakers and mentioned that some of the domains of language and literacy were more challenging than others, such as writing. This program offered specialized workshops and seminars to deepen their understanding of Spanish language across all of the domains, including reading, writing, listening, and speaking.

USBCC implementation

Over the first few years of the USBCC program, the departments, degree levels, and opportunities for students to access the program grew. During the program's pilot in 2021, the university prioritized three departments with programs that already had embedded Spanish language and global engagement foci, specifically the Joint Doctoral Program in Education, Public Health, and Bilingual Teaching Credential Program. These programs exemplified centering and amplifying student identity and voice at an HSI. These examples also highlight the possibilities across different departments and degree levels, as it is important to provide multiple entry points to ensure equitable access to the recognition across the university.

Joint doctoral program in education

In the College of Education, one of the examples of USBCC programming is through the Joint Doctoral Program in Education. In collaboration with the International Affairs Office, faculty led a group of doctoral students to Oaxaca for a binational and bilingual seminar exploring topics related to social-political justice in education and recognizing Indigenous languages and cultures as assets. This in-person meeting in Oaxaca, Mexico was the culminating experience of a semester-long Collaborative Online International Learning (COIL) class developed in partnership with the University of La Salle Oaxaca, Mexico. The seminar focused on both language and culture-immersive learning experiences to prepare students to earn the USBCC. It included shared topics such as multilingual and social justice education, educational leadership, bilingual curriculum development, and political and educational systems. This academic global collaboration engaged multilingual, intercultural, and global perspectives to enhance doctoral students' linguistic and cultural competence. As a culminating research project, SDSU and La Salle University in Oaxaca co-authored a bilingual textbook that highlights their collaborative research projects (Broca Dominguez & Cappello, 2023).

Bilingual teacher preparation program

Another example of USBCC programming is through the Department of Dual Language in Education (DLE) in the College of Education, where students are prepared as K–12 bilingual teachers, the largest bilingual teacher preparation program in the state of California. SDSU International Affairs, in collaboration with DLE, created a pathway for bilingual teacher candidates to earn the USBCC to demonstrate their bilingual and intercultural competence and as part of their credentialing process that fulfills their language and cultural requirements. This program offers several language and cultural immersion pathways in Spanish-speaking countries as well as transborder experiences. It was an authentic pairing for the DLE to partner with International Affairs to offer the USBCC pathway for bilingual teacher candidates given that DLE's mission and vision is to prepare linguistically and culturally competent teachers with a critical global perspective.

Global health program in Oaxaca

Another example of USBCC programming is a six-week program that prepares bilingual health-care providers in the Public Health Department. Students are immersed in Oaxacan culture and language through Medical Spanish courses and living with a local family. Through this program, students join local health-care professionals and learn firsthand about primary care, hospital care, and preventive medicine. They complete rotations at community-level clinics and hospitals serving low-income populations. Within these rotations, students interact and learn from Indigenous healers and Indigenous ways of knowing. They learn about Mexico's three-tiered insurance system, its approach to the rapidly rising burden of noncommunicable diseases, and various efforts to address health inequities. In the city of Oaxaca, students explore museums and art galleries or hang out with locals in the vibrant Zócalo or main plaza. Students explore nearby destinations, such as the Zapotec ruins of Monte Albán, and visit the coastal town of Puerto Escondido as part of their cultural experience. This program provides participants with unique insight and linguistic and cultural competency when serving the growing Mexican immigrant population in the United States and abroad.

As the USBCC program at SDSU has grown, so have access and opportunity to the recognition. Following the initial pilot, the university continued to expand the efforts to additional departments and programs. By the third year of the USBCC, students enrolled across the university could obtain the recognition.

USBCC value

To measure progress toward meeting the goals of the USBCC, we developed a qualitative study, which was conducted in 2022–2024 after three years of full implementation. We began the research process by conducting bilingual focus groups and individual interviews for the first three cohorts or USBCC recipients. In addition to students, interviews were also conducted with faculty members who supported the program. The qualitative data served as evidence for both the process and purpose of the USBCC. At the time of this writing, over 350 students have obtained the USBCC. Most of their majors were in liberal arts and sciences (bilingual education), business administration and management, psychology, nursing, health care, criminal justice, engineering, and general studies.

Data collection included interviews and focus groups of students and program staff. We adopted a *testimonios* framework (Delgado et al., 2012) because "the genre of testimonio has deep roots in oral cultures and in Latin America Human Rights Struggles" (p. 363), and "it involves the participant in a critical reflection of their personal experience within particular sociopolitical realities" (p. 364). Guiding the format of interviews and focus groups, the testimonios framework allowed the students to be authentic, go across their linguistic repertoires, and share their stories. Student participation was encouraged with an incentive that covered the costs of the language exams. By removing this financial barrier, we also increased access to the program for many students.

The semistructured interview protocol included questions that were asked in both English and Spanish to all participants. Questions included: Why did you choose to pursue the USBCC? How has your self-identity been influenced by the USBCC process? How does obtaining the USBCC impact your college-to-career plans? Is there anything else you would like to share? Interviews and focus groups were conducted via Zoom and audio recorded to facilitate transcription for analysis. Deductive coding was used to analyze the bilingual testimonios from the USBCC participants. Literature from Yosso's (2005) tenet of linguistic capital, as well as Garcia's (2019b) work on embracing language and bilingualism, were used to analyze the data.

Students came to the focus groups with gratitude for the opportunity to enhance their college-to-career portfolio by earning official documentation of their language and culture competence through the USBCC university-wide program. Their testimonios fell into two powerful themes: (a) Embracing Language, Culture, and Identity and (b) Enhancing Students' Linguistic Capital Beyond the University.

Embracing language, culture, and identity

The first theme related to how the USBCC supported students in embracing their language, culture, and identity. As one student, Ricardo, stated, "*No nomás es mi lenguaje, es mi cultura, mi identidad*; It's not only my language, it's my culture, my identity." This student's statement encapsulated a powerful sentiment regarding the deep connection between language, culture, and identity. Ricardo, a Homeland Security Masters student, emphasized that language is not merely a tool for communication but rather an integral part of cultural heritage and fundamental to shaping identity and voice (Anzaldúa, 1987). When students lose a sense of who they are geographically, culturally, and linguistically, they may also have difficulty thriving in academic spaces (Alfaro & Gándara, 2021; García-Mateus et al., 2023). This testimonio emphasizes the notion that language is more than just a means of conveying information; it is a carrier of culture and a reflection of one's identity (Alfaro & Bartolomé, 2017; Hall, 2020; Nieto, 2001).

Throughout the focus groups, several students expressed that earning the USBCC validated their linguistic capital in a higher education environment (Yosso, 2005). The recognition prompted them to feel like their linguistic assets were finally recognized, validated, and certified in schooling, empowering their bilingual and multilingual identity. Students shared how the USBCC had significantly increased their language competencies while also influencing the way they saw themselves. Catalina, a Business College Undergraduate student, explained,

> I have come to realize that language loss carries a heavy emotional toll for those of us who experienced the shift to the dominant language (English) and were coerced to deny our native language in the process of schooling. Earning the USBCC has helped me to powerfully reclaim my language and my cultural identity.

Another student, a bilingual teacher candidate, expressed a similar sentiment. In Paloma's testimonio, she stated,

> I showed up to become a teacher with a load of language shame. I dedicated myself to reclaiming my Spanish heritage language and now that I have earned the University Seal of Biliteracy and Cultural Competence--I am proud to be a highly qualified Bilingual Teacher and grateful for my enhanced bilingualism and intercultural competence.

Paloma, a bilingual teacher graduate student, like many other students, experienced much of her secondary school years in silence and experienced what Anzaldúa (1987) coded as *Deslenguadas* (We are de-tongued). Given the shortage of qualified bilingual teachers, it is important to create sustainable and supportive pathways to both embrace and enhance students' Spanish language skills and cultural competence (Alfaro, 2018).

The USBCC embraces language and culture by acknowledging all of the linguistic and cultural assets that students bring with them to university. By allowing students to bring their full selves to the university, instead of denying their *linguistic genius*, it offers space for students to feel whole, and feel like they belong. Belongingness is essential as universities such as SDSU work toward servingness. Another way the USBCC embraces language and culture is through its understanding of the need and advantage linguistic and cultural competence play in the workplace. Helping students have a method of showcasing their linguistic and cultural talents reduces the barriers to them embracing and articulating their identity and voice.

Enhancing students' linguistic capital beyond the university

The second theme related to how the USBCC enhanced students' linguistic capital, even beyond their experience at the university. Beyond validating their linguistic capital, students also expressed the value of earning a USBCC for the job market. Marisol, a Liberal Arts Undergraduate student, explained,

> I can say I speak Spanish (to future employers, for opportunities), but like my mom always says: Papelito Habla (Paper Talks), so it's good to have a university certification that shows I passed a rigorous exam and am proficient in Spanish.

As this quote illustrates, the USBCC has emerged as a powerful tool that our graduates proudly document in their job applications and discuss with confidence and pride in their job interviews.

As Andrea, a doctoral student, eloquently explained,

> I grew up in a Spanish speaking household, but in school I only spoke English. I kept up with my Spanish heritage language because my mother instilled in me that I had to keep up with my Spanish because it was part of my cultura (culture) so she taught me at home. I had never taken an exam in Spanish until now. I now have the honor to graduate with my Ph.D. in Education and the University Seal of Biliteracy and Cultural Competence, this is a huge milestone for me and a point of pride for my familia.

In this testimonio, Andrea acknowledged the importance, for her and her family, of enhancing her heritage language at the university level. This enhancement and honor were bigger than her individual pride but extended to those in her community. She identified as a bilingual mujer Latina with a Ph.D. in education and with the degree and credentials to prove it. The USBCC program created this pathway for her and many other students like her. By acknowledging their bilingualism, the USBCC enhanced students' linguistic capital by offering support and guidance to elevate their biliteracy development. As Catalina explained,

> The opportunity to graduate with a Ph.D. in Bilingual Education and to also have evidence (University Seal of Biliteracy and Cultural Competence) of my bilingualism and biliteracy competencies is a dream of a lifetime--and a boost to my career as a bilingual educator.

Faculty's testimonios illustrated that the value of the USBCC went beyond just the recognition itself to the experiences that came along with it. For example, Dr. Cappello, the director of the doctoral program, stated, "This partnership with La Salle University in Oaxaca has been significant in so many ways; the opportunity to collaborate with our peers on the other side of the border has been amazing." As the director of the doctoral program in education, Dr. Cappello recognized the importance of intentionally preparing doctoral students with the linguistic and cultural competence necessary for globally and critically conscious leaders and scholars.

The following quote clearly illustrates that employers value and search for candidates who show evidence of their linguistic and cultural competence. As Xochil, a public health graduate shared,

> When I applied for my current job as a healthcare provider, for a clinic near the border, the competition was huge. My employer later shared with me that when all things were equal among the top job candidates, I stood out because I had evidence (USBCC) of my language skills and cultural competence.

Once again, this quote depicts the importance and value of preparing linguistically and culturally sensitive global-ready graduates regardless of their major or degree.

In sum, not only does the USBCC embrace and enhance language and culture, but it enriches the dynamic and ongoing relationship one has with language and culture. By tailoring programs and support services directly to the Latine student populations and by curating cultural trips, experiences, and career development opportunities, the program expands the learning experiences, cultural competence, and linguistic immersion during students' university to career trajectories.

Conclusion and implications for Hispanic-serving institutions

In this chapter, we highlighted examples of work being done in a university-wide USBCC program and provided details about three specific programs that highlight the necessity and expansion of USBCC efforts: the doctoral education program, the bilingual teacher education program, and the public health program. We chose to begin with these three programs for distinct reasons. As nationwide efforts are currently underway to improve bilingual teacher preparation practices related to teaching academic content in Spanish, we knew it was important for us to work with this department. We concur that such efforts are important; however, we maintain that it is insufficient and inappropriate to strengthen prospective bilingual teachers' Spanish language competence without also addressing intercultural competence. Moreover, given the hegemonic nature of these issues, many prospective teachers have likely not had the opportunity to embrace and enhance their Spanish language and deepen their cultural competence. Given this, teacher candidates typically enter bilingual teacher credential programs without ever having had the opportunity to deconstruct their unconscious minds from hegemonic teaching and learning practices. Moreover, it is essential that teacher candidates engage in an immersive cultural experience to deepen their understanding of the relationship between language, culture, and power. The same could be argued for future professionals across industries, including business, medicine, and public safety. The other program that we highlighted was the doctoral education program. While USBCC started as a way to extend language learning past the high school level, working with the doctoral program was an additional opportunity to value lifelong language learning, even past the four-year university model. Finally, it goes without saying that the health-care profession has an urgent need for bilingual, culturally sensitive providers. Therefore, we found it essential to highlight the Global Health program.

Universities must do more to serve Latine students. As the Latine population continues to grow rapidly in postsecondary institutions, the need to develop promising pathways within success-oriented environments for Latine students and professionals in higher education is more important than ever. When initiatives and programs are implemented in a culturally and linguistically affirming way, students can show up as their whole selves. By creating and sustaining programs that attend to their voice and identity, we truly serve them. The time has come to engage in a higher education renaissance movement theoretically grounded in the experiences of those who have been pushed to the margins and whose heritage language and culture have been devalued (García et al., 2023).

With this work, we contend that IHEs must be reconceptualized in ways that reconstitute lenses regarding language, culture, and identity in ways that support students' heritage languages and cultures. For students to engage in globally conscious education and deep language learning opportunities, IHEs must intentionally invest and develop programs that will support student interest and engagement that value the linguistic and cultural repertoire they show up with (Monto, 2022). The goals and objectives of the USBCC are positioned to intentionally advance and enhance programming and opportunities for Latine students, both on campus during their undergraduate and graduate tenure and beyond, in the workplace, and in their communities. Future research should bridge the gap in how we prepare students for a global multilingual and more peaceful world.

College and university stakeholders can take tangible actions to initiate this work at their own institutions. For others wishing to create a similar program, we have published an implementation handbook. The handbook was written to offer practical guidance and best practices for developing, implementing, and sustaining a seal program tailored to the unique needs and goals of individual IHEs. It provides IHE faculty and staff members with the knowledge and tools to navigate the various aspects and stages of program development, from initial planning to ongoing assessment and sustainability. The handbook is broken up into three sections: *Before the Seal*, *The Pilot Year*, and *Sustaining the Seal*. Each section is designed to offer definitions and examples of building the program at a university site. The handbook also offers challenges and considerations that we learned through implementation at SDSU. The handbook aims to provide valuable insights into the process and outcomes of SDSU's successful and impactful USBCC program. By leveraging the experiences and lessons from SDSU's program, the handbook provides valuable recommendations and strategies to support the development and success of new USBCC programs at other IHEs. It includes important considerations for the long-term establishment and sustainability of future university programs. The USBCC handbook is available in print and online (Alfaro et al., 2023).

Engaging multilingualism, cultural humility, and self-awareness frameworks in higher education can equip students with a better understanding of the intersections between language, culture, and identity as critical concepts for strengthening students' knowledge and experience from college to career (Caffrey et al., 2005; Nguyen et al., 2021; Tervalon & Murray-García, 1998). In addition to the work being done at SDSU, we recognize the need to build networks of IHEs to support higher education USBCC implementation at HSIs and other institutions interested in embracing and enhancing language and culture competence. Using this and other chapters in this volume, we hope that readers work within their contexts to support students' cultural and linguistic identity building, as well as forge collaborations across institutions to support this important work of recognizing students' linguistic and cultural assets.

References

Alfaro, C. (2018). The sociopolitical struggle and promise of bilingual teacher education: Past, present, and future. *Bilingual Research Journal*, *41*(4), 413–427. https://doi.org/10.1080/15235882.2018.1540367

Alfaro, C., & Bartolomé, L.I. (2018). Preparing ideologically clear bilingual teachers to recognize linguistic geniuses 1. In B.R. Berriz, A.C. Wager, & V.M. Poey (Eds.), *Art as a way of talking for emergent bilingual youth* (pp. 44–59). Routledge.

Alfaro, C., & Bartolomé, L. (2017). Preparing ideologically clear bilingual teachers: Honoring working-class non-standard language use in the bilingual education classroom. *Issues in Teacher Education*, *26*(2), 11–34. https://files.eric.ed.gov/fulltext/EJ1148247.pdf

Alfaro, C., Barton, R., & Castro, A. (2022). Lengthening the language line: University global Seal of Biliteracy. *Multilingual Educator*, Spring, 15–19. https://www.gocabe.org/wp-content/uploads/2022/04/ME-2022-Revised.pdf

Alfaro, C., Barton, R., Castro, A., Perez, L., & Gustafson-Corea, J. (2023). *University seal biliteracy & cultural competence handbook* (1st ed.). San Diego State University.
Alfaro, C., & Gándara, P. (2021). Binational teacher preparation: Constructing pedagogical bridges for the students we share. In P. Gándara & B. Jensen, *The students we share: Preparing US and Mexican educators for our transnational future*, 45–69. SUNY Press.
Alfaro, C., & Hernández, A. (2023). Dual language bilingual teacher preparation: The braided relationship of ideology, identity, language and culture. In J.A. Freire, C. Alfaro, & E. de Jong (Eds.), *The handbook of dual language bilingual education* (pp. 597–610). Routledge.
Anzaldúa, G. (1987). *Borderlands/La frontera: The new mestiza*. Aunt Lute Books.
Broca Dominguez, L.C., & Cappello, M. (Eds.). (2023). *Seminario de investigación binacional Oaxaca - San Diego: Un espacio intercultural*. La Salle University, A.C. Press.
Caffrey, R.A., Neander, W., Markle, D., & Stewart, B. (2005). Improving the cultural competence of nursing students: Results of integrating cultural content in the curriculum and an international immersion experience. *Journal of Nursing Education*, *44*(5), 234–240. https://doi.org/10.3928/01484834-20050501-06
Delgado Bernal, D., Burciaga, R., & Flores Carmona, J. (2012). Chicana/Latina testimonios: Mapping the methodological, pedagogical, and political. *Equity & Excellence in Education*, *45*(3), 363–372. https://doi.org/10.1080/10665684.2012.698149
Falcón Orta, V., & Orta Falcón, A. (2018). The transborder identity formation process: An exploratory grounded theory study of transfronterizo college students from the San Diego-Tijuana border region. *Journal of Transborder Studies–Research and Practice*, *4*(1), 1–26.
Garcia, G.A. (2019a). *Becoming Hispanic-serving institutions: Opportunities for colleges and universities*. Johns Hopkins University Press.
Garcia, G.A. (2019b). *Defining "servingness" at Hispanic-serving institutions (HSIs): Practical implications for HSI leaders*. American Council on Education.
García, O., Alfaro, C. & Freire, J., (2023). Theoretical foundations of dual language-bilingual education. In J.A. Freire, C. Alfaro, & E. de Jong (Eds.), *The handbook of dual language bilingual education* (pp. 13–32). Routledge.
García-Mateus, S., Nuñez, I., & Urrieta, L., (2023). Identity construction and students in DLBE classrooms. In J.A. Freire, C. Alfaro, & E. de Jong (Eds.), *The handbook of dual language bilingual education* (pp. 373–392). Routledge.
Hall, S. (2020). Old and new identities, old and new ethnicities. In *Theories of race and racism* (pp. 199–208). Routledge.
Heineke, A.J., & Davin, K.J. (Eds.). (2020). *The Seal of Biliteracy: Case studies and considerations for policy implementation*. Information Age Publishing.
Hernández, A.M., & Alfaro, C. (2020). Naming and confronting the challenges of bilingual teacher preparation: A dilemma for dual language education in California–lessons learned. *NABE Journal of Research and Practice*, *10*(2), 31–46. https://doi.org/10.1080/26390043.2019.1653053
Monto, C. (2022). Bringing the state Seal of Biliteracy to higher education: A case for expansion. *Foreign Language Annals*, *55*(1), 35–53. https://doi.org/10.1111/flan.12597
Nguyen, P.V., Naleppa, M., & Lopez, Y. (2021). Cultural competence and cultural humility: A complete practice. *Journal of Ethnic & Cultural Diversity in Social Work*, *30*(3), 273–281. https://doi.org/10.1080/15313204.2020.1753617
Nieto, S. (2001). *Language, culture, and teaching: Critical perspectives*. Routledge.
San Diego State University International Affairs. (2023). *Global learning outcomes*. https://www.sdsu.edu/international-affairs/events-and-initiatives/global-learning-outcomes
Tervalon, M., & Murray-García, J. (1998). Cultural humility versus cultural competence: A critical distinction in defining physician training outcomes in multicultural education. *Journal of Health Care for the Poor and Underserved*, *9*(2), 117–125. https://doi.org/10.1353/hpu.2010.0233
U.S. Department of Education. (2023, February 23). *Remarks by U.S. secretary of education Miguel Cardona at the National Association for Bilingual Education (NABE) 52nd Annual international bilingual and bicultural education conference* (U.S. Dept of Education). https://www.ed.gov/news/speeches/remarks-us-secretary-education-miguel-cardona-national-association-bilingual-education-nabe-52nd-annual-international-bilingual-and-bicultural-education-conference
Yosso, T.J. (2005). Whose culture has capital? A critical race theory discussion of community cultural wealth. *Race, Ethnicity, and Education*, *8*(1), 69–91. https://doi.org/10.1080/1361332052000341006
Macedo, D., Dendrinos, B., & Gounari, P. (2003). *Hegemony of English*. Routledge.

6

THE B3 SCHOLAR SEAL

Designing and implementing an alternative to the SoBL at a Hispanic-serving institution in south Texas

Katherine Christoffersen and Dania López García

Introduction

The University of Texas Rio Grande Valley (UTRGV) is situated along the U.S.–Mexico border in South Texas. UTRGV, founded in 2015, represents the coming together of two legacy institutions: the University of Texas Brownsville (UTB) and the University of Texas–Pan American (UTPA). Approximately 66 miles from each other, both campuses are situated along the U.S.–Mexico border in South Texas. The Brownsville campus is directly adjacent to the border with Matamoros, Tamaulipas, while the Edinburg campus is approximately 21 miles from Reynosa, Tamaulipas. Both campuses are part of the region known as the Rio Grande Valley (RGV), which consists of four counties in South Texas that border Mexico. According to recent census data, the RGV is 91.8% Hispanic (U.S. Census Bureau [USCB], 2022b), and 76.8% of the population speaks Spanish (USCB, 2022a). As UTRGV primarily draws students from the local community, its students reflect similar demographic and linguistic characteristics. According to the recent fall 2022 UTRGV Enrollment Profile, approximately 90.9% of UTRGV students are Hispanic (Office of Strategic Analysis and Institutional Reporting [SAIR], 2022).

Upon the founding of UTRGV, the UT System Board of Regents called on the institution to explore bilingualism, biculturalism, and biliteracy as key parts of its new fabric (Office for Bilingual Integration, 2024a, para. 1). This prompted the university to form a Bicultural Studies Working Group which met from spring 2013 until January 2014. As a part of this work, the group traveled to the University of Ottawa in November 2013 to learn about how that institution implemented bilingual language policies. In January 2014, the working group drafted a report including a series of recommendations. Based on that report, the B3 Institute was created to facilitate the process through which UTRGV would become a bilingual, bicultural, and biliterate (B3) university. Once the universities came together, a steering group developed a proposal that included the structure. The B3 Institute[1] would work collaboratively with (a) the Center for Bilingual Studies, (b) the Center for Mexican American Studies, and (c) the Translation and Interpreting Office.

DOI: 10.4324/9781032667249-8

Over the years, the B3 Institute has worked to fulfill its mission

> to participate in the transformation of the Rio Grande Valley by building and promoting a bicultural, bilingual, and biliterate teaching, research, and service environment through engaged practices with the community that lead to healthy and sustainable regional development.
>
> *(Office for Bilingual Integration, 2024f, para. 1)*

This work has been extensive and multifaceted. As just a sampling of this wide-ranging work, the B3 Institute has engaged in (a) developing and fostering partnerships with the community; (b) organizing cultural community events; (c) promoting and supporting the K–12 dual language education pipeline; (d) providing translation and interpreting services for students, families, and the community; (e) developing Spanish courses for faculty and staff to enable them to connect with students and the community; and (f) supporting the development of courses across diverse disciplines taught fully in Spanish or bilingually. It is this last initiative that is most relevant to the current chapter.

UTRGV and legacy institution UTB have offered courses taught in Spanish and bilingually for years. These go beyond bilingual/Spanish language programs such as bilingual education, Spanish, and translation and interpreting to include classes taught across a broad range of different disciplines, such as philosophy, biology, mathematics, astronomy, anthropology, and many others. Since the founding of UTRGV in 2015, 74,467 students have taken courses taught fully in Spanish or bilingually, with an average of 3,188 students enrolled in these courses per semester and a total of 4,850 course sections taught bilingually or in Spanish by 395 faculty members. Out of an estimated undergraduate enrollment of 26,947, approximately 11.8% of the total UTRGV student population has been enrolled in courses taught bilingually or in Spanish each semester. The previous numbers include programs that are inherently bilingual, such as Spanish, translation and interpreting, and bilingual education. If we exclude those courses to understand the amount of coursework offered across a broad range of disciplines, the numbers decrease, but the impact is still sizable. That is, since 2015, 21,592 students have taken bilingual or Spanish courses, with an average of 1,228 students per semester in a total of 1,140 course sections taught by 293 faculty in nonbilingual programs. So, approximately 4.6% of the UTRGV undergraduate student population are enrolled in Spanish and bilingual courses across diverse subject areas and nonbilingual programs (SAIR, 2022).

However, the language of these courses has never been formally recognized in any way upon graduation, as the course medium of instruction has not been encoded on transcripts. For this reason, the B3 Institute developed the B3 Scholar Seal to acknowledge UTRGV students' linguistic achievements in taking relevant bilingual and bicultural coursework in Spanish and English. The B3 Scholar Seal serves as an example of how universities may develop an alternative to the Seal of Biliteracy, which fits their own unique context.

Literature review

According to a 2019 report by the U.S. Census Bureau, 22.0% of the population (67.8 million people) over 5 years old spoke a language other than English at home, and this number tripled between 1980 and 2019 (Dietrich & Hernández, 2022, p. 2–3). Exponential growth in linguistic diversity throughout the United States and the world is reflected in higher education, where a growing number of college students are bilingual and/or multilingual. In response to this trend, universities have sought different ways to support students' home languages and cultures.

One recent way that higher education has supported students' home language abilities is through offering/awarding the Seal of Biliteracy (SoBL). These programs aim to disrupt the monolingual norm in higher education and honor the linguistic assets of students' home languages (Heineke et al., 2018). Typically including a proficiency test that aligns with a state's SoBL criteria, the SoBL confirms "an individual's ability to perform competently in English and a second language" (Monto, 2022, p. 36). In addition to a proficiency test, some of these programs include optional or required coursework as a part of the program. More examples and details on the incorporation of the SoBL in higher education are detailed in the other chapters of this volume.

Other universities support students' home language through the promotion of translanguaging (García & Li, 2014; Otheguy et al., 2015) and flexible bilingual pedagogies (Creese & Blackledge, 2010). These pedagogies encourage students to use their full linguistic repertoire for coursework, including any languages or language varieties they may speak. Translanguaging and flexible bilingual pedagogies have been implemented in diverse subject areas, including bilingual education and writing instruction (Rodríguez et al., 2021), sociolinguistics (Christoffersen & Regalado, 2021), biology (Feria Arroyo, 2021), engineering (Moya, 2021), and philosophy (Stehn, 2021). Translanguaging in higher education is not relegated to the United States but is increasingly present in global contexts including countries such as South Africa, Ukraine, and the United Arab Emirates, among others (Mazak & Carroll, 2017).

Heritage language education is another way that postsecondary education supports multi/bilingual students. Although originally developed in the field of Spanish as a Heritage Language by Dr. Guadalupe Valdés, this now diverse field aims to further develop students' languages in a way that is responsive to heritage communities and their unique linguistic and cultural assets (Carreira & Kagan, 2018). While still most common in Spanish language departments, there are programs for other heritage languages, such as Chinese, Korean, and Japanese (Kondo-Brown, 2003; Luo et al., 2019).

Other institutions offer language classes that are representative of the communities they serve. As one example, the Universidad Autónoma Benito Juárez de Oaxaca offers a class in Diidxazá/ Isthmus Zapotec, a local indigenous language. While not exclusive to heritage students, Zapotec heritage students who enroll in the course find it personally relevant and meaningful (De Korne et al., 2019).

Another way in which some institutions of higher education have supported students' home languages is through dual language education. Dual language education is a system in which students are taught academic content and subject areas in two languages (Christian, 2016). For instance, they may learn social studies or math in Spanish or bilingually. While dual language education is more common in elementary schools and increasingly in kindergarten through twelfth grade (K–12) contexts, it is rare in higher education, which largely follows an English-only monolingual norm (García & Li, 2014; Phillipson, 2009). Specific bilingual programs or certificates in areas such as speech pathology, counseling, or bilingual education are more common than expansive dual language programs where students can take courses in diverse disciplines such as biology, math, and philosophy in Spanish or bilingually.

The Honors College at Miami Dade College in Florida presents a noteworthy example of the latter (Baena, 2023).

Research on dual language classes in higher education has demonstrated their value for students. In a study on bilingual and Spanish medium instruction at the University of Puerto Rico, Mayaguez, Mazak et al. (2017) found that these courses leveraged students' bilingualism to improve learning of course content and allowed students to develop academic language in Spanish and English. Similarly, Chapman et al. (2022) revealed that students enrolled in bilingual sections of biology courses at UTRGV demonstrated significantly greater gains in learning than students in English sections.

In addition to seeking to support students' home languages, many colleges and universities seek to honor and support students' cultural heritages through coursework embodying culturally relevant, responsive, or sustaining pedagogies. Culturally sustaining pedagogies aim to develop/invoke cultural competency and critical consciousness. Paris and Alim (2014) explained that these pedagogies include "evolving community practices" and "youth cultural practices" (p. 86). In recent years, they have been increasingly integrated into diverse contexts in higher education. Just a few examples include teacher education programs in California (Rodríguez-Mojica et al., 2020), a learning community of Hispanic students in a community college in South Texas (Sarker & Paulson, 2023), and media and society courses in small colleges that serve significant populations of students who are underrepresented in higher education (Cole, 2017).

UTRGV's B3 Scholar Seal program supports students' home language and culture, offering any undergraduate student, regardless of major, an opportunity to earn this recognition for taking courses in diverse disciplines bilingually or in Spanish as well as courses taught with culturally sustaining pedagogy. These courses serve to celebrate and further develop UTRGV students' unique cultural and linguistic heritage.

B3 course designations and endorsements

Prior to the founding of UTRGV, certain courses from diverse disciplines were already taught in Spanish at the legacy institution UTB. In fact, UTB had already developed a dual language certificate for students who completed 18 hours of coursework in Spanish. The Spanish course designation was carried over to UTRGV. After coming together at UTRGV, Dr. Dania López García, then-Associate Director of the B3 Institute, designed and implemented a set of criteria for Spanish course designation and a short informal application process in 2017. The registrar already had a letter identifier system process in place, and the B3 Institute staff assisted in labeling these courses with the letter E (for español). In 2020, three years later, the B3 Institute bilingual course designation was developed in response to the desire to encourage the inclusion of Spanish in the classroom and support students' bilingual abilities. Offering courses bilingually provided greater flexibility to both students and faculty in the classroom. The B3 Institute also viewed these courses as a potential springboard for the future development of Spanish language classes. In this case, the registrar already had another course designation that used the letter identifier "B", so the bilingual courses were labeled with the letter "X" based on the availability of remaining letters in the coding system. The B3 Institute staff assisted in labeling these courses. In more recent years, the B3 Institute added the culturally sustaining pedagogy designation, as well as a flexible bilingual pedagogy endorsement.

In the following sections, we describe these three course designations (Bilingual, Spanish, and Culturally Sustaining) and one endorsement (Flexible Bilingual Pedagogy) developed by the B3 Institute.

Bilingual course designation

In 2021, Dr. Dania López García, then-Interim Executive Director of the B3 Institute, and Dr. Katherine Christoffersen, then-Associate Director of the B3 Institute, formed a working group to develop criteria and an application process for the bilingual course designation. Drs. López García and Christoffersen appointed Dr. Sandra Musanti (Professor, bilingual and literacy studies) and Dr. Mirayda Torres-Ávila (Lecturer, biology) to the working group based on the former's expertise in bilingual education and the latter's experience teaching bilingual courses in the sciences. The group met several times among themselves and with various stakeholders, including faculty teaching bilingual courses.

The development of Bilingual Course Designation Criteria for UTRGV was challenging. Some faculty did not want to require any written or spoken Spanish, while others wanted to require at least half or more of all content, assignments, and instruction in Spanish. Some faculty worried that students would be scared off from the course due to linguistic insecurity (Christoffersen, 2019; Ek et al., 2013; González, 2011; Martínez & Petrucci, 2004) and years of experience in an English-only school system. Ultimately, we decided that it was important that a bilingual course required students to write and speak some amount of Spanish. In part, this was because we were already working on developing a B3 Scholar Seal, and we felt this was necessary if these courses would count toward this requirement.

Additionally, we distinguished between a bilingual course and a course taught with flexible bilingual pedagogy (Creese & Blackledge, 2010) or translanguaging pedagogy (García & Lin, 2016; Otheguy et al., 2015). These two pedagogical approaches encourage students to use any and all of their languages, language varieties, or linguistic skills in the class. Unlike the bilingual course designation as defined by UTRGV, classes taught with flexible bilingual pedagogy or translanguaging pedagogy do not require students to speak or write in Spanish. To recognize and support these teaching practices, we created a separate flexible bilingual pedagogy endorsement for faculty who are able to allow/encourage (but not require) students to speak or write in Spanish during their course. (See the "Flexible Bilingual Pedagogy Endorsement" section for more details on this.)

The resulting Bilingual Course Designation Criteria includes three sections: an introductory section with a definition, a section on *Planning Your Course*, and a section on the *Application Process*. Due to the diverse needs of various disciplinary areas, the definition of a bilingual course is flexible:

> In order to qualify for the bilingual course designation, the course must include instruction and content/materials in both languages and require that all enrolled students write and speak some amount of Spanish during the course.
>
> *(Office for Bilingual Integration, 2024c, para. 2)*

The section on *Planning Your Bilingual Course* includes subsections for Instruction, Content/Materials, and Demonstrations of Learning (Student Work). The materials section clarifies that courses may include required textbooks in English since certain courses have pre-determined textbooks (i.e., some general education and science courses). *Demonstrations of Learning* emphasizes that written and spoken Spanish may be low-stakes assignments and may be graded for content rather than grammar, spelling, or accentuation.

Finally, the application process requests a curriculum vitae, a syllabus that includes a short bilingual teaching philosophy statement, and a *Bilingual Language Profile* to keep a record of instructors' language background and experiences for accreditation purposes (adapted from Birdsong et al., 2012). It also asks faculty to respond to predefined questions in Spanish: (a) Why should this course be taught bilingually? (b) How will students benefit from the course being taught bilingually? (c) How will both languages be represented in the course? (d) How will Spanish be represented in instruction, content/materials, and demonstrations of learning (student work)? The webpage includes a link to a Microsoft Form where faculty can submit their Bilingual Course Designation Applications.

Spanish course designation

After the completion of the Bilingual Course Designation Criteria and Application, Drs. López García and Christoffersen updated the Spanish Course Designation Criteria and Application Process. The Spanish course designation criteria were more straightforward than the bilingual designation. The reasoning for this is twofold. First, almost all faculty instruction, course materials, and student work in Spanish-designated courses were completely in Spanish, with few exceptions. These exceptions were most often related to course materials that were provided in English due to a lack of availability of Spanish language resources or program requirements, as in the case of a required textbook. Second, there was more variation in the way that bilingual courses were taught. Some included extensive amounts of Spanish instruction, materials, and coursework, more akin to a 50/50 dual language model or even beyond that. Others simply allowed or encouraged students to participate in discussions or submit assignments in Spanish. As mentioned previously, this wide variation led to the distinction between the bilingual course designation and the flexible bilingual pedagogy endorsement. (See more information on these distinctions in the "Flexible Bilingual Pedagogy Endorsement" section.)

The Spanish Course Designation Criteria and Application included the same three sections as the Bilingual Course Designation Criteria and Application. The introductory sections outline that "[i]n order to qualify for the Spanish course designation, the course must include instruction and content/materials in Spanish and all students will be required to write, speak, and read Spanish during the course" (Office for Bilingual Integration, 2024g, para. 2). However, just as in the Bilingual Course Designation Criteria, the section on *Planning Your Bilingual Course* allows for required textbooks in English and clarifies that written and spoken Spanish may be low-stakes assignments and may be graded for content rather than grammar, spelling, or accentuation. Faculty seeking the Spanish course designation follow the same application process; this time, the three questions refer to the instructor's reasoning for teaching a course in Spanish.

Culturally sustaining pedagogy designation

To honor the mission and vision of all three Bs (bilingualism, biculturalism, and biliteracy), we believed that it was also important that the B3 Scholar Seal include courses that develop students' cultural competency. Initially, we considered several other terms, such as *culturally relevant pedagogy* (Ladson Billings, 1994). We ultimately decided to create a designation based on *culturally sustaining pedagogy* (Paris, 2012; Paris & Alim, 2014). Whereas culturally relevant pedagogies often primarily view students' cultural practices as a means to gain access to and improve dominant practices, culturally sustaining pedagogies seek "not only for students to maintain their own practices, but also to grow more critically engaged with them, seeing them as worthy of study themselves, rather than only seeing them as a bridge" (Hughes-Hassell et al., 2019, Module 17, Introduction, para. 2). Additionally, the development of this course designation aligned with the receipt of a federal grant awarded to various UTRGV faculty to develop culturally sustaining pedagogy courses (Alvarez et al., 2023b).

The B3 Institute drafted criteria and an application form for the *Culturally Sustaining Pedagogy* course designation. The B3 Institute created a list of courses that may be taught in this way, including courses that comprise Texas's Common CORE curriculum (Texas Higher Education Coordinating Board, 2023). These courses were part of diverse majors across the university. We also included many courses from the Mexican American Studies Academic Program. As a part of the School of Interdisciplinary Programs and Community Engagement, the Mexican American Studies program offers a major, a minor, and a master's program. The B3 Institute is responsible for contacting faculty prior to and at the beginning of each semester to ensure that their courses are correctly designated.

The Culturally Sustaining Pedagogy Course Designation Criteria and Application currently defines these courses as

> courses in which students 1) develop/maintain cultural competency and 2) develop/invoke a critical consciousness. As a part of the B3 Scholar Seal, we define these courses as relating to Mexican American culture/community. These courses should view cultural backgrounds as a resource and asset and incorporate assignments and activities which draw upon these resources to promote student success.
>
> *(Office for Bilingual Integration, 2024d, para. 2)*

While all B3 Institute course designation criteria and application processes are living documents, this is especially true for the culturally sustaining pedagogy course designation, as we look forward to collaborating with professional development opportunities provided by the recent federal PUENTES grant mentioned earlier.

Unlike the bilingual and Spanish course designations, Spanish is not required in these courses; rather, the instruction, content/materials, and demonstrations of learning should be related to the Mexican American community and develop/invoke cultural competency and a critical consciousness. For the application process, faculty are asked to submit a CV and a syllabus with a short statement on culturally sustaining pedagogy and answer the following questions: (a) Why should this course be taught with culturally sustaining pedagogy? (b) How will culturally relevant pedagogy be represented in the course? How will culturally relevant pedagogy be represented in instruction, content/materials, and demonstration of learning (student work)? It is important to note that courses may simultaneously have two designations since they may be designated as Spanish or bilingual, as well as culturally sustaining pedagogy.

Flexible bilingual pedagogy endorsement

As mentioned earlier, the B3 Institute decided to create a "Flexible Bilingual Pedagogy Endorsement" to acknowledge the work that students and faculty do in courses where faculty encourage students to speak or write in Spanish as a part of their coursework. This endorsement is not a part of the B3 Scholar Seal requirements since students in these courses have the option to not use Spanish. While similar in meaning, we opted to use the term *flexible bilingual pedagogy* (Creese & Blackledge, 2010) rather than *translanguaging* (García & Lin, 2016; Otheguy et al., 2015) since the wording may feel more comprehensible and less intimidating to faculty from diverse subject areas. However, our description certainly draws from important insights and work on translanguaging pedagogy. We define flexible bilingual pedagogy as any course

> which incorporates the intentional and purposeful use of English and Spanish in flexible and dynamic ways. Professors and students may use Spanish as a resource in varied ways to embrace students' full linguistic repertoires and unique linguistic resources. In these classes, the use of Spanish by students may be encouraged but not required.
>
> *(Office for Bilingual Integration, 2024e, para. 2)*

To apply for the flexible bilingual pedagogy endorsement, faculty must submit their CV and syllabus with a short bilingual pedagogy statement. They also answer the following questions: (a) Why should this course be taught with flexible bilingual pedagogy? How will students benefit from the course being taught with flexible bilingual pedagogy? (b) How will both languages be represented in the course? How will Spanish be represented in instruction, content/materials, and/or demonstration of learning (student work)?

The development of these three course designations and endorsement, including the criteria and application processes, provided the foundation and framework for the development and subsequent promotion of the B3 Scholar Seal.

Designing the B3 Scholar Seal

In actuality, the B3 Institute was interested in developing a seal or certificate program to recognize students taking bilingual and Spanish language courses for many years. However, while the letter identifiers (E, X) allowed the B3 Institute to track the courses, these letters were not encoded on students' transcripts due to space limitations. After multiple meetings with University Registrar Sofia Almeda and her team in the fall of 2023, we were able to find a solution to track students taking bilingual (X) and Spanish (E) courses through a new *attribute* system in the student scheduling software program *Assist* or *Banner*.

The attribute system is the new preferred method to identify course designations for several reasons. First, the attributes are much clearer and more transparent in describing aspects of the course. For example, students more easily understand when a course shows up as "taught bilingually or in Spanish" rather than when it includes an "X" after the section number. Secondly, there were many letter identifiers for different designations, such as "service learning" (SL) or course modalities, such as "online" (90L) or "hybrid" (O1R). Due to limited space in the course scheduling system, there would only ever be enough space for one letter identifier. For these reasons, the registrar began to phase out the course letter identifier system (E, X, etc.) for course designations and replace it with the *attribute* system in 2023.

The B3 Institute worked with the registrar to create two *attributes*: "culturally sustaining pedagogy" and "taught bilingually and/or in Spanish". These attributes align with our course designations described earlier. Each semester, the B3 Institute sends a list of courses with course designations in a spreadsheet to Associate Registrar for Academic Scheduling and Course Updates Michelle Madrid, who then adds the attributes to the courses in the scheduling system. This attribute is searchable in the course catalog by faculty, staff, and students, and it can be used to track students' completion of B3 Scholar Seal requirements.

With the good news that it would finally be possible to create a seal or certificate, the B3 Institute met with multiple stakeholders and parties to discuss the development of a new B3 Scholar Seal. The team first considered calling it a SoBL. However, through their research, the team found that all instances of something called a SoBL included a proficiency exam (Alfaro et al., 2022; Monto, 2022). B3's goals were distinct: to recognize how our students were already developing their bilingualism and biliteracy in existing bilingual and Spanish language courses across diverse disciplines and colleges.

The B3 Institute then decided on the requirements for students to earn the B3 Scholar Seal. We decided that students would need to successfully complete five distinct courses (or 15 credit hours), which is typical for certificate programs. Of these five courses, students had to complete at least three bilingual or Spanish language courses and at least one course taught with culturally sustaining pedagogy. Once we had determined the requirements, Vice Provost for Curriculum and Institutional Assessment in the Division of Academic Affairs Dr. Laura Sáenz assisted in bringing the B3 Scholar Seal to the Undergraduate Curriculum Committee in spring 2023, where it was officially approved and determined that it would be awarded upon graduation.

During the soft launch and initial rollout of the B3 Scholar Seal in the summer and fall semesters of 2023, students had several questions. They wanted to understand whether courses that they had taken in high school might count toward the seal. For example, they asked about dual enrollment Spanish classes, also called "dual credit". According to the Texas Higher Education Coordinating Board, "dual credit is a system in which an eligible high school student enrolls in college course(s) and receives credit for the courses from both the college and high school" (Texas Education Agency, 2023, para. 1). The B3 Institute decided to accept dual enrollment Spanish language classes at 2000-level or higher. Another common question was whether Advanced Placement (AP) credit would count toward the seal. In most cases, the eligible AP credit for the B3 Scholar Seal was earned from high school students taking AP exams. For this, the B3 Institute followed university policy by which a score of 3 or higher on a Spanish AP exam counted as the equivalent of two courses. Students also asked if Spanish courses transferred from other colleges or universities would count, and B3 Institute decided to allow these as well. However, the B3 Institute decided to count a maximum of two courses combined from dual enrollment courses, Spanish AP credit, and transferred Spanish courses since the B3 Scholar Seal is primarily meant to reflect an experience at UTRGV. We clarified these questions in a Frequently Asked Questions (FAQ) document distributed to students who completed the 'Intent to Pursue the B3 Scholar Seal' form. We also added an FAQ page on the website with the answers to these questions, among others.

The B3 Institute then needed to decide how students would be recognized for earning the B3 Scholar Seal. We determined that it would be acknowledged with a B3 Scholar ceremony at the end of the spring semester, a symbol in the graduation program, official notation on student transcripts, and a digital B3 Scholar certificate in both Spanish and English.

The B3 Institute honored the first cohort of B3 Scholars during a pinning ceremony on April 17 on the Edinburg campus and April 18 on the Brownsville campus during spring 2024. The event was attended by faculty, students, and their families. Program Manager for the B3 Institute Mercedes Torres was the master of ceremonies for the event. Dr. Joy Esquierdo, Vice Provost for the Office for Bilingual Integration, offered a welcome to all attendees, and Dr. Juliet García, Former President of UTB, was the distinguished speaker for the historic moment. Drs. López García and Christoffersen distributed the pins to the B3 Scholars, and a student offered a short speech on each campus. At the end of the ceremony, B3 Scholars were asked to invite someone who had been meaningful to their B3 Scholar journey to pin them. With over 600 total attendees at both campuses combined, the event was a momentous and beautiful occasion. Before the ceremony, students were asked to answer the question "¿Qué significa para ti ser un(a) Académico de B3?/What does it mean to you to be a B3 Scholar?'" Student responses in Spanish, English, and both languages were displayed before and during the event, providing a powerful testimony to this work.

After graduation, we collaborated with the Office of the Registrar to add a notation on students' transcripts as an institutional honor. For this process, B3 reviews student records after grades are finalized and degrees awarded three times a year (spring, summer, and fall) and then sends a list of student names and student IDs to Associate Registrar for Records and Data Control Esteban Martínez to add the notation to the student transcripts. Finally, the B3 Institute distributes a B3 Scholar certificate to eligible students.

Promoting the B3 Scholar Seal

The B3 Institute created a B3 Scholar Seal website which described the program as well as the requirements. B3 also created several dropdown menu items for the website, including a webpage on the benefits of earning the B3 Scholar Seal, a short *Intent to Pursue the B3 Scholar Seal* form, student testimonials, and a page listing B3 courses. The benefits web page includes a bulleted accordion list with the following five major headings:

- B3 Scholars are prepared to contribute to the RGV and beyond.
- B3 Scholars have cognitive advantages.
- B3 Scholars have social and emotional advantages.
- B3 Scholars have academic advantages.
- B3 Scholars have economic advantages and are more competitive in the job market.

When a viewer clicks on each of these headings, they see relevant research and statistics on the benefits of bilingualism, biculturalism, and biliteracy in each of these areas. Our page of student testimonials includes quotes from students talking about their positive experiences in bilingual, Spanish, and culturally sustaining pedagogy courses.

The short *Intent to Pursue the B3 Scholar Seal* form is integrated into the website and asks students to submit their names, student IDs, email, intended date of graduation, and any B3 coursework they know they have taken. Students may also request a meeting. By December 2023, only six months after the creation of the form, over 150 students had completed the *Intent to Pursue* form, and most of those students had requested to meet with the B3 Institute. To field questions, we held informational sessions and office hours. We also met with advising to help inform them about the program so that they could assist students in earning the B3 Scholar Seal. Finally, we created a B3 courses webpage to guide students to all B3 courses available in upcoming semesters and explain how they could find these courses by searching for attributes in the course catalog.

The B3 Institute met with University Marketing and Communications to create the B3 Scholar Seal graphic and accompanying marketing campaign. In addition to the creation of the actual seal image, the team worked with University Marketing to create a flyer, web slider (for the student my.utrgv.edu website), social media template graphics, eblast template graphics, and B3 Scholar certificates. Naturally, all these materials were created in Spanish and English. More recently, we have been working with University Marketing on developing a promotional video about the B3 Scholar Seal. We also created course designation and endorsement certificates for professors following the branding theme.

The B3 Institute also worked with the director of undergraduate recruitment to present at various summer student orientation and family orientation events. At several of these events, the rooms were packed, and students showed great interest in earning the B3 Scholar Seal. We used the promotional material created with University Marketing to develop the *Somos B3* newsletter to inform faculty about programming and opportunities for involvement in the work of the B3 Institute, professional development opportunities, and the B3 Scholar Seal and course designations. The team also sent emails to students and faculty and presented at meetings with deans and chairs.

Professional development for developing B3 courses

In general, faculty professional development for teaching in higher education is lacking and in need of greater support and focus (Altbach, 2011; Healey, 2000; Sorcinelli et al., 2006). This is especially true for dual language, bilingual, Spanish immersion, culturally sustaining, and flexible bilingual pedagogies, which are less commonly integrated into instruction at the university level. The B3 Institute has worked to provide training for faculty to develop B3 courses.

In spring 2022, the B3 Institute partnered with the Center for Teaching Excellence at UTRGV to offer a Faculty Learning Community entitled the *Bilingualism, Biculturalism, and Biliteracy (B3) Teaching and Learning Community*. Ten faculty from diverse colleges worked toward preparing to teach bilingual courses with a faculty facilitator, Dr. Ryan Bessett. In July 2022, the B3 Institute partnered with the Center for Teaching Excellence at UTRGV to offer a *B3 Course Designation Workshop for Gen Ed Core Courses* led by Dr. Alex Stehn. Twelve faculty participated in this workshop with the end goal of designating their courses as Spanish or bilingual. Then, in spring 2023, we secured a small internal Faculty Research Seed Grant to assess B3 teaching at UTRGV. In part, this funding was used for a *B3 Course Designation Workshop* led by Dr. Sandra Musanti in June 2023, wherein ten faculty designated their courses as bilingual or Spanish. We have had positive feedback from these workshops, and they have proven to be an effective method for preparing faculty and increasing bilingual, Spanish, and course designations. Faculty who participate in these workshops receive mentorship and support and become among our strongest advocates for B3 teaching at UTRGV. However, there are not always funds available to offer these workshops, which provide faculty with modest stipends to compensate for the time, work, and energy devoted to designing and developing these courses.

Over the years, we have partnered with the Center for Teaching Excellence and various other groups on the UTRGV campus to provide shorter professional development experiences, offered as one-hour virtual *Teaching Conversations*. During the academic year of 2023–2024, we worked with the Center for Teaching Excellence to organize a series of talks entitled *Becoming B3: Best Practices for Teaching Bilingual, Spanish, and Culturally Sustaining Courses* (Center for Teaching Excellence, 2023). The series was composed of six one-hour Zoom sessions, three per semester, with two to four panelists in each session. These sessions included an introductory session, panels on each of the course designations and the endorsement, and a final session on student perceptions about B3 courses. These sessions were recorded and posted on the Center for Teaching Excellence's webpage and YouTube channel (UTRGV Center for Teaching Excellence, 2023).

In spring 2023, the B3 Institute conducted an assessment of bilingual and Spanish language courses with the support of an internal seed grant with two main goals. First, this assessment allowed us to improve the teaching of bilingual and Spanish language courses based on what we learned about student experiences. Second, we used these findings to apply for a larger federal grant to support the professional development of bilingual and Spanish language courses at UTRGV. This study involved the distribution of a survey to students currently taking these courses, the distribution of a second survey to former students who had previously taken these courses, an analysis of average grade point averages for students who had taken these classes compared to students who had not taken these courses, and an analysis of course evaluations in Spanish/bilingual sections compared to their monolingual counterparts. Students overwhelmingly reported positive experiences in bilingual and Spanish-designated courses. Ninety-two percent of current students expressed that they were extremely or somewhat satisfied with the bilingual or Spanish aspect of the course. Ninety-one percent stated that they would take more courses designated as Spanish or bilingual, 96% would recommend that others take bilingual or Spanish courses, and 96% stated that they believed more courses should be taught bilingually or in Spanish at UTRGV (Christoffersen et al., 2023a; Christoffersen et al., 2023b). As a seed grant, this project provided valuable pilot study data for a larger grant proposal to support professional development for bilingual and Spanish language courses, thus complementing the professional development of culturally sustaining pedagogy provided through the PUENTES grant (Alvarez et al., 2023b).

Partnerships involved in developing the B3 Scholar Seal

The success of a university-wide program such as the B3 Scholar Seal requires support and buy-in from various stakeholders across campus. Even though teaching B3 courses takes more time and energy, our faculty are remarkably committed to providing these learning opportunities for our students. Each time we offer a workshop, we have more applicants than those we can fund, which demonstrates the expansive interest in developing and offering bilingual, Spanish, and culturally sustaining coursework.

In addition to providing professional development opportunities for faculty, we have presented for deans and chairs meetings to inform them of the different designations and opportunities for faculty. In the future, we look forward to the opportunity to meet with individual deans and chairs to discuss strategies for integrating the B3 curriculum into their specific coursework where it would be the most relevant for particular degree programs.

The support and buy-in from various stakeholders across campus were also critical to the development and success of the B3 Scholar Seal program. As previously mentioned, the B3 Institute worked collaboratively with the Office of the Registrar to find a way to track students taking B3 coursework. Our Then-Executive Vice President and Provost, Dr. Janna Arney, supported the development of the B3 Scholar Seal. To support our efforts, she asked Associate Vice President for Institutional Accreditation, Program Development, and Analysis Dr. Christine Shupala to assist in meetings with the registrar.

In addition to our collaboration with University Marketing and Undergraduate Recruitment, we also met with other groups across campus. During fall 2023, we held a meeting with advising where we were met with excitement and interest in the program. In that meeting, we brainstormed ways that we could flag students attempting to earn the B3 Scholar Seal so that advisors could help steer them toward B3 coursework. The Office of Enrollment Systems and Analysis assisted in flagging students who have completed the *Intent to Pursue the B3 Scholar Seal* form in EAB Navigate, a student advising software platform, to enable advising to track student progress. Each month, B3 sends a list of students who have responded to the *Intent to Pursue the B3 Scholar Seal* form, and they are flagged with the code B3Intent in the system.

Also, during fall 2023, we met with Financial Aid, who helped to clarify student questions on whether B3 courses would be covered under their financial aid package. As expected, any coursework fitting into students' degree programs, including open electives within the range of hours specified and required core education courses, were covered. This information allowed us to work strategically with departments and programs to ensure that students across majors were able to earn the B3 Scholar Seal. The Financial Aid staff also assisted in revising the response to this question on the FAQ list and associated web page.

We also work extensively with the Office of Strategic Analysis and Reporting (SAIR) to run reports to track students who have completed relevant coursework and will be graduating in that semester. This is no small feat, as they must take into account the minimum and maximum number of bilingual/Spanish and culturally sustaining courses, course level versus instructor-level courses for the culturally sustaining pedagogy designation, and a maximum number of two courses counted from Spanish dual enrollment, AP Spanish credit, and transferred Spanish courses. During the first year, Director of SAIR Mario Salinas worked with B3 to develop and refine this reporting process. In addition to identifying each semester's cohort of B3 Scholars, SAIR also assists in running reports of students who have taken fewer bilingual, Spanish, and culturally sustaining pedagogy courses. This allows us to contact students and assist them in pursuing the seal by suggesting relevant coursework, for example.

One recent exciting development has been the College of Liberal Arts (CLA) B3 Subcommittee, which is a subcommittee of the Committee for Undergraduate Advancement and Growth. The CLA B3 Subcommittee works toward "establishing the CLA as the leading college of Bilingual, Bicultural, Biliterate initiatives by having all programs meaningfully embed B3 into their curriculum," as outlined in the CLA Strategic Plan (Alvarez et al., 2023a, p. 3). The subcommittee contacted CLA department chairs, who appointed a faculty liaison from their department. As an initial step toward this goal, the faculty liaisons created a CLA Curriculum Map where they checked to ensure that courses that are taught bilingually, in Spanish, or with culturally sustaining pedagogy are designated as such. They then created a strategic plan for increasing B3 course offerings, and three of the faculty members drafted and submitted a proposal for a CLA B3 Course Designation Workshop with cost-sharing among CLA departments, the college, and the B3 Institute. As a result of this proposal, the CLA funded ten faculty in a B3 Course Designation Workshop during June 2024. B3 envisions this hub-and-spoke model as a way forward in expanding the B3 mission and vision across the UTRGV campus as we continue to work with faculty members, department chairs, and college deans.

The B3 Institute is also very appreciative of the broad institutional support from UTRGV leadership since its founding, and most recently from Provost and Senior Vice President for Academic Affairs Dr. Luis Zayas, who appointed Dr. Joy Esquierdo as the new Vice Provost for the Office for Bilingual Integration. We look forward to this new chapter in building upon the current programming to expand the impact and reach of B3 across the university.

Discussion

The B3 Scholar Seal is a local alternative to the SoBL; the SoBL traditionally assesses students' bilingualism by way of a proficiency exam. Instead, the B3 Scholar Seal "serves to *develop* undergraduate students' bilingualism, biculturalism, and biliteracy in Spanish and English through relevant coursework and formally acknowledge these skills through a certificate program" (Office for Bilingual Integration, 2024b, para. 1). To earn the B3 Scholar Seal, students successfully complete a combination of courses taught in Spanish, bilingually, and with culturally sustaining pedagogy. In this way, the B3 Scholars program enables students to develop college-level, discipline-specific subject area knowledge and expertise in Spanish and English. This rare example of dual language education in higher education breaks the English-only monolingual norm that dominates higher education (García & Li, 2014; Phillipson, 2009).

While this program is groundbreaking and important in any context, it is especially powerful within the context of South Texas, with its predominantly Hispanic and Spanish-speaking population (USCB, 2022a; USCB, 2022b). We understand that an expansive Spanish-English dual language education program accessible to undergraduate students across all majors may not be possible at all institutions of higher education due to a variety of factors, including the linguistic profiles of students and faculty. Still, the B3 Scholar Seal demonstrates one example of how universities may develop an alternative to the SoBL to fit their own unique context.

The B3 Scholar Seal and its associated information and programming are best conceived of as living documents and programs. It is a dynamic program that will continue to take shape and be revised for the benefit of students at UTRGV as student and community needs evolve. We also have many plans for future directions. These plans include the development of a B3 Scholars community of students and faculty through various events such as open houses, office hours, and a B3 Scholars Newsletter. Spring 2024 marked the first year that we included B3 Scholars in the Torneo de Ortografía, the Spanish Spelling Bee. This annual event hosted at UTRGV typically includes students in local K–12 school districts (Center for Bilingual Studies, 2023). We look forward to growing the participation of B3 Scholars in this event to show K–12 students, teachers, and the community how the B3 Scholar program offers students the opportunity to continue to develop their bilingualism and biliteracy at the college level. We will continue to work with colleges, departments, programs, and faculty members to expand B3 course offerings and provide professional development opportunities to assist faculty in designing and developing these courses. The B3 Institute has also had productive discussions with the Office of Engaged Scholarship and Learning and the Office of Global Affairs, and we look forward to including community engagement and service learning activities, as well as study abroad opportunities, as possibilities for inclusion in the B3 Scholar Seal. These are just a few of the many exciting opportunities for expansion and elaboration of the B3 Scholar Seal in the years ahead.

The journey to the B3 Scholar Seal has certainly not been quick, easy, or straightforward. At times, progress has been incremental and has taken much longer than expected. This work has been carried out by many individuals and their generous investment of time and energy into expanding the mission of B3 at UTRGV. Everyone who has contributed to the work of the B3 Institute over the years has done so for our students and our community. Gloría Anzaldúa was a scholar of Chicana cultural theory, feminist theory, and queer theory who was born and raised in the RGV and attended the legacy institution UTPA. In essence, we are following Anzaldúa, who called on scholars to become scholar-activists and "do work that matters. Vale la pena, it is worth the pain" (Anzaldúa, 2005, p. 102).

Note

1 During the drafting and review of this chapter, the B3 Institute transitioned to the Office for Bilingual Integration under the direction of Vice Provost for Bilingual Integration Dr. Joy Esquierdo, appointed by Provost Dr. Luis Zayas. Mentions of the B3 Institute are maintained, as they represent the name and leadership at the time of the writing of this chapter. The citations from the website have been updated; however, it is possible that the website may continue undergoing changes. In that case, we direct the reader to the general page of the Office for Bilingual Integration: https://www.utrgv.edu/bilingualintegration/index.htm.

References

Alfaro, C., Barton, R., & Castro, A. (2022, March). Lengthening the language line from high school to higher education: Global Seal of Biliteracy. *Multilingual Educator*, *13*, 15–18.

Altbach, P.G. (2011). Harsh realities: The professoriate in the twenty-first century. In P.G. Altbach, P.J. Gumport, & R.O. Berdahl (Eds.), *American higher education in the twenty-first century* (3rd ed., pp. 38–69). Johns Hopkins University Press. https://doi.org/10.2147/PRBM.S215912

Alvarez, S., Atisa, G., Bruehoefner, F., Dávila-Montes, J., Donner, W., Lemanski, J., Monty, R., Rodríguez, L., & Saenz, O. (2023a). *College of liberal arts strategic planning committee proposal.* College of Liberal Arts. University of Texas Rio Grande Valley.

Alvarez, S., Martínez, J., Cavazos, A., Pérez, E., Feria, T., & López, S. (2023b). *Puentes: A cultural wealth model for student success.* U.S. Department of Education. Developing Hispanic Serving Institutions. ($2.9 million). https://www.utrgv.edu/puentes/index.htm

Anzaldúa, G. (2005). Let us be the healing of the wound: The Coyolxauhqui imperative—La sombra y el sueño. In C. Joysmith & C. Lomas (Eds.), *One Wound for Another/Una herida por otra: Testimonios de Latin@s in the U.S. through Cyberspace* (pp. 120–122). Centro de Investigaciones Sobre América del Norte, Universidad Nacional Autónoma de México, with Colorado College and Whittier College.

Baena, E. (2023, June 12). How Miami Dade College teaches students to learn, live in a bilingual world. *The World.* https://theworld.org/stories/2023-06-13/how-miami-dade-college-teaches-students-learn-live-bilingual-world

Birdsong, D., Gertken, L.M., & Amengual, M. (2012). *Bilingual language profile: An easy-to-use instrument to assess bilingualism.* COERLL, University of Texas at Austin. https://sites.la.utexas.edu/bilingual/.

Carreira, M., & Kagan, O. (2018). Heritage language education: A proposal for the next 50 years. *Foreign Language Annals*, *51*(1), 152–168. https://doi.org/10.1111/flan.12331

Center for Bilingual Studies. (2023). *Programs & activities.* University of Texas Rio Grande Valley. https://www.utrgv.edu/center-for-bilingual-studies/en-us/programs-and-activities/index.htm

Center for Teaching Excellence. (2023). *Becoming B3.* University of Texas Rio Grande Valley. https://www.utrgv.edu/cte/programs/becoming_b3/index.htm

Chapman, A., Weimer, A.A., Torres-Avila, M., Trejo, C., & Racelis, A. (2022). The effects of teaching undergraduate freshmen biology courses in Spanish and English. *SN Social Sciences*, *2*(11), 248. https://doi.org/10.1007/s43545-022-00551-0

Christian, D. (2016). Dual language education: Current research perspectives. *International Multilingual Research Journal*, *10*(1), 1–5. https://doi.org/10.1080/19313152.2016.1118666

Christoffersen, K. (2019). Linguistic terrorism in the borderlands: Language ideologies in the narratives of young adults in the Rio Grande Valley. *International Multilingual Research Journal*, *13*(3), 137–151. https://doi.org/10.1080/19313152.2019.1623637

Christoffersen, K., & Regalado, K. (2021). "Toda lengua es válida aquí en esta clase": Translanguaging pedagogy and critical language awareness in sociolinguistics courses on the U.S.-Mexico border. *Journal of Bilingual Education Research and Instruction*, *23*(1), 45–71.

Christoffersen, K., López García, D., & Cavazos, J. (2023a). *How does dual language bilingual education in higher education impact student success and student experiences?* Annual Meeting of the Linguistics Association of the Southwest.

Christoffersen, K., López García, D., Pérez, K., Dearth, R., Torres-Hostos, L., González Núñez, G., Musanti, S., & Cavazos, J. (2023b). *Follow up report: Assessing the impact of B3 teaching at UTRGV* [Unpublished Manuscript]. University of Texas Rio Grande Valley].

Cole, C.E. (2017). Culturally sustaining pedagogy in higher education: Teaching so that Black Lives Matter. *Equality, Diversity and Inclusion: An International Journal*, *36*(8), 736–750. https://doi.org/10.1108/EDI-01-2017-0005

Creese, A., & Blackledge, A. (2010). Translanguaging in the bilingual classroom: A pedagogy for learning and teaching? *Modern Language Journal*, *94* (1), 103. https://doi.org/10.1111/j.1540-4781.2009.00986.x

De Korne, H., López Gopar, M.E., & Rios Rios, K. (2019). Changing ideological and implementational spaces for minoritised languages in higher education: Zapotequización of language education in Mexico. *Journal of Multilingual and Multicultural Development*, *40*(6), 504–517. https://doi.org/10.1080/01434632.2018.1531876

Dietrich, S., & Hernández, E. (2022). *Language use in the United States: 2019*. American Community Survey Reports. U.S. Census Bureau. https://www.census.gov/library/publications/2022/acs/acs-50.html

Ek, L.D., Sánchez, P., & Quijada Cerecer, P.D. (2013). Linguistic violence, insecurity, and work: Language ideologies of Latina/o bilingual teacher candidates in Texas. *International Multilingual Research Journal*, *7*(3), 197–219. https://doi.org/10.1080/19313152.2013.768144

Feria Arroyo, T.P. (2021). Aprendizaje activo y pedagogía culturalmente relevante en STEM: Tres lecciones aprendidas dentro y fuera del aula. *Journal of Bilingual Education Research and Instruction*, *23*(1), 72–88.

García, O., & Li, W. (2014). *Translanguaging: Language, bilingualism and education*. Palgrave Macmillan.

González, G. (2011). *Spanish heritage language maintenance: The relationship between language use, linguistic insecurity, and social networks*. [Doctoral dissertation, The University of Arizona]. UA Campus Repository.

Healey, M. (2000). Developing the scholarship of teaching in higher education: A discipline-based approach. *Higher Education Research & Development*, *19*(2), 169–189. https://doi.org/10.1080/072943600445637

Heineke, A.J., Davin, K.J., & Bedford, A. (2018). The Seal of Biliteracy: Considering equity and access for English learners. *Education Policy Analysis Archives*, *26*, 99. https://doi.org/10.14507/epaa.26.3825

Hughes-Hassell, S., Rawson, C.H., & Hirsh, K. (2019). Module 17: Culturally sustaining pedagogy. In S. Hughes-Hassell, C.H. Rawson, & K. Hirsh (Eds.), *Project READY: Reimagining equity and access to diverse youth*[online curriculum]. https://ready.web.unc.edu/section-2-transforming-practice/module-17/

Kondo-Brown, K. (2003). Heritage language instruction for postsecondary students from immigrant backgrounds. *Heritage Language Journal*, *1*(1), 1–25. https://doi.org/10.46538/hlj.1.1.1

Ladson-Billings, G. (1994). Toward a theory of culturally relevant pedagogy. *American Educational Research Journal*, *32*(3), 465–491. https://doi.org/10.3102/00028312032003465

Luo, H., Li, Y., & Li, M.Y. (2019). Heritage language education in the United States: A national survey of college-level Chinese language programs. *Foreign Language Annals*, *52*(1), 101–120. https://doi.org/10.1111/flan.12378

Martínez, G.A., & Petrucci, P.R. (2004). Institutional dimensions of cultural bias on the Texas-Mexico border: Linguistic insecurity among heritage language learners. *Critical Inquiry in Language Studies: An International Journal*, *1*(2), 89–104. https://doi.org/10.1207/s15427595cils0102_2

Mazak, C.M., & Carroll, K.S. (Eds.). (2017). *Translanguaging in higher education: Beyond monolingual ideologies* (Vol. 104). Multilingual Matters.

Mazak, C.M., Mendoza, F., & Mangonéz, L.P. (2017). Professors translanguaging in practice: Three cases from a bilingual university. In C.M. Mazak & K.S. Carroll (Eds.), *Translanguaging in higher education: Beyond monolingual ideologies* (pp. 70–90). Multilingual Matters.

Monto, C. (2022). Bringing the state Seal of Biliteracy to higher education: A case for expansion. *Foreign Language Annals*, *55*(1), 35–53. https://doi.org/10.1111/flan.12597

Moya, H. (2021). El español en los Estados Unidos como recurso para le educación de hispanos en ingeniería. *Journal of Bilingual Education Research and Instruction*, *23*(1). 33–44.

Office for Bilingual Integration. (2024a). *About: Overview and purpose*. University of Texas Rio Grande Valley. https://www.utrgv.edu/bilingualintegration/about/mission/index.htm

Office for Bilingual Integration. (2024b). *B3 Scholar Seal*. University of Texas Rio Grande Valley. https://www.utrgv.edu/bilingualintegration/b3-scholar-seal/index.htm

Office for Bilingual Integration. (2024c). *Bilingual course designation*. University of Texas Rio Grande Valley.https://www.utrgv.edu/bilingualintegration/course-designations-and-endorsements/bilingual-course-designation/index.htm

Office for Bilingual Integration. (2024d). *Culturally sustaining pedagogy course designation*. University of Texas Rio Grande Valley. https://www.utrgv.edu/bilingualintegration/course-designations-and-endorsements/culturally-sustaining-pedagogy-designation/index.htm

Office for Bilingual Integration. (2024e). *Flexible bilingual pedagogy endorsement*. University of Texas Rio Grande Valley. https://www.utrgv.edu/bilingualintegration/course-designations-and-endorsements/flexible-bilingual-pedagogy-endorsement/index.htm

Office for Bilingual Integration. (2024f). *Mission*. University of Texas Rio Grande Valley. https://www.utrgv.edu/bilingualintegration/about/mission/index.htm

Office for Bilingual Integration. (2024g). *Spanish course designation*. University of Texas Rio Grande Valley. https://www.utrgv.edu/bilingualintegration/about/mission/index.htm

Office of Strategic Analysis and Institutional Reporting. (2022). *UTRGV enrollment profile fall 2022*. University of Texas Rio Grande Valley. https://www.utrgv.edu/sair/data-reports/fall-2022-student-profile.pdf

Otheguy, R., García, O., & Reid, W. (2015). Clarifying translanguaging and deconstructing named languages: A perspective from linguistics. *Applied Linguistics Review*, *6*(3), 281–307. https://doi.org/10.1515/applirev-2015-0014

Paris, D. (2012). Culturally sustaining pedagogy: A needed change in stance, terminology, and practice. *Educational Researcher*, *41*(3), 93–97. https://doi.org/0.3102/0013189X12441244

Paris, D., & Alim, H.S. (2014). What are we seeking to sustain through culturally sustaining pedagogy? A loving critique forward. *Harvard Educational Review*, *84*(1), 85–100. https://doi.org/10.17763/haer.84.1.982l873k2ht16m77

Phillipson, R. (2009). English in higher education: Panacea or pandemic? In P. Harder (Ed.), *In English in Denmark: Language Policy, Internationalization and University Teaching*. (pp. 29–57). Museum Tusculanum Press.

Rodríguez, A.D., Musanti, S.I., & Cavazos, A.G. (2021). Translanguaging in higher education in the US: Leveraging students' bilingualism. *Critical Inquiry in Language Studies*, 1–22. https://doi.org/10.1080/15427587.2021.1893730

Rodriguez-Mojica, C., Muñoz-Muñoz, E.R., & Briceño, A. (2020). Preparing bilingual teachers to enact Culturally Sustaining Pedagogy. *Handbook of research on diversity and social justice in higher education*. 202–221. IGI Global. https://doi.org/10.4018/978-1-7998-5268-1.ch012

Sarker, A.L., & Paulson, E.J. (2023). Texas community college students' perceptions of culturally sustaining pedagogy in a learning community at a Hispanic Serving Institution. *Journal of College Reading and Learning*, 1–21. https://doi.org/10.1080/10790195.2023.2201828

Sorcinelli, M.D., Austin, A.E., Eddy, P.L., & Beach, A.L. (2006). *Creating the future of faculty development: Learning from the past, understanding the present*. Anker Publishing Company, Inc.

Stehn, A. (2021). Philosophizing in tongues: Cultivating bilingualism, biculturalism, and biliteracy in an introduction to Latin American philosophy course. *Journal of Bilingual Education Research and Instruction*, *23*(1), 12–32.

Texas Education Agency. (2023). *Dual credit.* https://tea.texas.gov/academics/college-career-and-military-prep/dualcredit#:~:text=The%20Texas%20Higher%20 Education%20Coordinating,the%20college%20and%20high%20school

Texas Higher Education Coordinating Board. (2023). *Texas core curriculum (TCC).* https://www.highered.texas.gov/our-work/supporting-our-institutions/institutional-resources/transfer-resources/texas-core-curriculum/

U.S. Census Bureau. (2022a). *Community facts.* http://data.census.gov

U.S. Census Bureau. (2022b). *Quick facts.* http://www.census.gov/quickfacts

UTRGV Center for Teaching Excellence. (2023). Becoming B3 Series. https://www.utrgv.edu/cte/programs/becoming b3/index.htm

García, O., & Lin, A. M. (2016). Translanguaging in bilingual education. *Bilingual and multilingual education*, 117–130. https://doi.org/10.1007/978-3-319-02324-3_9-1

PART III

Awarding College Credit for Biliteracy Attainment

7

SEALS OF BILITERACY

Initial rewards for freshmen and attractive bonuses for seniors

Grant D. Moss and James A. Gambrell

Introduction

This chapter explores how modern languages (ML) departmental faculty at Pittsburg State University (Pitt State) began to award credit to incoming students with a Seal of Biliteracy (SoBL) as well as to award the Global Seal of Biliteracy (GSoBL) to outgoing students. Like many other Institutions of Higher Education (IHEs), Pitt State has aligned with national trends of steady declines in undergraduate enrollment resulting from the COVID pandemic, as well as a demographic decline in college-age students (Kansas Board of Regents [KBOR], 2022). Undergraduate enrollments at Pitt State over the past five years have declined, with data showing that from 2015 to 2021, students decreased in number from 6,782 to 5,415. Enrollments, specifically within the humanities, have also declined, and these numbers also compare similarly to national trends (Heller, 2023).

In 2018, the ML department began to offer credit to SoBL recipients to encourage more students to pursue a major or minor in ML. Students who had obtained the SoBL in high school could enroll directly in the fifth-semester language course and, upon successful completion of the course, could earn all credits for the prior four semesters, which translated into 15 credit hours total. After initial success with these efforts, ML faculty determined that they could also award the GSoBL to majors who reached the required level of proficiency. This curricular innovation allowed students to focus on proficiency instead of solely grades. The implementation of these two measures has kept declared majors and minors steady despite the decrease in enrollments at the institution overall, the decrease in enrollment in the program overall, and the decreasing number of faculty in the program.

In this chapter, we explore how SoBL implementation has begun to address enrollment declines. We begin by describing the context including the background on the State SoBL (SSoBL) in Kansas. Next, we center on SoBL curricular innovations at Pitt State. We subsequently outline the benefits and curricular challenges to SoBL implementation. Finally, we consider the implications, conclusions, and possible next steps to enhance and more efficiently imbed the SoBL at Pitt State.

DOI: 10.4324/9781032667249-10

Context

Pitt State is a midsize regional comprehensive state public university, categorized as a four-year, primarily residential, high undergraduate enrollment institution (American Council on Education, 2023). The student-to-faculty ratio is 15:1 (US News, 2023). Pittsburg is located in the southeast corner of Kansas and has in-state tuition for many counties from adjoining states: Missouri, Oklahoma, and Arkansas. Regarding world language curriculum and instruction, there is no language course requirement for graduation at Pitt State.

For incoming Pitt State freshmen, no placement test exists in the ML Program. For over 20 years, the Pitt State ML retro-credits program has rewarded students for prior language experience, such as high school coursework or languages used at home. Students who desire credit for language proficiency that they acquired before attending Pitt State consult with ML faculty about which course to take. ML faculty encourage students to sign up for the next class in the sequence. For example, if a student has taken Spanish I and Spanish II in high school, they are encouraged to enroll in Spanish III.[1] When students earn an A, B, or C in the Pitt State course, they receive retro-credits for previous coursework or language experience.

For example, students with one to two years of prior language experience enroll in the second-semester class, and once they earn an A, B, or C, they receive three credit hours for the first-semester class (six credits in all). Students with two to three years of prior language experience enroll in the third-semester class, and once they earn an A, B, or C, they receive six credit hours for the first- and second-semester class (nine credits in all). Students with three to four years of prior language experience enroll in the fourth-semester class, and once they earn an A, B, or C, they receive nine credit hours for the first-semester class, the second-semester class, and the third-semester class (12 credits in all).[2] Nonetheless, in the past, academic advisors have routinely enrolled students in Spanish I, despite the fact that students had prior experience in high school because Spanish I is on a list of possible courses for general education.

Background on the SSoBL in Kansas

The Kansas SSoBL was implemented in 2016 after a recommendation from the World Language Advisory Council that developed the parameters of the recognition. It began with two tiers: Gold and Platinum. Gold meant that learners had reached a minimum level of proficiency equivalent to Intermediate-Mid on the ACTFL Proficiency Scale on an approved language-proficiency assessment, and Platinum meant that learners had reached an equivalent of at least Advanced Low (ACTFL, 2012). In 2022, in response to confusion between Gold and Platinum, the Kansas State Department of Education (KSDE) changed to a Silver designation for learners at Intermediate-Mid and Gold for learners at Advanced Low. In Kansas, the number of students earning the SoBL has increased each year, from 200 in 2016–2017 to 870 in 2022–2023, providing increased opportunities for students to graduate from high school with an additional credential (KSDE, 2024).

The first author of this chapter, Dr. Grant Moss, professor of Spanish at Pitt State in the Department of English and Modern Languages, often leads and contributes to (inter) national, regional, state, and community language efforts, such as serving as an IHE representative on the Kansas World Language Advisory Council (2015–2016). Although discussions primarily centered on kindergarten-through-grade-12 (K–12) education in the advisory council meetings, Moss wondered how IHEs could reward Pitt State students for putting forth effort through their K-12 experience to earn the SSoBL (see also Heineke et al., 2018). In subsequent years, he began to think about how to tap into the growing number of high school students earning the SoBL to encourage students to build on that credential and increase their level of language proficiency. He also wondered how there could be more articulation between K–12 and IHEs in Kansas, which prompted exploration into ways to recognize students for their biliteracy.

SoBL curricular innovations at Pitt State

The curricular innovations of the SoBL at Pitt State can be separated into two spheres: (1) innovations for those who came to Pitt State with a SSoBL or a GSoBL and (2) innovations for those who major in ML and can earn the GSoBL during their senior year, whether or not they entered the program with the SoBL. In this section, we discuss each in turn.

Innovation 1: Accepting SoBLs from incoming high school students

Scant empirical evidence or policy briefs exist on how universities accept and incorporate the SoBL. Illinois and Minnesota were the first states to adopt legislation requiring public IHEs to award college credit for the SoBL (Davin & Heineke, 2017). Rhode Island followed suit in 2023. To date, no such legislation exists in Kansas. The Kansas Board of Regents (KBOR) governs six state universities (the University of Kansas, Kansas State University, Wichita State University, Fort Hays State University, Emporia State University, and Pitt State) and supervises Washburn University and community and technical colleges in the state (KBOR, n.d.). Because no such legislation exists in Kansas, KBOR institutions who wish to offer credit to SSoBL or GSoBL recipients must determine their own policies.

In 2018, Pitt State became the first university in Kansas to offer credit to SoBL recipients, which included the SSoBL and GSoBL. At the time of publication of this volume, Kansas IHEs took varying approaches to the SoBL, according to university websites and discussions with program coordinators. The University of Kansas (University of Kansas, 2023), Wichita State University (Wichita State University, 2023; personal communication, 2023), and Emporia State University (Emporia State University, 2023) did not offer credit for the SoBL. Kansas State University had followed in the footsteps of Pitt State and offered similar retro-credit rewards for the SoBL. At Kansas State, students with the Kansas Silver SoBL began in the fourth semester of their retro-credits, and those with the Kansas Gold SoBL began in fifth-semester courses (Kansas State University, 2023; personal communication, 2023).

Fort Hays State University offers credit for the first two courses (10 credit hours) in the non-English language(s) for the SSoBL from Colorado, Kansas, and Missouri (Fort Hays State University, 2023). Washburn grants credit for the first semester for the Silver SoBL and credit for both the first and second semesters of the Gold SoBL (Washburn, n.d.). Depending on the test students take for the SoBL (e.g., AAPPL, STAMP), proficiency levels may vary (see challenges section). However, despite possible proficiency discrepancies, students have successfully completed the fifth-semester Pitt State Spanish course regardless of the test(s) they took to obtain the SoBL in high school. As word gets out about the SoBL credits, many freshman students (and their families) are excited to see how Pitt State recognizes their high school and prior sociolinguistic experience.

Innovation 2: Offering the GSoBL to graduating university seniors

In 2019, the ML faculty decided to also implement the GSoBL to address issues of equity and access with the SSoBL. Because of a lack of federal funding and voluntary participation (Wiley & García, 2016), significant discrepancies exist among state requirements for how students prove their second language (L2) proficiency (e.g., grade point average, language exam, portfolio, cultural competency in real-life communities; see Davin et al., 2022). Some states, such as North Carolina, have additional requirements for students labeled as English learners (Cervantes-Soon et al., 2021; Heineke et al., 2018).

One of the biggest critiques of the SoBL is the question of *for whom* and *by whom* they are created (Freire et al., 2022; Tuck & Yang, 2014). Many states do not explicitly address English learners in the framing behind the purpose of the SoBL (Heineke et al., 2018). Indeed, Subtirelu et al. (2019) question issues of access: "While it has been widely celebrated as a positive development in U.S. educational language policy, it is important to consider to what extent marginalized students benefit from this initiative" (p. 371). They further argue that the framing around *foreign* language development (most states have the SoBL under foreign or world language departments) benefits White, English-dominant students (see also Blanton et al., 2021; Dorner et al., 2023; Gambrell et al., 2016). In addition, schools in areas with large concentrations of students of color or linguistically-minoritized students have significantly less access to programs that endorse the SoBL (Cervantes-Soon et al., 2017; Valdez et al., 2016b). Other issues of inequitable access include disparities in which schools offer the SoBL (Valdez et al., 2016a), the expense of tests required to determine world language proficiency (Subtirelu et al., 2019), and the lack of availability of assessments for some less commonly taught and tested languages (Gambrell & Freire, 2017).

In response to these critiques, Avant Assessment designed the GSoBL to expand access (see Chapter 2). The purpose was to provide an alternative recognition for individuals of any age located anywhere in the world to earn a credential showing their multilingualism. The GSoBL thus provided a way for private, home, and charter schools to offer students a similar credential to students in public schools.

Since the GSoBL is available to anyone who reaches a proficiency level equivalent to Intermediate-Mid or Advanced Low, Moss thought that the GSoBL might inspire more students to focus on their own proficiency once they began their studies at Pitt State (especially since a modified ML senior assessment required the ACTFL Oral Proficiency Interview – Computer [OPIc] and the Writing Proficiency Test [WPT] – both of which can be used to obtain a GSoBL). Initially, Moss reached out to the Global Seal to inquire about what documentation of the OPIcs and the WPTs was necessary to obtain the GSoBL certificate. In response, the Global Seal asked for the corresponding WPT and OPIc assessment results. Once the Global Seal organization received the results, they verified them, sent the GSoBL certificates, and ML staff awarded the certificates. Pitt State is currently the only institution in Kansas that offers the GSoBL to graduating seniors. The results also give Pitt State ML faculty a better idea of how our courses contribute to students' proficiency levels.

Benefits of SoBL implementation

In this section, we discuss the benefits of SoBL implementation at Pitt State. First, we talk about increased enrollment in upper-level Spanish courses. Then we note that despite drops in overall enrollments at Pitt State, we have maintained steady enrollment in Spanish majors and minors. Additionally, the implementation of the SoBL has attracted Spanish heritage speakers whom we did not consistently see in the program previously. Plus, we have experienced improved end-of-program senior assessments as we have included the GSoBL, resulting in a greater curricular focus on Spanish proficiency from the beginning to the end of the program.

Increased enrollment in upper-level Spanish courses

ML faculty's initial reasoning for offering the GSoBL was to attract students who already had demonstrable experience and who met or exceeded the expectations for the mid-program assessment. ML faculty hoped that more students would declare majors in ML since major enrollment was used to determine program viability.[3] With the retroactive SoBL credit policy, after successful completion of the fifth-semester course (15 hours in all), students had completed 45% of the major, 63% of the minor, or 100% of the Spanish certificate. Since students at Pitt State want to be full-time students to take advantage of the flat-rate tuition policy, many choose to take an ML class each semester until they graduate so that they can earn a major. In addition, ML faculty regularly visit local high schools to promote retro-credits and send retro-credit information to other feeder schools to strengthen partnerships and boost enrollment. It is important to note that as ML faculty have implemented the SoBL in addition to the retro-credits program, enrollments in Spanish level I have decreased (see challenges section), but enrollments in the third-, fourth- and fifth-semester courses have increased, which we will discuss in detail in the implications section.

The decline, both in classes offered and in enrolled students, should also suggest that the program minors and majors would also go down proportionately. However, enrollment in Spanish 358 (the fifth-semester class), the first class for those who earned the SSoBL in high school, *increased* in the first year of implementation and has continued to increase despite overall trends of decreasing numbers of students over the past five years. As seen in Figure 7.1, Spanish 358 enrollment in academic year 2015 was 15; in 2016, 16; and in 2017, 11. In 2018, ML faculty began to extend credits for the SSoBL earned in high school, and Spanish 358 enrollment increased to 30 students. Although subsequent years did not increase as dramatically, the steady Spanish 358 enrollment (i.e., 22 in 2019, 22 in 2020, 26 in 2021, 22 in 2022) despite decreasing enrollment at the university represents a significant accomplishment that stems from awarding retro-credits for the SoBL.

Figure 7.1 displays the increase in Spanish majors over the same five-year period. Even though the number of students who enter the program with an SSoBL might seem small, they have had a positive impact on the number of declared majors since 2018. As seen in Figure 7.1, no students completed the Spanish major in 2015 due to programmatic adjustments at the university. In 2016, five students completed a Spanish major, followed by three in 2017. In 2018, when ML faculty began awarding retro-credits for the SSoBL, nine students completed the Spanish major: six in 2019, nine in 2020, nine in 2021, and six in 2022.

Steady numbers of declared Spanish majors and minors

Along with the increase in overall credit hours, another benefit that ML faculty notice is an increase in students who enroll in the Spanish major or minor due to the SoBL credits. Tied to credit hours/classes, students only need six classes (18 credit hours) after their initial

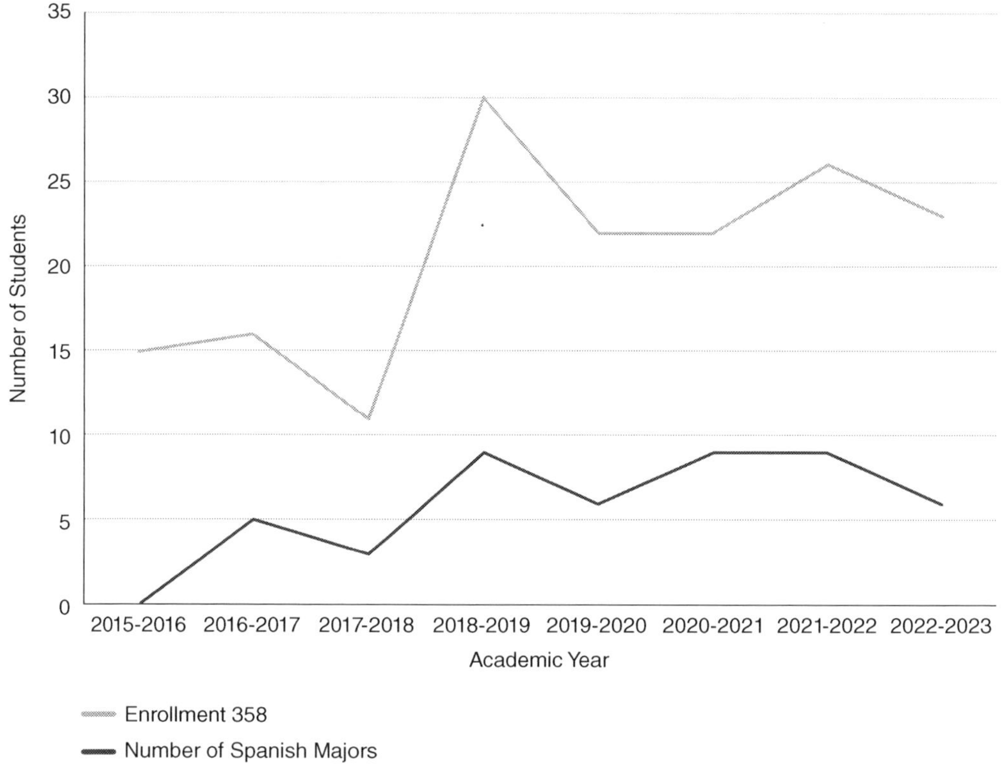

FIGURE 7.1 Numbers of enrollment in Spanish 358 and Spanish majors.

enrollment in the fifth-semester course in order to obtain a Spanish major. These credits allow incoming students to enroll full-time during their junior and senior years instead of having to find classes that are unrelated to their areas of study. Thus, they can take ML classes and declare a major in ML, and they only need to take 21 hours in all (18 credits plus the three-credit-hour, fifth-semester course), which is fewer credit hours than many minors on campus.

Attracting Spanish heritage speakers

Retro-credits are also meaningful for heritage speakers to see that a credential in their home language also contributes to building their professional linguistic repertoire. When heritage speakers discover they can continue to build up their linguistic proficiency through a formal university Spanish program, many are excited to enroll in Spanish majors or minors. The asset-based framing of the SoBL at Pitt State contributes to the dismantling of the oft-repeated false narrative that heritage speakers already speak the language, so they do not need additional study (MacGregor-Mendoza, 2020). The SSoBL and the GSoBL are reminders that L2 acquisition is, in reality, just like any other field. For example, L1 speakers of English typically do not assume that because they are proficient in English, they can teach English without a credential.

Greater focus on Spanish proficiency

Since the ML Program adopted the SoBL as part of retro-credits, ML faculty considered ways to encourage students to continue on their pathway to proficiency. In 2018, we made modifications to our senior assessment, changing it from an in-house writing assessment to the OPIc and the WPT. Students in the last semester of their coursework for the major in ML now take the OPIc and the WPT, the same evaluative instruments also qualify them for the GSoBL, provided they meet the required levels of proficiency. Since both of these tests qualify for the GSoBL, we began reporting the results to the nongovernment organization that sponsors the GSoBL so that students could get an additional credential (The Global Seal, 2023). ML faculty hoped that our learners could use the GSoBL as another credential for future employers to demonstrate their language proficiency beyond grades.

Similar to innovations of the SoBL for incoming students, the GSoBL for graduating seniors encourages students and instructors to focus on language proficiency and not solely on grades throughout the entire program. Both rewarding incoming students' SoBLs so that they can enroll in the fifth-semester course and rewarding seniors with the GSoBL at the end of the major encourages students and instructors to think about and talk about proficiency levels more openly. Faculty can promote proficiency and that focus can continue through the major until students take the senior assessment (the OPIc and the WPT). The GSoBL is a way to see where students have grown in proficiency from the mid-program assessment to the senior assessment.

Improved end-of-program senior assessments

At Pitt State, the benchmark for mid-program assessment during the fourth-semester ML course is Intermediate-Low (IL) on the *Oral Proficiency Guidelines* (ACTFL, 2012) to meet expectations. Given that Intermediate-Mid (IM) exceeds expectations for the mid-program assessment, ML faculty believed that students with a SoBL could be successful in the fifth-semester course. ML faculty wanted to reward students who obtained an SSoBL or a GSoBL since both credentials demonstrate their proficiency level. Although states have varying SoBL requirements, ML faculty decided to award retro-credits for an SSoBL from any state or a GSoBL.

After the end-of-program assessment, ML faculty can determine if the ML Program is helping students to increase their proficiency. Although students who already have an SSoBL may not necessarily need the GSoBL, one of the benefits for majors is that those who had not earned an SSoBL prior to their enrollment at Pitt State can seek the GSoBL. KBOR wants all Kansans to earn some kind of credential; the SoBL is similar to other kinds of certificates offered in the state of Kansas and other states that promote industry-ready credentials (KBOR, 2020). Anecdotally, ML faculty have noticed that encouraging students to obtain another credential through the GSoBL is attractive at graduation because it encourages learners' success beyond the classroom in our globalized world.

Curricular challenges

However, implementation was not without challenges. These fell into two categories: (1) challenges for accepting SoBLs that students earn in high school and (2) challenges for those who earn the GSoBL as graduating seniors at Pitt State.

Challenges of accepting SoBLs from incoming freshmen

Enrollments in Spanish 154 (Spanish I) have declined in a comparable fashion to overall student enrollment during the past five years (see Figure 7.2). Although the trends are similar, in the fall of 2019, when ML faculty put into place the SoBL as part of retro-credits, they also reduced the number of Spanish I courses offered so that advisors would enroll students in the course that matched their prior linguistic experience. As seen in Figure 7.2, in 2015–2016, there were 10 sections of Spanish I with 191 enrollments. In 2016–2017, there were also 10 sections of Spanish I with 165 enrollments. In 2017–2018, there were 11 sections with 182 enrollments. In 2018–2019, there were 159 students enrolled in eight sections. In 2019–2020, the first year of implementation of the SoBL in retro-credits, six sections had 95 enrolled students (in spring 2020, the pandemic began after spring break). In 2020–2021, with modified course delivery because of the pandemic, there were five classes and 62 students enrolled. In 2022–2023, we had only five sections with 60 students enrolled.

An additional challenge for the ML Program at Pitt State was the limitation of only being able to award retro-credits to incoming students who earned the SoBL in Spanish or French. Since college credit for the SoBL can only be accessed if a student earns an A, B, or C in fifth-semester classes, and those are not available for other languages, we have not yet been able to award credits to students for SoBLs in other languages. Some departmental faculty have considered possibly providing ways to recognize SoBLs in other languages, such as counting the SoBL as a general education course for ML. But others are concerned that because we do not offer classes in those languages, we might lose enrollments in ML courses. Such decreases in student enrollment might put the ML Program in the crosshairs of KBOR given that policy allows administrators to deprogram lower-enrolled majors.

A third challenge is that we offer the same fifth-semester placement to Silver SSoBLs, Functional GSoBLs, Gold SSoBLs, and Working GSoBLs, which may not fully acknowledge prior experience or proficiency differences of learners who arrive at Pitt State. This placement,

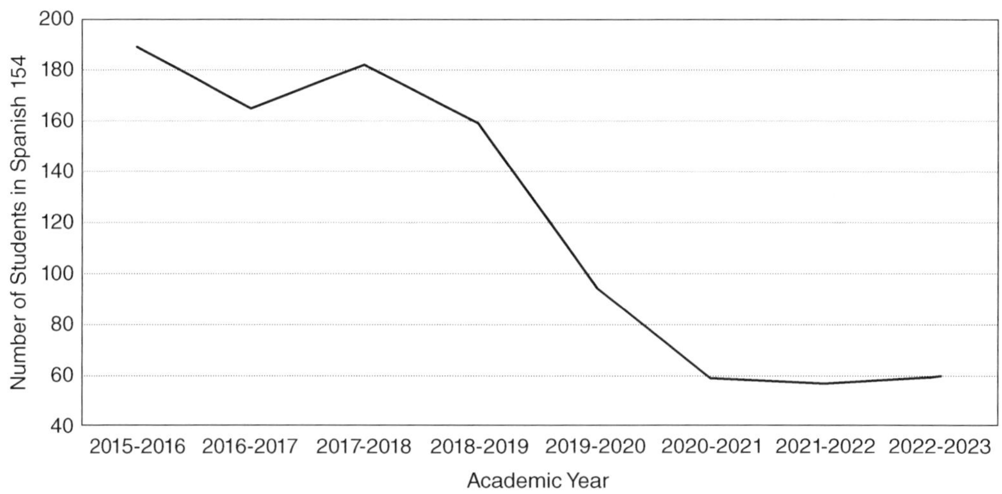

FIGURE 7.2 Enrollments in Spanish 154 (level 1).

regardless of the type of SoBL, leads to another challenge: the ML major and minor are set up with a core set of classes, which ends with the fifth-semester class; in this way, access to all other Spanish major or minor courses rests on the student's successful completion of the fifth-semester class.

Challenges resulting from awarding GSoBLs to graduating seniors

Although Pitt State is one of the 60+ universities in the United States (and one of two in Kansas) that offer students the opportunity to earn the GSoBL, the ML Program only offers the GSoBL in Spanish or French because only ML majors participate in the ML senior assessment (OPIc and WPT). ML faculty have considered a similar end-of-program assessment leading to the GSoBL for minors, but the department lacks funds to support the requisite testing.

Another concern for evaluating program effectiveness is ML faculty currently do not have sufficient longitudinal data to determine which students enter with a first- or second-tier SoBL and whether or not incoming students with SoBLs choose majors (33 credit hours), minors (24 credit hours), or certificates (15 credit hours). Finally, one of the biggest challenges is that ML faculty hoped to encourage learners who speak Spanish at home and who did not earn the SSoBL in high school so that they could earn a credential to justify their language proficiency to future employers, but many heritage speakers, unfortunately, do not choose to finish the major but rather cease their ML education with either a Spanish minor or a certificate. Nevertheless, ML faculty are encouraged by the initial response to SoBL recognition.

Implications

Despite overall decreases in student enrollment at Pitt State, the number of students who take the fifth-semester Spanish 358 course and complete Spanish majors and minors has remained steady or increased. We attribute this increase to the fact that students who earn a SoBL in high school can take advantage of the additional retro-credits. The enrollment trends at Pitt State have resulted in fewer offerings of introductory Spanish courses, which have been compounded by an unfortunate but cost-saving measure that has reduced the number of ML faculty from five in 2015 to three in 2022. Furthermore, since ML faculty offer the GSoBL as a reward for program completers, student enrollments have remained steady or increased in 300-, 400-, and 500-level courses. Both the retro-credits for the SoBL students earned in high school and offering the GSoBL for majors were faculty-designed curriculum advances that were applauded by Pitt State administrators. In addition to increased student enrollment, this process has strengthened bottom-up shared governance, benefiting students, faculty, and administrators alike. The true win is for Pitt State students: through the SoBL, they profit from better placement and more engagement. A win for students, though, is also a win for faculty through better-engaged students, maintained major numbers, and a win for administrators because of fewer sections overall and reduced spending.

Programmatically speaking, we believe minors and majors will remain steady in the long run despite overall enrollment declines at the university. Additionally, one seemingly simple yet long-term effect of offering rewards for the SoBL to incoming students and to program completers is that among colleagues and students, the SoBL and its corresponding proficiency levels have become part of the language that we use as a program. We focus on language proficiency as an asset. We value bilingualism and biliteracy, which was the original intention of the SoBL. Of note for ML faculty, of the heritage Spanish-speaking students who have taken advantage of the SoBL so far, three have declared a major in Spanish, and four have declared a minor. Although KBOR focuses on the number of majors and does not keep track of minors, the ML Program has kept track of those who entered with a SoBL and the credential they earned at graduation. We would like to continue to see the number of enrolled heritage Spanish-speaking students increase through the incorporation of both the SSoBL and GSoBL.

Conclusions and next steps

We believe that language creates an opportunity for shared human experience, which is necessary in this world in need of more dialogue and human interconnectivity. Currently, Pitt State offers a native speaker ML major. With this shared human experience in mind, we believe the next steps include reframing that major. Building on our successes in using the SoBL to shift departmental discourse and decision-making to center on proficiency, we plan to move in the direction of focusing on students' linguistic assets recognized in a second-tier state SSoBL or a Working GSoBL, provided that those SoBLs also require a minimum level of proficiency equivalent to Advanced Low. The shift in language to proficiency levels instead of *native* could also contribute to more of a focus on what students can do with the language instead of on *nativeness* or *heritageness* and would therefore create more equity among students (MacGregor-Mendoza, 2020). It might also reduce the possible tension between sequential bilingual learners (those who acquire one language first and another later on) and simultaneous bilingual learners (those who acquire two languages from birth). Such a shift might encourage program instructors to reevaluate their practices for both sets of learners.

Another possible future action could be providing additional program funds for increased access for the necessary assessment to award the GSoBL to students who declared minors, in addition to the declared majors who currently take the requisite assessments described earlier. If students minoring in Spanish reach the proficiency level on the OPIc and WPT assessments (IM for each), then minors could also earn a GSoBL. At the same time, this increased assessment funding could provide data as to possible proficiency level differences (if any) between those who earn minors and those who earn majors. ML faculty, in turn, could improve the curriculum based on the findings.

We propose that proficiency is a gateway, not an end, and, therefore, the SoBL for incoming freshmen and GSoBL for graduating university students reminds learners, instructors, and administrators that L2 acquisition is not a grade but an asset toward human connectedness (Davin & Heineke, 2018). We value the assets and prior language experience that students have when they enter college, and the SoBL exemplifies that experience. So, instead of granting credentials based solely on classroom performance, we build on what they bring with them and encourage more development of proficiency. Such development reminds students, teachers, and administrators that we incorporate history, culture, linguistics, and deeper thinking beyond superficial notions of grammar and vocabulary. We, like Motha (2014), struggle with the idea of framing language solely as something to be learned, but we hope to empower L2 acquisition through the SoBL as an entryway to business, sciences, travel, and shared human understanding.

Notes

1 Although the Pitt State ML Program offers majors in Spanish and French, this chapter will solely focus on Spanish due to a lack of student enrollment data for French during the period of time covered in this chapter.
2 There is even a retro-credit option for *native* speakers designed for learners who earned their high school diploma in a Spanish-speaking country. They only need to take 15 hours of coursework in the language to earn the major.
3 KBOR sets the bar at ten graduates per year per major.

References

American Council on Education. (2023). *Pittsburg State University*. Carnegie classification of Institution of Higher Education. https://carnegieclassifications.acenet.edu/institution/pittsburg-state-university/

ACTFL. (2012). *ACTFL proficiency guidelines 2012*. ACTFL.

Blanton, A., Kasun, G.S., Gambrell, J.A., & Espinosa, Z. (2021). A Black mother's counterstory to the Brown-White binary in dual language education: Toward disrupting dual language as White property. *Language Policy, 20*, 463–487. https://doi.org/10.1007/s10993-021-09582-4

Cervantes-Soon, C.G., Dorner, L.M., Palmer, D., Heiman, D., Schwerdtfeger, R., & Choi, J. (2017). Combating inequalities in two-way language immersion programs: Toward critical consciousness in bilingual education spaces. *Review of Research in Education, 41*(1), 403–427. https://doi.org/10.3102/0091732X17690120

Cervantes-Soon, C., Gambrell, J.A., Kasun, G.S., Sun, W., Freire, J., & Dorner, L. (2021). "Everybody wants a choice" in dual language education of el Nuevo Sur: Whiteness as the gloss for every*body* in media discourses of multilingual education. *Journal of Language, Identity, & Education, 20*(6), 394–410. https://doi.org/10.1080/15348458.2020.1753201

Davin, K.J., & Heineke, A.J. (2017). The Seal of Biliteracy: Variations in policy and outcomes. *Foreign Language Annals, 50*(3), 486–499. https://doi.org/10.1111/flan.12279

Davin, K.J., & Heineke, A.J. (2018) The Seal of Biliteracy: Adding students' voices to the conversation, *Bilingual Research Journal, 41*(3), 312–328. https://doi.org/10.1080/15235882.2018.1481896

Davin, K.J., Heineke, A.J., & Hancock, C.R. (2022). The Seal of Biliteracy: A 10-year retrospective. *Foreign Language Annals, 55*(1), 10–34. https://doi.org/10.1111/flan.12596.

Dorner, L.M., Moon, J.M., Freire, J.A., Gambrell, J.A., Kasun, G.S., & Cervantes-Soon, C. (2023). Dual language bilingual education as a pathway to racial integration? A place-based analysis of policy enactment. *Peabody Journal of Education, 98*(2), 185–204. https://doi.org/10.1080/0161956X.2023.2191566

Emporia State University. (2023). *Placement testing*. https://sites.goog.e.com/g.emporia.edu/modern-languages-program/confirm-your-placement?authuser=0

Fort Hays State University. (2023). *Credit by documentation*. https://www.fhsu.edu/cpl/documentation

Freire, J.A., Gambrell, J.A., Kasun, S.G., Dorner, L., & Cervantes-Soon, C. (2022). The expropriation of dual language bilingual education: Deconstructing neoliberalism, whitestreaming, and English hegemony. *International Multilingual Research Journal, 16*(1), 27–46. http://doi.org/10.1080/19313152.2021.1929762

Gambrell, J.A., Bright, A., & De La Vega, E. (2016). ¿Para quién son los estándares curriculares? Revisión de un programa educativo multilingüe. [Standards for whom? Re-visioning a multilingual education program]. In M.J. Bolarín Matinex, M. Porto Currás, & L. García Hernández (Eds.), *Evaluación e identidad del alumnado en educación superior, 3* (pp. 193–196). Ediciones de la Universidad de Murcia.

Gambrell, J.A., & Freire, J.A. (2017). Una contextualización lingüística, racial y política de la evaluación de los programas de magisterio en Estados Unidos [Assessment in United States teacher preparation programs: Exploring linguistic, racial, and political contexts]. In A. Rivera (Ed.), *Miradas a la evaluación en la diversidad cultural: Brasil, España, EU, Venezuela y México*. (pp. 69–92). Castellanos Editores.

The Global Seal. (2023). *Global seal colleges and universities*. https://theglobalseal.com/higher-education

Heineke, A.J., Davin, K.J., & Bedford, A. (2018). The Seal of Biliteracy: Considering equity and access for English learners. *Education Policy Analysis Archives, 26*(99), 1–12. http://doi.org/10.14507/epaa.26.3825

Heller, N. (2023). The end of the English major. *The New Yorker*, 27.

Kansas Board of Regents. (n.d.). *A brief history of the Kansas board of regents system.* https://www.kansasregents.org/about/history

Kansas Board of Regents. (2020). *AO-K to work program rules and regulations - 88-25-2 AO-K career pathways; Industry-recognized credentials.* https://www.kansasregents.org/about/rules-regulations/ao-k-to-work?start=2

Kansas Board of Regents. (2022). *Institutional profiles: Pittsburg State University.* https://www.kansasregents.org/resources/PDF/Data/2022_State_University_Data_Book/PSU.pdf

Kansas Department of Education. (2024). *Seal of Biliteracy: Guidance, direction and documentation.* https://www.ksde.org/Agency/Division-of-Learning-Services/Career-Standards-and-Assessment-Services/Content-Area-M-Z/World-Languages/Seal-of-Biliteracy

Kansas State University. (2023). *Language placement information.* https://www.k-state.edu/languages/prospective/index.html

MacGregor-Mendoza, P. (2020). Language, culture, and Spanish heritage language learners: Reframing old paradigms. *Dimension*, *55*(1), 19–34.

Motha, S. (2014). *Race, empire, and English language teaching.* Teachers College Press.

Subtirelu, N.C., Borowczyk, M., Thorson Hernández, R., & Venezia, F. (2019). Recognizing whose bilingualism? A critical policy analysis of the Seal of Biliteracy. *The Modern Language Journal*, *103*(2), 371–390. https://doi.org/10.1111/modl.12556

The University of Kansas. (2023). *Credit and exemption for high school work.* https://admissions.ku.edu/apply/credit-transfer/high-school

US News. (2023). *Pittsburg State University.* Best colleges. https://owl.purdue.edu/owl/research_and_citation/apa_style/apa_formatting_and_style_guide/reference_list_electronic_sources.html

Tuck, E., & Yang, K.W. (2014). R-words: Refusing research. In D. Paris & M.T. Winn (Eds.), *Humanizing research: Decolonizing qualitative inquiry with youth and communities* (pp. 223–248). Sage Publications.

Valdez, V.E., Delavan, G., & Freire, J.A. (2016a). The marketing of dual language education policy in Utah print media. *Educational Policy*, *30*(6), 849–883. doi:10.1177/0895904814556750

Valdez, V.E., Freire, J.A., & Delavan, M.G. (2016b). The gentrification of dual language education. *The Urban Review*, *48*(4), 601–627. doi:10.1007/s11256-016-0370-0Wentworth

Washburn University. (n.d.). *Modern languages program quality indicators.* https://www.washburn.edu/academics/college-schools/arts-sciences/departments/modern-foreign-languages/quality-indicators.html

Wichita State University. (2023). *Spanish placement exam.* https://www.wichita.edu/academics/fairmount_college_of_liberal_arts_and_sciences/mell/Languages/Spanish/Spanish_Placement_Exam.php

Wiley, T.G., & García, O. (2016). Language policy and planning in language education: Legacies, consequences, and possibilities. *The Modern Language Journal*, *100*(S1), 48–63. https://doi.org/10.1111/modl.12303

8

REDUCING OPPORTUNITY GAPS AND PROMOTING ENROLLMENT THROUGH CREDIT BY EXAMINATION FOR THE SEAL OF BILITERACY

Jesse Gleason, Sobeira Latorre, and Resha Cardone

Introduction

Given a historic decline in enrollment and the reduction or elimination of university language requirements, language departments are striving to reinvent and bolster recruitment to survive (Looney & Lusin, 2019; Lord, 2020; Modern Language Association (MLA), 2007; Murphy et al., 2022). Generally speaking, public regional comprehensive universities seek to provide educational opportunities to student populations who have been historically marginalized, including first-generation students (i.e., the first in their families to attend college), bilingual learners who speak languages other than English, and individuals from ethnic minority communities (Excelencia in Education, 2020). Institutions of higher education (IHEs) have often given the message, either directly or indirectly, that students' home languages and cultural backgrounds are more of a hindrance than an asset (Baker & Wright, 2017; Rabe Thomas, 2017). Whereas using languages other than English at home has traditionally been viewed as a deficit that educational institutions must correct, the Seal of Biliteracy (SoBL) places value on students' bilingualism and biliteracy by awarding them a seal affixed to their high school diploma (Davin & Heineke, 2022).

Offering university learners Credit by Examinination(CBE) (e.g., by demonstrating bilingualism and biliteracy using valid proficiency-based assessments) provides an opportunity to reduce the total number of credits that bilingual students have to take toward completing their degrees and potentially incentivizes their continued study of a language through upper-level university courses. This chapter describes an evolving partnership between a Regional Public University (RPU) and a Neighborhood Public School District (NPSD) to grant university credits to high school graduates based on their documented language proficiency. Part of a larger data set including additional languages, we explore how this partnership may have impacted Spanish SoBL students' decision to pursue a minor or major in Spanish, as well as their experiences around receiving university language course credit for their SoBL. We focus on Spanish due to the importance of the language at RPU, whose Latinx students represent close to 25% of the student body and, in this particular state, whose Hispanic and Latinx population comprises nearly 20% of the state population (Willner, 2022), as is the case in the United States more broadly.

DOI: 10.4324/9781032667249-11

Background and context

Granting university credit for the SoBL in a time of declining language enrollments

By offering college-level credit to bilingual students who can certify their proficiency using SoBL-approved language proficiency assessments, IHEs have the potential to change a language-as-deficit message, thus working to reduce opportunity gaps or the differences in student achievement based on structural inequalities that have disadvantaged historically marginalized populations (Subtirelu et al., 2019). By acknowledging the importance and value of bilingual students' cultural and linguistic capital, IHEs can create policies that provide bilingual students with a structural advantage (Baker & Wright, 2017; Santos, 2022). Assigning academic value to bilingual students' existing language competencies helps IHEs to potentially disrupt deficit-based educational policies that have traditionally disadvantaged students from homes where languages other than English are spoken.

By granting students credit based on language proficiency via the SoBL, IHEs potentially incentivize systemically underserved bilingual students, in particular Latinx learners, to continue to develop their home languages. Recognizing the SoBL at IHEs also has the potential to encourage second language learners, those who have developed bilingualism through prior academic learning, to continue language study at the university level. With this in mind, faculty recognize the SoBL as having the potential to (a) bolster otherwise declining language enrollments, (b) incentivize adjacent programming, such as study abroad and global studies, (c) increase students' intercultural awareness and bilingual competence, (d) augment global consciousness among learners, and (e) provide opportunities for relationship-building and community formation among the speakers of the languages in contact.

The other possible outcome of granting students university CBE is that they may choose not to continue their language study. Over the past decade, the number of university students taking language classes has dropped for reasons including a (a) lack of availability of courses in a language students desired to learn (e.g., Korean), (b) decrease or elimination of general education language requirements, and (c) perceived lack of direct link with students' overall career goals (Diao & Liu, 2020). Some IHEs may be reluctant to grant students CBE due to a fear of fewer students enrolling in language classes, thus exacerbating the enrollment crisis. Decades of erosion of university language requirements and declining resources have left language departments on the defensive. According to Looney and Lusin (2019), student enrollment in university language classes dropped by 9.2% between 2013 and 2016. Between 2016 and 2021, they dropped an additional 16.6% (Lusin et al., 2023). According to Lord (2018, 2020), this marked decline is in great part due to the cutting or elimination of language requirements within the general education curriculum across IHEs. Looney and Lusin (2019), for example, found that between the MLA survey of 1993–1994 and 2009–2010, there had been a 17% decline in the number of four-year institutions with language requirements (67.5% in 1994–2005 to 50.7% in 2009). Of the smaller sampling of universities that Lord (2018) surveyed in 2017, 30% no longer had language requirements, and close to 40% had requirements recently eliminated.

Given changes to university language requirements and precipitous declines in language enrollment, it is only natural that faculty feel cautious about granting credit to students who hold the SoBL. Many learners who come to the university having proven language proficiency by examinations such as the Advanced Placement (AP), College-Level Examination

Program (CLEP), or International Baccalaureate (IB) are already entitled to receiving university credit, and many decide not to continue language study (Murphy et al., 2022). The difference between students who hold the SoBL and those who are entitled to university credit by examinations such as AP, CLEP, and IB is oftentimes a matter of opportunity. Students coming from better-resourced school districts that offer AP classes may have greater access to earning college credit in high school than those from less-resourced schools (Davin & Heineke, 2022). Many SoBL recipients come from lower-income school districts, which may not offer AP classes, and many of these learners are heritage or native speakers of a language who have acquired and developed the languages spoken in their homes (Subtirelu et al., 2019). By failing to offer university credit for language proficiency documented by the SoBL, IHEs may inadvertently add to institutionalized inequities.

On the other hand, providing opportunities for students from households where languages other than English are spoken to earn the SoBL for university credit may potentially reduce opportunity gaps between higher- and lower-resourced students. Institutions of Higher Education may empower bilingual students to minor or major in another language by situating their bilingualism as an asset rather than a deficit (Baker & Wright, 2017; Morgan, 2012; Thompson, 2017). This requires taking into account their identity and agency, thus granting them university credit for what they already can do with a language. This is particularly true if university language departments, in turn, can overhaul their curricula and pedagogies to recognize the heritage learners and native-speaker populations recruited through CBE tools like the SoBL. Whereas some university language curricula may have traditionally catered to English-dominant students of world languages over time, granting credit for proficiency may increase the recruitment of bilingual learners, necessitating changes to curricula to address and take account of their implicit language knowledge. Many world language departments have not adapted their curricula sufficiently to cater to heritage and native-speaker students and hence may be recruiting and retaining fewer bilingual students than if they were to deliberately serve bilingual students. While, indeed, some departments offer a few specialized courses designed for heritage and native-speaker students, by and large, world language curricula continue to be rooted in the historic assumption that students learning languages at the university are English-dominant. This perspective fails to recognize that regional public universities are intentionally accessible and thus serve more heritage and native-speaker students than they had when these curricular norms were established. This shift requires an asset-based approach that recognizes that heritage learners and native speakers have a different—and oftentimes less academic—relationship with the language. This would be in line with the changing demographics of students attending regional public comprehensive universities today.

Partnership between a regional public university and a neighboring public school district

We now describe three distinct phases of a partnership between a Regional Public University (henceforth referred to as RPU) and a Neighboring Public School District (henceforth NPSD) to award university credit to bilingual students who held the SoBL. The first phase, occurring between academic year (AY) 2018–2019 and AY 2020–2021, involved forming a partnership agreement between the then-chairperson of the Languages Department at RPU (henceforth Chairperson A) and the NPSD and implementing the initiative at RPU. The second phase, occurring between AY 2021–2022 and AY 2022–2023, came one year after a transition in departmental leadership that prompted modifications to the partnership and changes to the advising process. The third and final phase, beginning in the fall of 2023, eliminated several steps involved in the first two phases, namely the requirement that students must meet and have a conversation with the department chairperson. As such, the process was streamlined, and the number of university credits that students who held the SoBL received was standardized. It should be noted that IHEs have used several approaches to determine if university credit should be granted to students with the SoBL: (a) granting credit based on a proficiency testing mechanism, (b) granting credit based on a proficiency testing mechanism only after students place into and successfully complete a language class at the university, (c) granting credit only if the student declares a major or minor in the language, and (d) not granting credit (Davin, 2021).

Phase one: Initial partnership (2018–2021)

Conversations regarding awarding incoming students with credit for the Connecticut State SoBL (SSoBL) began in 2017. A state-level bill, signed into law by the Governor in June 2017, required the State Board of Education to develop criteria by which a local or regional board of education could award the SSoBL to a student who had achieved a high level of proficiency in English and one or more additional languages. To prepare for the first high school recipients of the SoBL who graduated in spring 2018, Chairperson A and the NPSD World Language (WL) supervisor met multiple times during AY 2017–2018. They discussed the possibility of the RPU awarding college credit to SoBL recipients, especially those from the NPSD language programs that the supervisor directly oversaw.

Because RPU already had a language requirement in place, awarding students with credit for the SSoBL was a simple decision. RPU's language requirement stipulated that each student successfully complete a third-semester language course or demonstrate proficiency equivalent to an Intermediate-Low level (ACTFL, 2012) on an external proficiency assessment, such as the Standards-based Assessment Measurement of Proficiency (STAMP) or the ACTFL Assessment of Performance Toward Proficiency in Languages (AAPPL). Alternatively, RPU also offered the STAMP for a nominal fee so that students could receive CBE through on-campus proctoring services in the Language Department's open lab. However, this requirement of Intermediate-Low was one sublevel lower than that required to earn an SSoBL in Connecticut (i.e., Intermediate-Mid level or higher). Thus when the legislation became state law, RPU faculty realized that SSoBL recipients would have already met and exceeded RPU's proficiency requirement.

Despite this realization, during AY 2017–2018, faculty in RPU's Languages Department agreed to recognize the SoBL for university credit at the same level as students testing out of the language requirement. In this way, SoBL recipients received nine credits (or the first three semesters of language coursework), which was in line with the credits given to students who took STAMP and provided the equivalence to their university language requirement. But given that the Intermediate-Mid level required to earn the SoBL equated to the targeted benchmark for students completing the fourth-semester language class, SoBL recipients technically should have been entitled to 12 university credits. Nonetheless, because some states do not require formal proficiency assessments to earn a SoBL (see Davin 2021), instead allowing for world-language seat time—for example, faculty opted to continue with only nine language credits.

A critical component of this new process was advertising. In the fall of 2017, Chairperson A and the WL supervisor created a pamphlet to distribute to all NPSD students who received or were considering the SoBL (see Table A8.1). During that time, NPSD students took the STAMP test to earn the SoBL, although they later transitioned to the AAPPL. The flier described the Languages Department's degree offerings and the process for receiving nine credits in the language for which they achieved their SoBL. The pamphlet emphasized that nine university language credits constituted half of those needed to complete a language minor (18 credits) and would serve to fulfill the university's general education language requirement. Additionally, the flier showcased the various RPU language major and minor offerings. Lastly, the document alerted students to schedule an appointment with the Languages Department chairperson to provide evidence of their SoBL.

The meeting with the department chairperson served several purposes. During these one-on-one appointments, Chairperson A would (a) validate the student's SoBL, (b) award them nine university-level language credits (the equivalent of first-, second-, and third-semester language courses), and (c) discuss the advantages of majoring or minoring in the language. Chairperson A explained to students that (a) all credits earned through the SoBL counted toward their degree, (b) earning the SoBL demonstrated that language learning constituted an area of strength for students (i.e., an asset), and (c) it was possible to complete the minor by taking only three additional courses in the language, which in the case of Spanish and several other languages, also counted toward additional general education requirements beyond RPU's language requirement. Faculty deliberately structured the minor so that students could take courses that met multiple university requirements, subsequently reducing educational costs and time to graduation.

Phase two: Evolving partnership (2021–2023)

In Phase Two of the partnership, several changes occurred. In the fall of 2021, Chairperson A fulfilled their leadership term, and faculty elected a new chairperson (Chairperson B). During this transition in leadership, which also coincided with ongoing pandemic conditions and many curricular/modality modifications, the RPU-NPSD partnership evolved. First, Chairperson B began conversations with department faculty regarding the number of credits that students were receiving through the CBE process. Discussions focused on the possible impact of waiving credits on the department's enrollment. The new chairperson suggested that SoBL recipients should receive only three credits to meet the university's general education language requirement but that they could earn additional credits only if they declared a minor or major in that language. Incoming students with the SoBL who came in with the understanding that they would receive nine credits, the equivalent of first-, second-, and third-semester language courses, found that the former policy was no longer in place. During this second phase of the partnership, not all students with the SoBL received consistent advising or credit allocation.

Another rationale for not automatically granting nine credits to students with the SoBL was the implementation of new financial aid guidelines. Automatically granting credits to SoBL recipients could be detrimental to certain students if those credits would reduce their limited number of elective credits. This could cause some students to exhaust their elective credits with no way to complete major (or required course) prerequisites as part of their degree requirements.

Finally, another challenge encountered during the second phase of the partnership related to the requirement that students must meet with the department chair to receive credit for their SoBL. This was challenging because of the lack of clarity around how policies had changed under new department leadership, mixed messages regarding the amount of credit students would receive, and a lack of an updated written policy. As will be shown in the following section, a written policy published on the university website would have helped students understand the rules and self-advocate.

Phase three: Current partnership (2023–onward)

The third phase of the RPU policy on awarding university credit to SoBL recipients represented a standardization in the number of credits awarded. SoBL recipients became eligible to receive six university language credits for the second and third semesters of a language, which satisfied both RPU's language requirement and an additional distribution requirement within the university's general education curriculum. It should be noted that beginning in this semester, the university decided via referendum to lower its general education language requirement to two semesters rather than three semesters, so incoming students only needed to take up to the second-semester language course, corresponding to a level of Novice-High proficiency (ACTFL, 2012).

The streamlining of the credit allocation process also made it possible to eliminate the requirement that SoBL earners meet with the department chairperson. Instead, they were required to send a photo of their high school diploma to RPU's Admissions Office, which then granted credit in the language for which the student held the SoBL.

Given the evolution in RPU policies and the NPSD partnership, our study aimed to answer the following questions:

1 How many university credits did participants receive for their SoBL in 2018–2023 during the different phases of the RPU-NPSD SoBL partnership?
2 Was there an observable connection between the different stages of the RPU-NPSD SoBL partnership, the credits awarded for the SoBL, and the number of students who decided to major or minor in Spanish?
3 How did various stakeholders (e.g., students, staff, community partners) perceive and/or experience the distinct phases of the RPU-NPSD SoBL partnership (2018–2023)?

To answer these questions, we recruited 56 NPSD students who graduated high school between the years of 2018–2023 and enrolled at RPU as full-time students. In addition, we interviewed seven key stakeholders who were instrumental in understanding the impact of the RPU-NPSD partnership: the WL supervisor at NPSD, the RPU director of first-year admissions, the RPU director of the First-Year Program, and the past chairperson (Chairperson A, also Author 3), current chairperson (Chairperson B) of the RPU Languages Department, and two professors within the Spanish section of the Languages Department (Author 1 and Author 2). A total of four students were also interviewed: one from the first phase, two from the second phase, and one from the third and final phase of the partnership. All student participants who agreed to participate in the study signed informed consent documents protecting their privacy and confidentiality. Table 8.1 shows the pseudonyms and demographic information of the students (first four rows), as well as the demographic details for the other stakeholder participants.

TABLE 8.1 Participants

Pseudonym or Role	*First Year at RPU*	*Age*	*Gender Identity*	*Major/Minor*	*Ethnicity*
Maria	2020	21	Female	Interdisciplinary	Latina
Nelly	2021	19	Female	Sociology	Latina
Grace	2021	20	Female	Communications	Latina
Dana	2023	18	Female	Child Rec/Leisure	Latina
NPSD WL Director	–	–	Female	–	White
Director, First-Year Program	–	–	Female	–	White
Director, First-Year Admissions	–	–	Male	–	Latino
RPU, Chairperson 1 (Author 3)	–	–	Female	–	White
RPU, Languages Chairperson 2	–	–	Male	–	Latino
RPU, Spanish Faculty (Author 1)	–	–	Female	–	White
RPU, Spanish Faculty (Author 2)	–	–	Female	–	Latina

Data were both quantitative and qualitative and were analyzed using a mixed-methods design (Creswell, 2007). Quantitative data were drawn from a larger pool of 460 NPSD graduates who obtained the SoBL between the years 2019 and 2023. Of these graduates, 9% ($n = 56$) had been accepted to RPU. Descriptive statistics using Excel were conducted on the quantitative data.

Qualitative data consisted of semi-structured interviews. Nine focal participants, four students and five key stakeholders, were interviewed, totaling approximately four hours and 27 minutes of audio recordings. The recordings were transcribed and analyzed using Grounded Theory (Charmaz, 2006; Glaser & Strauss, 1967). Three independent coders corroborated, and several major themes emerged. Each theme was supported through multiple participant quotes and references as presented in the following section.

Findings

To answer the first research question, descriptive statistics were performed on the total number of university credits awarded over the five-year period. Table 8.2 shows how the number of university credits that participants received for their SoBL steadily increased during the years of 2019–2022. Students received the largest number of credits (i.e., 6.5 per student) in AY 2021–2022 when 75% of participants with the SoBL received university credit. In AY 2022–2023, the percentage of students who received credit for their SoBL (29%) declined, and the average number of credits students received dropped to 4.8 per student. In AY 2023–2024, the percentage of students who received credit increased to 44%, but the average number of credits dropped to an all-time low (2.7%). These data justified the need for the third phase of the partnership, in which students automatically received university language credit for their SoBL.

TABLE 8.2 Students who received university language credit for their SoBL

AY	*Number of Students with the SoBL* (n = *112)*	*Percentage (%) of Sts Who Received Credit*	*Average Number of Credits Sts Received (0–9)*
2019–2020	6	33	3.6
2020–2021	12	58	3.8
2021–2022	12	75	6.5
2022–2023	17	29	4.8
2023–2024	9	44[a]	2.7

Note:

[a] Although 100% of students became eligible to receive credit for their SoBL during the 2023–2024 academic year, they did not automatically receive credit for reasons that will be discussed.

TABLE 8.3 Number and percentage of students who completed a Spanish major or minor

AY	*Total Undergraduate Enrollment*	*Number of Spanish Majors (%Total)*	*Number of Spanish Minors (% Total)*
2019–2020	7,665	22 (0.29%)	58 (0.76%)
2020–2021	7,458	27 (0.36%)	74 (0.99%)
2021–2022	6,759	26 (0.38%)	69 (1.0%)
2022–2023	6,423	30 (0.47%)	58 (0.90%)
2023–2024	6,405	36 (0.56%)	60 (0.94%)

To answer the second research question regarding trends across partnership phases, the number of Spanish majors and minors over the five-year period was collected. Table 8.2 illustrates the steady increase in the number of Spanish majors, from 22 in AY 2019–2020 to 36 in AY 2023–2024. It is important to note that to address declining enrollment, in 2021, the Languages Department rolled out a new bachelor of science (BS) degree in Spanish with three workforce-applicable concentrations (i.e., teacher certification, translation studies, and Spanish for health and human service professionals) and a fourth concentration in Hispanic Studies. This degree replaced the Bachelor of Arts (BA) in Spanish and allowed the approximately 70% of RPU students who held a BS degree to pair it with the BS in Spanish. In this way, the increase in majors was likely influenced by an increase in the perceived applicability of the new BS degree to students' chosen career paths, their ability to double major in Spanish and their primary degree, as well as an incentive to continue with formal language study from receiving university language credit for their SoBL (Table 8.3).

The number of Spanish minors also fluctuated over the five-year period. The largest number (i.e., 74) occurred in AY 2020–2021. With overall university enrollments declining over the five-year period, a small decline in minors might not have necessarily indicated that recruitment efforts were less successful. Moreover, RPU offered two Spanish minors: a general minor and a medical Spanish minor, which faculty created to appeal to the growing number of students at RPU majoring in health and human service fields. Given the time difference between when students received university credit for their SoBL and when they graduated with a major or minor, it was difficult to prove a direct correlation between students receiving credit for their SoBL and their decision to minor or major. Nonetheless, it is likely that the factors described earlier influenced students' decision to minor or major in Spanish, including (a) incentivized to come to RPU while still in high school thanks to the partnership with NPSD, (b) receiving university language credit for their SoBL upon arrival, and (c) receiving social and emotional support and recognition for their language proficiency as acknowledged by the SoBL. The sense of belonging cultivated during Chairperson A's one-on-one meetings with students, the partnership with NPSD, and the encouragement to continue with formal language study at RPU may all have played a role in students' decisions to minor and major in the language.

To answer our third question regarding stakeholder perceptions and experiences, we documented five themes from the analysis of the interviews with students, staff, and community stakeholders. The themes paint an illustrative picture of the multiple aspects at play when examining the SoBL as a tool for remedying disparate opportunity gaps. We examine each in some detail.

Theme 1: Differing perspectives on credit by examination (CBE)

Different perspectives emerged around the practice of granting CBE through the SoBL. Some stakeholders held an optimistic stance. For example, the Supervisor of WL Programming at NPSD stated that she expected the SoBL recognition to help enrollments by offering students with higher proficiency a clear path into upper-level classes that counted toward a minor or major. She asserted, "I don't believe that in the long run giving credit is going to hurt your programs at all...you might not have as many level 1 or 2, but you're going to have these beautiful high level language classes". Other stakeholders expressed some apprehension that the practice of awarding credit through the SoBL could be detrimental. Chairperson B stated, "Since we give them so many credits for the basic [language classes], we're actually not encouraging them to go beyond 200 and 301". These two contrasting viewpoints dominated discussions regarding the allocation of credits within language departments.

Theme 2: Need for greater clarity in policy

The theme of clarity and empowerment came up numerous times in stakeholder and student interviews. Nelly, a 19-year-old Latina sociology major, reflected:

> I know a lot of people who have the SoBL...most of them are first generation and probably like me, don't know a lot about it [the SoBL]. Putting your office out there and saying bring the Seal to us and not only that, but maybe encourage them to take a minor or a major.

Nelly's statement revealed her desire for greater clarity around the SoBL process. She alluded to the fact that first-generation college-goers might not have the knowledge of how to earn credit for their SoBL. Similarly, Dana stated, "I feel like if I would have talked to someone I would have declared it [the Spanish minor] right away instead of overthinking it". Although Dana did ultimately declare a Spanish minor, she indicated how useful it would have been for her to have the opportunity to speak with someone in the Language Department about her SoBL. These students' sentiments were also reflected by the views of the director of the First-Year Program, who was emphatic about the need for clarity in order to empower students to take responsibility for their college experiences. Overall, the need for clear written policies arose repeatedly across interviewees.

Theme 3: SoBL as a tool for recruitment

Interviewees expressed that awarding credit for the SoBL served as a tool for the recruitment and retention of bilingual university students. As the director of first-year admissions remarked,

> "I think the Seal...[represents] a group of students who can increase minor enrollment...because number one they showed an interest in it already to be able to get into these levels and number two the amount of credits left for them is lower than in other minors".

This sentiment was echoed by Grace, a 20-year-old Latina, who stated,

> [The advisors] didn't convince me, but they recommended that I could have a minor because it would save me money...and because I already had many credits. Also, with the credits I was going to get from my AP Spanish, I only had to take two classes. I ended up needing three. Now I'm going to take my last two classes. But, in reality, I saved money and didn't have to take the other classes because I already had the SoBL. After that.... I thought about doing a double major, but then I decided not to.
>
> *(Translation from Spanish)*

As multiple stakeholders pointed out, recruitment through CBE was a win-win scenario for institutions and language departments that have been grappling with decreasing language enrollments for decades.

Theme 4: Financial and enrollment considerations

Various stakeholders perceived the SoBL CBE policy as important, considering the rising cost of education. Increasing cost is an ongoing concern and part and parcel of the mission of RPUs that wish to increase access. As Grace pointed out, "I'm sure that any student will want to save time and money" (Translated from Spanish). Similarly, the director of first-year admissions remarked, "Early college credit...saves time, it saves money...you can really leverage these areas". CBE allowed students to save money by offering them the opportunity to either test out of costly requirements or continue to effectively pursue their language study at the level that is most appropriate for their ability, thereby potentially remedying preexisting opportunity gaps, such as those exacerbated by the lack of availability of AP credit in some school districts.

It is important to acknowledge the relationship between CBE and the reduction of the cost of education and time to graduation; thus, allocation of credits can save a student time and money. Furthermore, encouraging a student to pursue a language is not the same as holding their language credits hostage. This relates to the importance of clear policies surrounding CBE. As the director of FYE stated, "Students don't necessarily know there's something wrong with [their not being granted credit]". She went on to tell the story of a student who spoke four African languages but struggled to have his language requirement waived, going on to say, "I don't think that [student] fully understood that he could just say no [to taking additional language classes]". RPUs, especially those with clear social justice missions, have an obligation to ensure that their faculty and midlevel administrators implement clear policies that, at the very least, do not hinder students' progress and path toward graduation. Holding these students' credits hostage (i.e., not consistently awarding CBE based on students' language ability and, in certain cases, placing barriers to timely graduation) is a disservice to students, programs, and university missions. Although some faculty may worry that granting CBE will decrease language enrollment, it may actually encourage students to take courses at their appropriate level of ability and incentivize their efficient path toward minoring or majoring in a language.

Theme 5: Student- versus program-centered

In a climate of declining enrollments, it would be naive to assume that students' academic, professional, and personal livelihoods are the only administrative considerations. In a campus climate where humanities, more broadly, and language departments, more specifically, have been reduced or eliminated, there are equally pressing concerns. One concern is the assessment of program success based purely on quantitative numbers. As Chairperson B remarked, "The bottom line, the department [is] only [as] strong as the number of majors that we have, so I think that one of my efforts for now is to increase the number of majors". Atrophy of resources and the perceived nationwide devaluation of language programs have led language departments to fear for their own survival. "I'm not married to either giving [students credit] or not, but I think my decision is always based on what is best for...the department. I assume that what's best for the department is best for the students" (Chairperson B). Indeed, without support from university administration, students may no longer have language programming, which is often deemed costly and unrelated to students' future professional careers.

Implications

Based on our collective experiences in the RPU-NPSD partnership around the SoBL credit policy, we argue that granting students CBE should include policies that advantage bilingual learners through the SoBL. Although stakeholders may disagree about how to offer CBE to SoBL recipients, doing so puts universities in a unique position to engage in student success initiatives aimed at reducing opportunity gaps, such as decreasing time to graduation and increasing graduation rates of bilingual students. This should include the (a) targeted advising of Spanish majors and minors, (b) formal and informal mentorship of students by faculty and peers, and (c) deliberate creation of a sense of belonging at universities through event programming and initiatives founded to provide a broad range of resources, such as, but not limited to, supports for undocumented students, like scholarships.

While awarding university language credit for students who hold the SoBL has the potential to create more equitable structures for bilingual students at IHEs, it also has the danger of reproducing existing inequities (Davin & Heineke, 2022). As the SoBL and CBE become vehicles to recruit students for university language programs, faculty must also consider programmatic changes. Traditional university language departments formed as an institutional mechanism to promote and nurture elite bilingualism in IHEs, meaning programs targeting primarily English-dominant students who were learning a foreign language as part of a classic liberal arts education (Subtirelu et al., 2019). It is important to acknowledge that universities now serve considerable numbers of heritage Spanish learners and native Spanish speakers; therefore, it follows that universities will need to adapt their practices to effectively prepare these students to develop their language skills in the workplace and beyond (Davin & Heineke, 2022).

If language programs risk losing bilingual students in lower-division courses because of SoBL and other CBE policies, then IHEs ought to consider ways to preserve and protect language departments, recognizing the important role they serve in furthering their access mission. Administrators, in particular, can help by allocating resources to programs that recruit bilingual students into the minor and major, as well as engaging in other student success initiatives, such as strategically decreasing time to graduation through CBE to serve the increasingly dense population of heritage and native-speaker students. The fight-or-flight response that many language departments may feel at the constant erosion of their programs may lead to an ever-increasing sense of hostility and defensiveness (Lord, 2020). University administrations interested in maximizing student success through strategies such as implementing a SoBL policy should recognize these inherent vulnerabilities and the risk that new approaches to recruitment may involve for language departments.

Conclusions and next steps

The practice of awarding credit for the SoBL and language proficiency tests, along with the strategic recruitment of students by counting courses for other general requirements, holds the potential to recruit heritage learners and native speakers of Spanish into university language study. As evidenced in this chapter, active recruitment of students to attend universities that offer language credit for the SoBL and clear advertisement of the SoBL credit policy can lead to increased enrollment and potentially grow the number of students who pursue a major or minor. On the other hand, CBE policies that fail to acknowledge students' bilingualism as an asset and rather view general education language requirements as merely another hoop for students to jump through disincentivize enrollment and add to growing concerns for the future of university languages and humanities (Looney & Lusin, 2019; Lord, 2020; Lusin et al., 2023). Partnerships such as the one described in this chapter incentivize bilingual students to continue formal language study and have the potential to bolster recruitment and retention of students from local high schools.

Bilingualism as either an asset or a deficit is a theme that has been well documented in the literature (Baker & Wright, 2017). Power differentials between professors and students must be taken into account. As the director of the First-Year Program stated,

> "We should start celebrating that credential the way we celebrate students coming in with early college credits and they get all that hype but like the Seal of Biliteracy...which really works against that stigma of the old like ESL student as opposed to the bilingual".

By choosing to honor students' language proficiency through the SoBL, the message can be made clear that faculty see their bilingualism as an asset. By choosing not to honor it, or by putting up roadblocks, or lack of clarity, universities and departments might send the message to bilinguals that their bilingualism is unimportant or unvalued. In the case of heritage and native Spanish speakers, it may allude to the possibility that their particular variety of the language is not appreciated or welcome in academic spaces.

Since students are rightfully preoccupied with choosing majors that hold clear career outcomes, and because language and culture fluency are 21st-century skills, language departments stand to benefit by helping students articulate how their learning and credentials prepare them for success in their chosen career paths. While it feels like a discouraging time for language departments, this moment of transition also offers opportunities for creativity, growth, innovation, reinvention, and a recommitment to the foundational values of the discipline.

Appendix

TABLE A8.1 Original partnership agreement between RPU and NPSD

Earn World Language Credits for your Seal of Biliteracy!
If you received the Seal of Biliteracy, then YOU can qualify for language credits at RPUU!

If you tested in Spanish, Italian, Chinese, French or German, you will receive 9 credits at the 100 and 200 level if you are accepted at Regional Public University.
If you tested in another language, you will receive 9 generic language credits.

What does that mean?

You will already have 9 college credits on your transcript as you begin your university years!
You will have fulfilled your graduation requirement for RPU in world languages!
If you would like to pursue a minor or major in world languages, you are well on your way!

You should also consider...

- **A Minor in Spanish, Medical Spanish, Italian, Chinese, French or German!** With the 9 credits you will earn, you only need 9 more credits during your time at RPU to achieve the Minor.
- **A Major in Spanish, Italian or French!** With the 9 credits you earn, you only need 21 more credits during your time at RPU to achieve the Major.
- **Becoming a teacher of Spanish, Italian, or French!** World language positions are called a "shortage area" in Connecticut because there are so few qualified candidates. RPU offers certification in all three of these languages and can guide you through the process from day one!

How do I make it happen?

- Ask your high school teacher to print a copy of your "Score Report" from the test you took for the Seal of Biliteracy.
- The school or district must stamp the report with a school seal or stamp indicating the school or district.
- Your teacher or principal must sign and date the report with BLUE ink to verify its authenticity.
- After you are accepted to RPU, you must submit the report to the chairperson of the World Languages Department in person.

For more information on transferring your Seal of Biliteracy scores for credits at to RPU, please talk to your world languages teacher or supervisor to be sure you follow the directions above.
For information on *applying to RPU in the World Languages department, please contact Dr.* …
For information on *applying to RPU*, go to …

References

ACTFL. (2012). *ACTFL Proficiency guidelines*. ACTFL.
Baker, C., & Wright, D. (2017). *Foundations of bilingual education and bilingualism* (6th edition). Multilingual Matters.
Charmaz, K. (2006). *Constructing grounded theory: A practical guide through qualitative analysis*. Sage.

Creswell, J.W. (2007). *Qualitative inquiry and research design: Choosing among five traditions* (2nd ed.). Sage.

Davin, K. (2021). The Seal of Biliteracy: College credit and placement. *The Language Educator*, *16*(2), 32–34.

Davin, K.J., & Heineke, A.J. (2022). *Promoting multilingualism in schools: A framework for implementing the Seal of Biliteracy*. ACTFL Press.

Diao, W., & Liu, H.Y. (2020). Starting college, quitting foreign language: The case of learners of Chinese language during secondary-postsecondary transition. *Journal of Language, Identity & Education*, *20*(2), 75–89. https://doi.org/10.1080/15348458.2020.1726753

Excelencia in Education. (2020). *Ensuring America's future: Benchmarking Latino college completion to 2030*. Excelencia in Education. https://www.edexcelencia.org/research/latino-college-completion/connecticut

Glaser, B., & Strauss, A. (1967). *The discovery of grounded theory*. Aldine Publishing Company.

Looney, D., & Lusin, N. (2019). *Enrollments in languages other than English in United States institutions of higher education, summer 2016 and fall 2016: Final report*. Modern Language Association. www.mla.org/content/download/110154/2406932/2016-Enrollments-Final-Report.pdf

Lord, G. (2018, January 6). *What is the status of the foreign language requirement in higher education?* New York City: MLA Annual Convention.

Lord, G. (2020). Is the sky falling (again)? Observations on the language requirement in U.S. higher education. *ADFL Bulletin*, *46*(1), 114–122.

Lusin, N., Peterson, T., Sulewski, Z., & Zafer, R.. (2023). *Enrollments in languages other than English in US institutions of higher education, Fall 2021*. Modern Language Association of America. https://www.mla.org/content/download/191324/file/Enrollments-in-Languages-Other-Than-English-in-US-Institutions-of-Higher-Education-Fall-2021.pdf

MLA. (2007). *Foreign languages and higher education: New structures for a changed world*. MLA Ad Hoc Committee on Foreign Languages. www.mla.org/flreport

Morgan, J.L. (2012). Background and motivation of students studying a Native American language at the university level. *International Journal of Literacy, Culture, and Language Education*, *1*, 27–49. https://doi.org/10.14434/ijlclc.v1i0.26826

Murphy, D., Sarac, M., & Sedivy, S. (2022). Why U.S. undergraduate students are (not) studying languages other than English. *Second Language Research & Practice*, *3*(1), 1–33. https://doi.org/10125/69866

Rabe Thomas, J. (2017, July 31). *In their words: English learners share their stories about school*. Connecticut Mirror. https://ctmirror.org/2017/07/31/in-their-words-english-learners-share-their-stories-about-school/

Santos, V. (2022). *Psychometric evidence for the validity of STAMP 4S assessments*. Avant Assessment, LLC. https://avantassessment.com/research

Subtirelu, N.C., Borowczyk, M., Hernández, R.T., & Venezia, F. (2019). Recognizing whose bilingualism? A critical policy analysis of the Seal of Biliteracy. *Modern Language Journal*, *103*(2), 371–390. https://doi.org/10.1111/modl.12556

Thompson, A. (2017). Language learning motivation in the United States: An examination of language choice and multilingualism. *Modern Language Journal*, *101*(3), 483–500. https://doi.org/10.1111/modl.12409

Willner, C. (2022, October 14). *Celebrating Connecticut's Hispanic and Latino residents*. CT Data Collaborative. https://www.ctdata.org/blog/celebrating-connecticuts-hispanic-and-latino-residents/

PART IV

Recruiting Biliterate Individuals into Higher Education

9

EXPLORING THE RECRUITMENT POTENTIAL OF THE SEAL OF BILITERACY FOR HIGHER EDUCATION

Results of a pilot initiative

Janet Eckerson and Christopher Jacobs

Introduction

Over the past two decades, increasingly fewer students participating in postsecondary language programs has become a cause for concern amid widespread declines in overall higher education humanities enrollments (Heller, 2023; Lusin et al., 2023). In particular, midsize and smaller institutions of higher education (IHEs), especially those located outside major population centers, have seen fewer language majors and minors, as well as the reduction or elimination of language programs. As a result, many postsecondary language departments have doubled efforts to attract students, from the creation or redesign of programs to outreach efforts directed at future students now in kindergarten through 12th grade (K–12) schools (see Uebel et al., 2023). The emergence of the Seal of Biliteracy (SoBL) educational policy initiative across the United States can be seen as a promising aid in the effort to recruit students to postsecondary language study.

The notion of targeting students with existing language skills as undergraduate language majors or minors is hardly novel, given that such students have traditionally constituted a sizable portion of language department enrollments (Winke et al., 2020). Students with existing language skills may view language degree programs as more accessible or attractive because they have made progress toward completion, unlike novice-level or first-year students. SoBL recipients, depending on varying state policy benchmarks, typically demonstrate at least ACTFL Intermediate-Mid to Intermediate-High language proficiency (Black et al., 2020), which corresponds to second—or even third—year university language study (Winke et al., 2020). For this reason, the Modern Languages Department at the University of Nebraska at Kearney (UNK; henceforth referred to as "the Department") hypothesized that adopting placement and academic credit policies for SoBL recipients would help recruit these students to language study.

Some states' SoBL policies (e.g., Illinois, Minnesota, Rhode Island) mandate via legislation that at least some public IHEs award credit to SoBL recipients (Davin & Heineke, 2017). However, in most states, the creation of such credit policies falls on individual institutions, as is the case in Nebraska. Adopting such policies, we argue here, is crucial to leveraging

DOI: 10.4324/9781032667249-13

the SoBL to recruit language students. As will be detailed in the subsequent section, the Department modeled SoBL placement and retroactive credit policies on existing policies for placing students with Advanced Placement (AP) or International Baccalaureate (IB) exam scores. In fact, AP or IB exam scores are one of the ways SoBL candidates can demonstrate sufficient proficiency in languages other than English (LOTE) to qualify for the Nebraska SoBL. Otherwise, Nebraska students can demonstrate LOTE proficiency through commercial proficiency tests, such as the AAPPL or STAMP 4S, or coursework in dual, heritage, or native-speaker language courses. These measures serve as a reliable proxy for language placement tests at the postsecondary level.

The potential of the SoBL as a recruitment tool in higher education is complicated by the reality of unequal access to the recognition among potentially eligible secondary students. Critiques of the SoBL and its implementation in a variety of contexts have called attention to the various ways in which state policies and practices tend to reproduce existing inequalities (e.g., Burnet, 2017; Castro, 2020; Schwedhelm & King, 2020; Subtirelu et al., 2019). For instance, students labeled as English learners (ELs), speakers of less commonly taught languages, and students in rural and under-resourced schools may not have the same access to the language instruction and assessments needed to qualify for the SoBL. In rural contexts, there are fewer opportunities for advanced language study, such as fifth-year, AP, and IB course offerings or heritage or native-speaker courses (Chen et al., 2010). At the same time, outside of advanced language study, access to information about proficiency assessments and resources to cover the fees associated with the latter presents significant obstacles for eligible students whose school districts or buildings do not facilitate the SoBL award process.

Greater equity and access in the implementation of state SoBLs (SSoBLs) is in the interest of postsecondary language departments aiming to increase enrollments. Studies of SoBL recipients have pointed to the role academic credit policies at colleges and universities play in encouraging students to pursue the SoBL in secondary school by taking advanced courses or sitting for exams (Davin et al., 2018; Eckerson & Jacobs, 2024). The promise of low-cost college credit engages a variety of stakeholders, including parents and administrators, who may then advocate for access to opportunities for their students. But adopting and communicating SoBL academic credit policies is only the first step for colleges and universities. Language departments can do more to connect with potential future students through the SoBL by leveraging institutional resources like language laboratories and admissions outreach to support SoBL implementation in underserved communities.

Background and context

The focal university

UNK is a midsize regional public university with about 4,200 undergraduate students (UNK Factbook, 2023a). UNK is in Kearney, a town of about 34,000 inhabitants in rural south-central Nebraska (US Census Bureau, 2023a). Nebraska is a large but sparsely populated state located in the middle of the United States that ranks 38th in population and 43rd in density among the 50 states. Nebraska's population is concentrated around its two largest cities, Lincoln and Omaha, which are both located in the southeast part of the state, a two-to-three-hour drive from Kearney. Denver and Kansas City, the closest major metros, are about five hours away.

As a regional public institution, UNK focuses on serving the surrounding communities (Ellyson, 2022b). Over 90% of UNK students come from Nebraska and neighboring states (i.e., Kansas, Colorado, Wyoming; UNK Factbook, 2023b). Seeing a continued statewide decline in the rural white population, juxtaposed with a rapidly increasing Latinx population (NBC 6 News, 2021), UNK has begun specific initiatives to increase its Latinx enrollments (Ellyson, 2022c). As a result, this group now constitutes a larger share of UNK enrollments than of the local community. About 15% of UNK undergraduates identify as Hispanic/ Latino (UNK Factbook, 2023b), while 10% of Kearney residents and 12% of Nebraska residents identify in the same way (US Census Bureau, 2023a, 2023b).

Students from rural Nebraska counties account for more than two-thirds of UNK's undergraduate enrollments (UNK Factbook, 2023b). In Nebraska, rural schools are less likely to offer LOTE coursework; in fact, over one-fourth of Nebraska high schools (27%) do not have a language teacher employed in the building (Liu, 2023). The most commonly taught language in Nebraska high schools is Spanish, constituting just over two-thirds of statewide LOTE enrollments (NDE, 2019). However, this figure probably approaches 80%–90% (or more) in rural Nebraska, where most UNK students reside and where most high schools offer no LOTEs other than Spanish (if any at all). As a result, Spanish is the most commonly studied LOTE at UNK.

The focal initiative

In 2021, the Department revised the existing course placement policy to accept the SSoBL for placement and retroactive credit. The Nebraska SSoBL has two tiers; the Gold award recognizes language proficiency at the level of ACTFL Intermediate-High, while the Silver award recognizes Intermediate-Mid. To demonstrate eligibility, Nebraska high school students complete an online application and submit scores from proficiency assessments such as the APPPL or STAMP 4S, or AP or IB exam results. Students may use secondary English Language Arts, dual immersion, and heritage/native-speaker course completion (with a grade better than C) in lieu of an assessment, provided that the transcript shows at least six semesters of this coursework. Traditional foreign language courses and English learner courses do not constitute evidence for the Nebraska SSoBL (Nebraska Department of Education, 2024). The existing departmental policy placed students with AP/IB exam scores into fifth- and sixth-semester courses. Following this precedent, students who received a Nebraska Gold SoBL were placed into an upper-division class, qualifying them for nine retroactive credits toward a 24-credit modern language minor. Those who earned Silver placed into the third class of the 24-credit minor sequence and were thus eligible for six retroactive credits. In both cases, retroactive credit was awarded when students passed their first UNK language class with at least a B−.

Unlike many other states, the Nebraska SSoBL is administered by the Nebraska Department of Education (NDE) and is independent of the local school administration. In other words, individual Nebraska students apply for the recognition with the NDE, often aided by a teacher, counselor, or parent, and the NDE determines eligibility and issues certificates and seals directly to the student. As such, any Nebraska student may receive the award independent of their school or district's participation in adopting a pathway or process. However, in practice, districts with large AP/IB and dual-language enrollments have been more likely to facilitate student access to the SSoBL, organizing assessments and/or aiding students in completing the online application.

Not immune to the general declines in enrollment impacting IHEs throughout the country, UNK has seen a slow but steady decline in undergraduate enrollments (Lusin et al., 2023; UNK Factbook, 2023a). In 2021, the Dean of the College of Arts and Sciences (henceforth referred to as "the Dean") responded to this situation by offering to support departments with ideas to boost enrollments in their programs and on campus more generally. Encouraged by the Dean's funding, and knowing the difficulty that area students might have in accessing the SSoBL award, the Department decided that it would provide SSoBL-qualifying testing on campus for high school students. The Department hoped that this would both expose more students to higher education and to the SSoBL, leading to higher overall and language class enrollments. Students who participated in language testing on campus would learn about the Nebraska SSoBL application process and receive a score report they could submit as evidence of their proficiency in their LOTE.

To recruit participants, with the help of student assistants, we emailed high school language teachers (including world language and EL teachers) who were within a two-hour drive of campus, thought to be the most likely to accept our invitation, to arrange campus visits. In coordination with UNK Admissions, dates were chosen for group testing visits on weekdays during the spring semester. School groups were responsible for their own transportation, and students were responsible for a $20 test fee, but UNK Admissions provided visiting students with campus tours and a free lunch. Some schools provided transportation by bus or school vehicle, and some nearby students arranged their own transportation to campus. As of the fall of 2023, seven different area schools had participated in group visits, and another five schools had sent individual students to test on campus. Group visits were organized to allow students to take a language test upon arrival, have lunch, go on a campus tour, and/or visit with the Office of Diversity and Inclusion, and then attend a presentation about the program offerings in the Department of Modern Languages.

The testing instrument was the Avant STAMP 4S test, chosen because of its low cost and wide selection of languages. As of April 2023, the STAMP 4S—which includes listening, speaking, reading, and writing—was offered in 14 modern spoken languages, including English and all the LOTEs that are most often studied in the US (Avant Assessment, 2023). Twenty-seven additional languages can be assessed with two- or three-skill STAMP tests. In the case of the current initiative, high school students took STAMP 4S tests in a university computer lab, where the tests were proctored by a research assistant, a faculty member, or one of the Department's student workers. The initial funding from the Dean's office allowed for a bulk purchase of testing licenses; the student testing fees replaced these funds, and the project has become self-sustaining.

The focal study

The data reported here were collected in the local impact evaluation phase of a larger educational design research study exploring the relationship between SSoBL awards and the pursuit of postsecondary language study in Nebraska (see Eckerson & Jacobs, 2023; Eckerson & Jacobs, 2024). Educational design research models bring design thinking to educational interventions (Bannan-Ritland, 2003); in this phase of the design project, we aimed to examine the effectiveness of the testing visits as a recruitment tool in our language department, as well as their impact on SSoBL implementation in our region. Specifically, we asked: *To what degree do the opportunities to test for the SoBL serve as a recruiting tool for the Department of Modern Languages? What role(s) could this university initiative play in improving access to the SSoBL?* IRB approval was obtained to interview high school teachers who had participated in the testing visits with their students and to use enrollment data that had been collected by the Department for the evaluation of the recruitment initiative.

Findings

UNK enrollment data for testing participants

As of October 2023, 182 high school students had taken a STAMP test on UNK's campus. All but one participant used Spanish as their LOTE, and one other participant took tests in two LOTE languages (including Spanish). Neither of the non-English, non-Spanish languages—both home languages—was taught locally. No teachers of other commonly taught world languages (e.g., French, German) have accepted the researchers' invitation thus far, so no students have taken a STAMP test in locally taught languages other than Spanish.

Table 9.1 presents STAMP 4S testing data by the academic year (AY) in which the participants took their test. The UNK AY runs from mid-August of one year to mid-August of the next. Composite data for the three AYs are also shown. For the purposes of this study, high school (HS) seniors included not only those in their last year of high school but also those who had graduated high school but were not yet enrolled in a postsecondary institution. In other words, HS seniors are those who were eligible to enroll in college within no more than a year of taking their STAMP test. Seven AY 2020–2021 test-takers had already graduated HS at the time they tested.

TABLE 9.1 STAMP 4S test-taking and UNK enrollment data by AY

AY	*Test-takers*	*Number and % of test-takers who were HS seniors*	*Number and % of test-taking seniors who enrolled at UNK*	*Number and % of test-taking seniors who enrolled at UNK and took a language class*	*Number and % of test-taking seniors who enrolled at UNK and took a language class and enrolled in a language major or minor*
AY 2020–2021	14	14 (100%)	9 (64%)	5 (56%)	2 (40%)
AY 2021–2022	76	57 (75%)	12 (21%)	7 (58%)	6 (86%)
AY 2022–2023	92	52 (57%)	10 (19%)	2 (20%)	1 (50%)
Total for three AY's	182	123 (68%)	31 (25%)	14 (45%)	9 (64%)

When compared to the general population at UNK, the data in Table 9.1 reveal the impact of the testing initiative. At first glance, a yield of nine language majors and minors from 182 test-takers may seem suboptimal, but it is worth remembering that many, perhaps most, HS senior test-takers had already decided if and where they would study in the coming fall when they came to UNK to test. Whereas only 5% (*n* = 197) of UNK undergraduates enrolled in a language class, 45% (*n* = 14) of students who tested at UNK as seniors and later enrolled there (*n* = 31) took a language class. Similarly, 29% (*n* = 9) of UNK-matriculated test-takers (*n* = 31) declared a language minor or major, compared to 3% (*n* = 117) of the general UNK undergraduate population (UNK Factbook, 2023a).

By this metric, UNK STAMP 4S test-takers (i.e., future SoBL recipients) were far more likely to take a language class than the average UNK student. In fact, the earlier figures regarding the general UNK population overestimate enrollments because UNK data do not allow for the separation of unique enrollments from duplicate enrollments (i.e., enrollment in one language class or program vs. enrollment in multiple). This means that SoBL recipients were even more likely than the average UNK student to take a language class or enroll in a language degree program than the data in 9.1 reflect.

Insignificant differences were found between test-takers residing within 60 miles of UNK, the distance within which UNK would be the nearest University of Nebraska campus, and those living farther away. (Table 9.1 does not distinguish between those over and those under 60 miles from UNK). Among those less than 60 miles from UNK, 28.05% (*n* = 23) of those who took a STAMP test as seniors enrolled at UNK, of which 39.13% (*n* = 9) took a UNK language class, and 66.67% (*n* = 6) declared a language major or minor. These yields were much like the yields for the whole sample.

The true picture of how many test-takers eventually enrolled in language courses, or chose majors or minors, has not yet emerged. For example, three AY 2022–2023 HS senior test-takers declared a Spanish minor, but as of the fall of 2023, they had yet to take a UNK language class. One AY 2021–2022 senior test-taker, counted once in the major/minor column, enrolled in both a Spanish minor and a French minor. Students enrolled in language classes as first-year students may not have declared a language major or minor yet but may do so in the future.

Given the large number of Spanish speakers who participated in the testing, it was useful to analyze data specifically for Spanish heritage language learners (HLLs) to consider the effectiveness of this intervention on a group of institutional interest. For this study, HLLs are individuals who hear or speak the LOTE in which they tested at home, while second language (L2) learners are those who do not. See Table 9.2 for data on HLLs and Table 9.3 for data on L2 learners.

Among HLLs of Spanish (Table 9.2), 40% (*n* = 10) of those who tested at UNK as seniors and later matriculated there (*n* = 25) enrolled in a language class. Twenty-eight percent (*n* = 7) of UNK-matriculated HLL senior test-takers (*n* = 25) declared a language major or minor. On the other hand, 67% (*n* = 4) of L2 Spanish learners who tested at UNK as seniors and subsequently matriculated there (*n* = 6) enrolled in a language class, while 33% (*n* = 2) of the same population (*n* = 6) declared a language major or minor. In other words, L2 learners were more likely to enroll in a college language class and declare a language major or minor than their HLL peers. However, the fact that four times more HLL senior test-takers than L2 senior test-takers (*n* = 25 vs. *n* = 6) enrolled at UNK complicates comparisons of course and degree program enrollments between HLLs and L2 learners.

TABLE 9.2 Test-taking and enrollment data for HLLs of Spanish

Academic year (AY)	*Test-takers who were HLLs*	*Number and % of HLL test-takers who were HS seniors*	*Number and % of HLL test-taking seniors who enrolled at UNK*	*Number and % of HLL test-taking seniors who enrolled at UNK and took a language class*	*Number and % of HLL test-taking seniors who enrolled at UNK, took a language class, and enrolled in a language major or minor*
AY 2020–2021	11 (79%)	11 (100%)	6 (55%)	3 (50%)	2 (67%)
AY 2021–2022	59 (78%)	45 (76%)	11 (24%)	6 (55%)	5 (83%)
AY 2022–2023	71 (77%)	42 (59%)	8 (19%)	1 (13%)	0 (0%)
Total for three AY's	141 (77%)	98 (70%)	25 (26%)	10 (40%)	7 (70%)

TABLE 9.3 Test-taking and enrollment data for L2 learners

Academic year (AY)	*Test-takers who were L2 learners*	*Number and % of L2 learner test-takers who were HS seniors*	*Number and % of L2 learner test-taking seniors who enrolled at UNK*	*Number and % of L2 learner test-taking seniors who enrolled at UNK and took a language class*	*Number and % of L2 learner test-taking seniors who enrolled at UNK, took a language class, and enrolled in a language major or minor*
AY 2020–2021	3 (21%)	3 (100%)	3 (100%)	2 (67%)	0 (0%)
AY 2021–2022	17 (22%)	12 (71%)	1 (8%)	1 (100%)	1 (100%)
AY 2022–2023	21 (23%)	10 (48%)	2 (20%)	1 (50%)	1 (100%)
Total for three AY's	41 (23%)	25 (61%)	6 (24%)	4 (67%)	2 (50%)

Fifty-nine of the 182 participants tested before they were HS seniors. Twenty of these were juniors who tested in AY 2021–2022 and likely graduated the following year. Two retook the test as seniors, matriculated at UNK, and enrolled in language classes in the fall of 2023. One has already declared a language minor. A third did not retake the test as a senior also enrolled at UNK. He has not taken a language class yet and is not counted in any of the enrollment columns in the tables. Current data do not tell what happened to the other 17 HS students who tested as juniors in AY 2021–2022, but one can assume that some matriculated at other institutions while others chose not to pursue postsecondary education—at least not yet.

Participating teacher interviews

To better understand the effectiveness of the recruitment initiative, the program evaluation included Summer 2022 interviews with four of the teachers who had brought students on testing visits during AY 2021–2022. After obtaining informed consent, the interviews were conducted via Zoom using a semi-structured interview protocol focused on the campus visit process and the SSoBL award more generally. Responses regarding the visit process are reported here. The four teachers—Carlos, Kate, Mary, and Sarah (all pseudonyms)—were HS teachers at schools within a two-hour drive of UNK's campus. Carlos, Kate, and Mary were Spanish teachers, while Sarah was an EL teacher.

The three Spanish teachers were familiar with the SSoBL, and both Carlos and Mary had aided some students in applying for the award in the past. They mentioned having learned of the SSoBL from the NDE or Nebraska International Language Association (NILA) communications. NILA is Nebraska's ACTFL-affiliated language teacher organization. For Sarah, the EL teacher, the email from the UNK language department was the first she had heard of the recognition. She recollected,

> [This was] the first time anybody here [at my school] had [heard of the SSoBL]. Well, I don't know if the counselors ever got information and didn't share it. But as far as the teachers go, we had never heard anything until we were reached out to from your department.

Sarah's lack of familiarity with the SSoBL as an EL teacher illustrates a challenge in Nebraska's implementation. The Nebraska world language specialist administers the program for NDE; thus, naturally, world language teachers have had greater access to information. Given that students apply as individuals, information about the recognition from the NDE needs to reach students, parents, and teachers, including and especially EL teachers like Sarah.

Kate had heard of the recognition in the past, sharing, "It [the SSoBL] was very intriguing, but a little bit overwhelming. There was a lot on my plate at that time, and I just kind of tabled that [SSoBL testing] as a goal". Then, Kate described how a colleague at a nearby school had mentioned that her students had earned a SSoBL, making her think, "I need to make sure that they [my students] have this opportunity". When she received the email invitation to bring students to campus for the test, she recalled, "It was just like, this [initiative] is what I need. I need somebody to hold my hand and help my students to be able to have this opportunity".

Classroom teachers and counselors are often bombarded with information and initiatives that go beyond their everyday instructional duties. The Department infrastructure was well positioned to support classroom teachers with the logistical and administrative tasks needed to implement the proficiency testing that provides access to the Nebraska SSoBL.

Carlos also expressed appreciation for the convenience of the testing experience on campus. He described having administered the STAMP 4S assessment at his school.

> The year before, when we did the Seal of Biliteracy, we were in charge of giving the test to our students. So, one night they got to stay for those three long hours, and I was there, and two people from our technology department were helping me with adding the test to their iPads and everything, all the process. So, we found it quite difficult for us to manage the technology part because we found some difficulties.... So the following

> year, when I got that email…telling us that we were able to do this at UNK, I thought, this is great. I mean it is—it is really convenient for us to have someone to—that has the knowledge already on how to deliver the test to students, and we don't have to worry about that part.

The initiative removed barriers to facilitating the SSoBL application for students. While larger school districts might support proficiency testing, in smaller schools, this work may fall to classroom teachers. The regional university partner, in this case, was able to step into the role that a larger district might have played in disseminating information about the award and application process and arranging for testing opportunities.

Sarah and Mary described the advantages they perceived in offering access to the SSoBL through proficiency testing outside of the HS course enrollment requirement. Sarah said that many EL students at her school had strong language proficiency but never enrolled in a Spanish class. Similarly, Mary suggested that the AP Spanish class at her school was not appealing to all students potentially eligible for the award. She explained,

> We kind of tried to catch those kids last year as seniors [to participate in the visit] who maybe would be phasing out and just give them the opportunity to earn this… and see if they would be interested in trying Spanish in college because they already have a skill that they didn't have to learn, but that they could earn credits for.

The testing visits provided students an opportunity to obtain evidence of language proficiency for SSoBL eligibility that was independent of their HS course enrollments.

All four teachers appreciated the "value-added" design of the visit that incorporated elements of a traditional admissions campus visit. Carlos, for one, said this helped him to recruit students to participate,

> I really love the way that you guys are setting up a whole day for our students (…) a tour around campus, and a free lunch, because when you tell the student as well, it's not just a test (…). You will get to see the dorms and some of the classrooms, and talk to some of the staff and department, and you are even getting a free lunch! I think we can still get more participants, you know, because the day is more attractive rather than just going to take the test and come back.

In this sense, the design of the testing visits served both the university partners, connecting admissions officials with the visiting students and also the participating teachers, who were able to leverage the multi-purpose visit to campus to increase participation.

Mary, Sarah, and Kate emphasized that the retroactive credit opportunities associated with the SSoBL at UNK and other Nebraska universities were the key point they emphasized in persuading students to participate in the visits. In short, Sarah explained, students should understand that with retroactive credit, "you get those credits for the lower levels, for free, basically. No time and no money spent on those". Mary connected the retroactive credit to making language minors more accessible as well:

> Money is a big thing at university, (…) then let's look at how many credits you have to take to have a Spanish minor, let's say. Now, let's look: If you could start at the 300 level instead

of the 100 level, and you could earn those retroactive credits at a UNK or UNL or Doane. What would that look like for your future? How many classes would you actually have to take?

The participating teachers' comments highlighted the power that retroactive credit or placement policies in language departments might have in recruiting undergraduate language majors and minors from HS language programs.

When asked how the visit experience could be improved, the only specific suggestion came from Mary, who said that having additional information about the format of the STAMP 4S assessment itself would have been helpful for "understanding the test a little bit better, so I can better prepare them without really like teaching to the test". She also explained that knowing how the assessment would be administered, specifically that all students would not be doing the speaking section at the same time, as they do in an AP examination, would help her prepare students who might have felt nervous about speaking during the assessment. Nonetheless, in general, the responses from all participants were overwhelmingly positive, with teachers describing the initiative and experience using adjectives like "perfect", "great", and "smooth".

Discussion and implications

Leveraging the SoBL to recruit undergraduate language students

The results of UNK's SSoBL-qualifying STAMP 4S testing initiative have proven promising as a recruitment strategy. The SSoBL recipients who tested at UNK enrolled in language courses at nine times the rate of UNK's general undergraduate population, while they enrolled in LOTE degree programs at ten times the rate of UNK's general undergraduate population. In a climate of declining enrollments and pressures on the language departments to ramp up recruitment efforts at this institution and others, leveraging the SSoBL testing opportunity helped create valuable connections for the Department with local language teachers and their students.

The initiative results have been encouraging enough for the Department to continue organizing campus visits. The overwhelmingly positive response from participating teachers and the growing interest from schools in the region reinforces the positive enrollment data. More HS students and recent graduates have taken the STAMP 4S test each year than the last. To date, about one-quarter of the HS seniors who have taken the STAMP 4S at UNK have enrolled there. This number would likely increase if high schoolers tested earlier in their senior years or even before. Under the current project, many high schoolers tested well into the spring of their senior year, when they had probably already decided on a college or decided not to attend college. In any case, it seems that this initiative is succeeding in encouraging language class and degree program enrollments, even if it does not impact students' decisions to enroll at UNK. The impact of the testing initiative on high schoolers' college decisions must be further investigated.

Among test-takers in this project, HLLs outnumbered L2 learners by nearly 4:1. However, HLLs appeared less likely to enroll in a language class or to declare a language major or minor than their L2 peers. Perhaps they saw less value than L2 learners in further studying Spanish because of their existing proficiency or because of societal pressure to favor English over Spanish. The present study did not examine learners' perceptions of languages or reasons for (not) enrolling in classes or degree programs. Nevertheless, the data suggested that both HLLs and L2 participants who enrolled in language classes at UNK continued their language studies and declared a related major or minor. Specifically, 70% (n = 7) of HLLs who took a UNK language class (n = 10) declared a language major or minor (Table 9.2), while 50% (n = 2) of L2 learners who took a language class (n = 4) did the same (Table 9.3). Small and imbalanced sample sizes, however, complicate comparisons between HLLs and L2 learners.

From a research methods perspective, the imbalance between HLLs and L2 learners in test-taking is not ideal, as it limits statistical comparisons, but it is perhaps unsurprising given that HLLs tend to start their language journeys at a much higher proficiency level than their L2 peers, leaving them more likely to take a STAMP 4S test and to obtain a SoBL. L2 learners of non-Spanish languages were poorly represented in the study due to the lower response rate to the researchers' invitations from teachers working in contexts with predominantly L2 learners. Perhaps teachers did not believe that their students' language levels were high enough, or perhaps they simply missed the emails or otherwise saw the visit opportunity as unfeasible or unworthwhile.

The present data do not explore why test-takers, turned likely SSoBL recipients, did (not) pursue college language study. However, there is reason to believe that the SSoBL, especially when paired with the tangible benefits of retroactive credit and advanced course placement, can motivate college language study. First, retroactive credit reduces the time and financial barriers to entry into language degree programs, making them seem more attainable for students pursuing them alongside other degree aims. Second, the "confidence boost" that many SoBL recipients describe in relation to the SoBL helps them believe in their language skills and the possibility of developing even stronger skills (Davin & Heineke, 2018; Eckerson & Jacobs, 2024; Castro, 2020; Monto, 2022).

Equity and access to the SoBL

An important outcome of this initiative is its impact on access to the Nebraska SSoBL award in the central Nebraska region that UNK serves. At least two of the teachers (Kate and Sarah) discovered a pathway for their students to earn the recognition, and the first students ever from their respective HSs qualified by testing at UNK. For Mary, the initiative broadened which students at her school could pursue the award, beyond AP Spanish Language and Culture course enrollments. For Carlos, the opportunity to test on campus resolved technical difficulties that might have dissuaded his continued work to provide language testing opportunities to his students. University campuses are perhaps better suited to facilitate the time, space, personnel, and technology needed to administer proficiency tests to students than some secondary schools, especially in rural areas.

Students in rural schools are more likely to lack access to advanced language course enrollments, like AP and IB, that offer testing opportunities (Chen et al., 2010). Students in these schools are also less likely to enroll in specialized Spanish for Spanish speakers or dual-language secondary coursework that would allow them to qualify for the Nebraska SSoBL using grades from those courses. This leaves commercial proficiency tests as the only avenue available to most rural students in the state. Buying test licenses in bulk allowed the Department to offer the test as economically as possible and to reduce the investment of the undoubtedly unremunerated time and energy classroom teachers might have invested in organizing tests for their students, as Carlos had done in the past.

Perhaps most critically, the initiative succeeded in bringing opportunities to earn the SSoBL to heritage speakers and ELs who were not world language students in the region, groups who are significantly underrepresented among Nebraska SSoBL recipients (NILA, 2021). By reaching out directly to the classroom teachers working with students, including EL teachers, the effort effectively expanded SoBL implementation/adoption in regional schools with large numbers of multilingual students. At the same time, by offering the "value-added" admissions visit and Office of Diversity and Inclusion meetings in conjunction with the test, the initiative contributed to broader equity goals of improving college access for historically underrepresented groups, roundly appreciated by the participating teachers.

In addition to these impacts, it is important to account for the extension and outreach-related outcomes that are especially meaningful for a public land-grant institution like UNK. The enthusiastic response from participating teachers, the admissions office, and even local news media (Ellyson, 2022a) is evidence of the general goodwill generated for the Department of Modern Languages by this effort. This is a so-called soft but not unimportant outcome.

Conclusions and next steps

As this project is ongoing, we will continue to monitor the enrollment trends of current participants while also recruiting new ones. As of October 2023, none of the testing participants have graduated from college, so there is still time to track how current participants' language course and degree program enrollments evolve. The Department will continue to reach out to Nebraska HS language teachers, including those with whom they have already made contact and others, to educate them on the benefits of the SSoBL and the possibility of earning it through UNK language testing. Due to UNK's institutional priorities, nearby teachers with many Spanish HLLs are of particular interest. Yet, they are not the only teachers of interest. The Department would also benefit from recruiting test-takers in French and German, two languages with regionally and nationally declining enrollments, that are taught in some regional HSs.

Outreach has targeted world language teachers and teachers of ELs in the region, but few EL teachers (aside from Sarah) have responded to the communications. No teachers of non-Spanish LOTEs have responded. Expanding efforts to contact counselors and/or administrators might aid in increasing participation. In practice, most of central Nebraska's ELs are Spanish speakers, but Middle Eastern, African, and Southeast Asian immigrant communities are growing. Some speak major world languages in which UNK offers coursework (i.e., French, Mandarin Chinese), but others speak less commonly taught languages (LCTLs) in which UNK does not.

With equity for speakers of LCTLs in mind, the Department is considering how to recognize proficiency in languages that they do not teach without exacerbating enrollment concerns. One possibility would be to award speakers of languages not taught at UNK retroactive credit via a catch-all language course as soon as they receive a B- or higher in any UNK language class—even a first-semester class. In this way, the Department would not entirely lose possible language enrollments, and students would still receive a tangible benefit for their language knowledge, no matter what that language might be. Perhaps some of those students would also continue to study their new language and even declare a major or minor in it, as this initiative aims to encourage them to do.

References

Avant Assessment. (2023). *STAMP FAQ*. https://avantassessment.com/stamp-frequently-asked-questions

Bannan-Ritland, B. (2003). The role of design in research: The integrative learning design framework. *Educational researcher*, *32*(1), 21–24. https://doi.org/10.3102/0013189X0320010

Black, C., Chou, A., & Hancock, C. (2020). *The 2018–19 National Seal of Biliteracy report*. https://sealofbiliteracy.org/research/2020-National-Seal-of-Biliteracy-Report

Burnet, M.M. (2017). *Signed, sealed, delivered: District-level adoption of the Washington State Seal of Biliteracy* (Doctoral dissertation). http://hdl.handle.net/1773/40446

Castro, A.C. (2020). Validating the linguistic strengths of English learners. In A. Heineke & K. Davin (Eds.), *The Seal of Biliteracy: Case studies and considerations for policy implementation* (pp. 121–137). Information Age.

Chen, X., Wu, J., & Tassof, S. (2010). *Academic preparation for college in the high school senior class of 2003–04*. National Center for Education Statistics. https://nces.ed.gov/pubsearch/pubsinfo.asp?pubid=2010169

Davin, K.J., & Heineke, A. (2017). The Seal of Biliteracy: Variations in policy and outcomes. *Foreign Language Annals*, *50*(3), 486–499. https://doi.org/10.1111/flan.12279

Davin, K.J., & Heineke, A.J. (2018). The Seal of Biliteracy: Adding students' voices to the conversation. *Bilingual Research Journal*, *41*(3), 312–328. https://doi.org/10.1080/15235882.2018.1481896

Davin, K.J., Heineke, A.J., & Egnatz, L. (2018). The Seal of Biliteracy: Successes and challenges to implementation. *Foreign Language Annals*, *51*(2), 275–289. https://doi.org/10.1111/flan.12336

Eckerson, J., & Jacobs, C. (2023). The Seal of Biliteracy as a recruitment opportunity. In Heidrich Uebel, E., Kronenberg, F.A., & Sterling, S. (Eds.), *Language program vitality in the United States*. Educational Linguistics (vol. 63), 315–319. Cham: Springer. https://doi.org/10.1007/978-3-031-43654-3_29

Eckerson, J., & Jacobs, C. (2024). The Seal of Biliteracy as a recruitment tool in postsecondary language study. *Foreign Language Annals*, *57*(3), 654–674. https://doi.org/10.1111/flan.12769

Ellyson, T. (2022a, May 5). *Biliteracy program brings high school students to UNK campus*. https://unk.ews.unk.edu/2022/05/05/biliteracy-program-brings-high-school-students-to-unk-campus/

Ellyson, T. (2022b, September 12). *UNK ranked 2nd in value, 7th-best public regional university by US News & World Report*. https://unk.ews.unk.edu/2022/09/12/unk-ranked-2nd-in-value-7th-best-public-regional-university-by-us-news-world-report/

Ellyson, T. (2022c, October 20). *UNK College readiness for Hispanics program receives Women Investing in Nebraska grant*. https://unk.ews.unk.edu/2022/10/20/unk-college-readiness-for-hispanics-program-receives-women-investing-in-nebraska-grant/

Heller, N. (2023). The end of the English major. *The New Yorker*. https://www.newyorker.com/magazine/2023/03/06/the-end-of-the-english-major

Liu, C. (2023, March). ESU 5: Addressing the teacher shortage through distance learning. *World Language Review*. https://docs.google.com/document/d/1NDxykTNzVm9SFiAO7W5DCIqtyUZbjYZ36cQEi42qXJM/edit

Lusin, N., Peterson, T., Sulewski, C., & Zafer, R. (2023). *Enrollments in languages other than English in US institutions of higher education, Fall 2021*. Modern Language Association of America.

Monto, C. (2022). Bringing the state Seal of Biliteracy to higher education: A case for expansion. *Foreign Language Annals*, *55*(1), 35–53. https://doi.org/10.1111/flan.12597

NBC 6 News. (2021, August 12). *Census: Metro populations grew, rural areas lost in Nebraska, Iowa*. https://www.wowt.com/2021/08/12/census-metro-populations-grew-rural-areas-lost-nebraska-iowa/

NILA. (2021). *Data on Nebraska Seal Recipients 2020–2022*. Nebraska International Language Association.

Nebraska Department of Education. (2019). *Language learning in Nebraska*. https://www.education.ne.gov/wp-content/uploads/2019/03/Languages-Learned-in-Nebraska-2019.pdf

Nebraska Department of Education. (2024). *Nebraska Seal of Biliteracy*. https://www.education.ne.gov/worldlanguage/nebraska-seal-of-biliteracy/#1659558008327-ac632a2c-b9cd

Schwedhelm, M.C., & King, K.A. (2020). The neoliberal logic of state seals of biliteracy. *Foreign Language Annals*, *53*(1), 12–27. https://doi.org/10.1111/flan.12438

Subtirelu, N.C., Borowczyk, M., Thorson Hernández, R., & Venezia, F. (2019). Recognizing whose bilingualism? A critical policy analysis of the Seal of Biliteracy. *The Modern Language Journal, 103*(2), 371–390. https://doi.org/10.1111/modl.12556

Uebel, E.H., Kronenberg, F.A., & Sterling, S. (2023) *Language program vitality in the United States: From surviving to thriving in higher education.* Springer. https://doi.org/10.1007/978-3-031-43654-3

UNK Factbook. (2023a). *Academic programs.* https://www.unk.edu/factbook/acad_prog.php

UNK Factbook. (2023b). *Fall headcount enrollment.* https://www.unk.edu/factbook/enrollment.php

US Census Bureau. (2023a) *QuickFacts: Kearney city, Nebraska.* Retrieved October 2023, from https://www.census.gov/quickfacts/kearneycitynebraska

US Census Bureau. (2023b) *QuickFacts: Nebraska.* Retrieved October 2023, from (https://www.census.gov/quickfacts/fact/table/NE/PST045222

Winke, P., Zhang, X., Rubio, F., Gass, S., Sonenson, D., & Hacking, J. (2020). The proficiency profiles of language students: Implications for programs. *Second Language Research & Practice, 1*(1), 25–64. http://hdl.handle.net/10125/69840

10

PIPELINES TO PRACTICE

Utilizing the Seal of Biliteracy in teacher education

Amy J. Heineke, Sarah L. Cohen, Eric Steinmiller, and Ji Won Lee

Globalization and immigration have drastically changed the landscape of the United States in recent decades, subsequently increasing the need for bilingual and biliterate individuals in all facets of the workforce (Gándara, 2014; Kroll & Dussias, 2017). Nonetheless, studies have indicated that only 20% of U.S. students study another language in kindergarten-through-twelfth-grade (K–12) schools, which deters from the competitiveness of the U.S. economy given the many countries across the world that prioritize multilingualism (American Councils for International Education [ACIE], 2017; Commission on Language Learning, 2017). Whereas world language study has been declining in institutions of higher education (IHEs), K–12 schools have increased and extended language programming (American Councils Research Center [ARC], 2021; Looney & Lusin, 2018; Met & Brandt, 2017). Up from approximately 1,000 dual-language immersion programs in U.S. public schools in 2010, there are now around 3,600 programs that provide at least 50% of daily instruction in another language (ARC, 2021). Spanish accounts for 80% of these programs, with the remaining 20% mediating bilingualism in 26 other languages, including both immigrant languages from around the world and Indigenous languages from within the United States. In addition to dual-language programs, K–12 world language programs have strengthened their curriculum to deepen language proficiency and expanded offerings in less commonly taught languages (Met & Brandt, 2017).

With expanding language programming across K–12 settings, paired with a national teacher shortage exacerbated by the COVID-19 pandemic, schools have encountered challenges in securing bilingual teachers (Garcia, 2017; Schmitt & deCourcy, 2022; Sutcher et al., 2016). In the 2022–2023 school year, 44% of U.S. public schools reported teaching vacancies, with 12% of those schools reporting vacancies for English as a Second Language (ESL) or bilingual education and 9% reporting vacancies for world languages (Institute of Education Sciences [IES], 2022). At schools with vacancies, 72% noted difficulties in filling ESL and bilingual teaching positions, and 78% noted difficulties in filling world language teaching positions with fully certified teachers. In the midwestern state of Illinois, which situates the bilingual teacher preparation pipeline program described in this chapter, language teachers comprised 56% of the unfilled teaching positions during the 2021–2022 school year,

DOI: 10.4324/9781032667249-14

including 20% ESL and bilingual and 36% world language (Beilstein & Withee, 2022). Ultimately, Illinois districts reported leaving 59% of ESL and bilingual and 56% of world language positions unfilled and hiring under-qualified, substitute, or outsourced teachers to fill the remaining 41% and 44% of openings, respectively. These troubling numbers demonstrate the urgent need to attend to the language teacher shortage with novel solutions to attract and recruit bilingual educators.

As the demand for language teachers has intensified, the state Seals of Biliteracy (SSoBL) have extended across the United States through grassroots policy and practice efforts (Davin et al., 2022). First initiated by language educators and bilingual education advocates in California, the SSoBL movement has spread across the country over the past 13 years, which currently encompasses all 50 states and the District of Columbia (DC; Olsen, 2020; Seal of Biliteracy, 2024). Though state policies differ in various ways, commonalities center upon the formal recognition of students' proficiency in two languages (Davin & Heineke, 2017). At the high school level, the SSoBL is typically affixed to graduating seniors' transcripts and diplomas to indicate bilingualism and biliteracy to potential employers and IHEs. As described in Chapters 8 and 9, the high school SSoBL has been utilized at certain IHEs to award college credit for K–12 biliteracy attainment and place students in appropriate levels of postsecondary language study. But the high school SSoBL has been used with less frequency at IHEs to recruit and prepare biliterate students within professional preparation programs, such as teacher education.

This chapter explores the potential of the SSoBL to support K–12 leaders and university-based teacher educators in collaboratively developing bilingual teacher pipelines. Given the widespread implementation of the SSoBL across the United States, we see this biliteracy recognition as assisting language teacher educators in recruiting and preparing teachers to meet the growing demand for bilingual educators in K–12 schools. Drawing from our collective experiences, we detail the partnership between one university and a regional network of urban public schools with predominantly Latinx students aiming to recruit and prepare Spanish-speaking bilingual teachers. Across the chapter, we describe how the SSoBL can facilitate the recruitment of high school students with requisite language proficiency into university language teacher education, followed by teacher educators recognizing and using candidates' experience with biliteracy development as a springboard to develop their expertise in language pedagogy. We first ground the chapter in the existing literature on bilingual teacher pipelines.

Responding to shortages: Recruiting and preparing bilingual teachers

Classrooms need teachers, but school and district leaders have faced increasing challenges in hiring qualified educators to fill teaching vacancies (Schmitt & deCourcy, 2022). Despite the overall shortage of teachers nationwide following the COVID-19 pandemic and the specific shortage of bilingual and world language teachers, K–12 language programs have increased and expanded to nurture students' language competencies in response to the growing demand for bilingual individuals (ACIE, 2017; ARC, 2021; Commission on Language Learning, 2017; IES, 2022; Met & Brandt, 2017). This context presents a conundrum for local stakeholders who need language teachers to offer language programming. In contexts that center on English language development, stakeholders have responded by preparing monolingual teachers and teacher candidates to scaffold and facilitate students' language development in English-medium classrooms (de Jong & Gao, 2023; Heineke & Giatsou, 2020). But bilingual and world language classrooms require teachers with bilingualism and biliteracy, which takes years to develop (Hakuta et al., 2000; Zhang et al., 2020). To recruit bilingual teachers, local stakeholders often seek out individuals in their communities who are already bilingual.

Grow Your Own (GYO) programs seek to extend and diversify the existing teacher workforce by tapping into local community members who wish to join the profession (Garcia, 2020; Gist et al., 2019). Typically emerging as grassroots efforts in response to local teacher shortages, GYO programs involve partnerships between stakeholders in school districts, IHEs, and community organizations, who then recruit and prepare high school students, paraeducators and noncertified school personnel, or community members. As described by Garcia (2020), these grassroots efforts in local communities have prompted state and national attention, evidenced by 27 states with policies that target GYO programs, 18 states with funding for GYO programs, and the inclusion of GYO programs in federal legislation (i.e., Classrooms Reflecting Communities Act, 2019; College Affordability Act, 2019). Whereas many programs have a broad scope to attract potential teachers reflective of the community, the GYO initiative holds specific promise for recruiting and preparing bilingual teachers. But GYO programs for bilingual teachers currently exist in just 11 states and DC (Garcia, 2020).

In a recent review of GYO programs in the United States, Garcia (2020) found that bilingual educator pipelines primarily target adults in schools and communities. This finding aligns with existing literature on bilingual teacher preparation pipelines, which documents efforts to recruit bilingual community members (Esparza et al., 2019; Garcia & Garza, 2019; Gross, 2018) and bilingual paraprofessionals and noncertified school personnel (Amos, 2013; Cramer & Ryan, 2023; Garcia, 2017; Garcia et al., 2019). Some programs require participants to have a bachelor's degree and bilingual proficiency prior to starting graduate-level teacher preparation coursework (e.g., Cramer & Ryan, 2023; Garcia & Garza, 2019; Gross, 2018), while others open the opportunity to all bilingual individuals with options for undergraduate coursework leading to teaching licensure (e.g., Esparza et al., 2019; Garcia, 2017). Whereas certain programs enroll bilingual educators from multiple language backgrounds (e.g., Gross, 2018), others target Spanish bilingual teachers and provide coursework and mentoring in Spanish (e.g., Esparza et al., 2019). Despite these differences reflective of unique local contexts, bilingual pipeline programs share similar features, including (a) mentorship from teacher education faculty, (b) apprenticeship from cooperating teachers in public school classrooms, (c) flexibly timed coursework responsive to work responsibilities, and (d) cohort models that bring together these nontraditional bilingual teacher candidates working in various schools.

The literature on broader GYO programming provides valuable insight into potential opportunities in recruiting bilingual high school students to become bilingual teachers. Whereas pathways for high school students are the most common type of GYO program to diversify the teaching force across the United States, they are not as customary in bilingual-specific pipelines, which tend to focus on adults within schools and communities (Garcia, 2020). Coffey et al. (2019) detail a partnership between education faculty at the University of North Carolina at Charlotte and leaders in the Charlotte-Mecklenburg school district, as they recruit students from this urban school district to attend UNC-Charlotte and provide targeted support and preparation via seminars, mentorships, and internships. Morales (2018) describes AccessUS, a collaboration between a midwestern university, two Hispanic-serving community colleges, and three Latinx-majority districts, which offers distance-delivered elementary teacher education to predominantly bilingual Latinas. With recruitment and programming focused on BIPOC individuals, these GYO programs create pipelines from high schools to colleges and universities, ultimately encouraging teachers to return to schools within their communities.

Merging the previously described substrands of the literature, we assert the potential value of bilingual teacher pipelines that begin with students in K–12 schools. Whereas GYO programs for bilingual paraprofessionals, noncertified school personnel, and community members can indeed recruit and prepare bilingual educators in response to shortages, schools need additional avenues to get bilingual individuals into bilingual and world language classrooms. Given the popularity of the SSoBLs, which have been enacted primarily in high schools spanning all 50 states and DC, we see this biliteracy recognition as the starting place for a new pipeline of bilingual teachers: (a) biliterate high school graduates are recruited into teacher education programs, (b) teacher educators prepare candidates as expert pedagogues in language education, and (c) teachers return to classrooms to promote their students' bilingualism. In this chapter, we describe one such effort to leverage the SSoBL initiative to create a bilingual educator pipeline spanning one urban public school district, community college, and university.

Leveraging the SSoBL: Developing a bilingual teacher pipeline

Situated in one of the most ethnically diverse neighborhoods in the Midwest, Clinton High School (pseudonym) serves approximately 1,000 students from an array of culturally and linguistically diverse backgrounds. Given the community has the highest percentage of foreign-born residents of any neighborhood in the focal city, Clinton students come from families who have immigrated from countries including Mexico, Guatemala, Ecuador, the Philippines, India, Korea, Cambodia, Somalia, Romania, Pakistan, and Iraq. Three-quarters of the students identify as Latinx, as well as 9% Asian, 9% Black, 6% White, and 1% multiracial; 88 percent of students are considered low-income (Source blinded, 2023). Over 80% of students attending this neighborhood public high school use languages other than English at home with over half of the student body labeled as English learners (ELs). Though Clinton students use a collective 35 languages, most students use Spanish, which requires the school to offer bilingual programming in line with Illinois state policy.

Located near Clinton High School, Loyola University Chicago implements a field-based teacher education program embedded in local schools and communities. Shifting from a traditional, university-based preparation model in 2013, the Teaching, Learning, and Leading with Schools and Communities (TLLSC) program has partnered with schools for over a decade to prepare teacher candidates in, with, and for urban schools and communities with culturally and linguistically diverse populations (Heineke & Giatsou, 2020). Candidates have five major options to deepen their professional expertise and fulfill state licensure requirements, including bilingual-bicultural education, elementary education, secondary education, special education, and early childhood special education. Because of the large and growing number of students labeled as ELs in partner schools like Clinton and others across the city, state, and nation, TLLSC embeds requirements for the state's ESL endorsement across all programs such that all teacher candidates graduate with both teaching licensure and their ESL endorsement. Given the overlap in ESL and bilingual endorsement requirements, teacher candidates can complete the requirements for the bilingual endorsement by adding one course, as well as demonstrating language proficiency and completing 100 clinical hours in the target language.

Loyola and Clinton stakeholders began partnering in 2013 through a grant-funded project called Language Matters, which sought to build capacity in partner schools with large numbers of students labeled as ELs. One of six initial partner schools, Loyola faculty provided professional development and university coursework to Clinton teachers and leaders to enhance EL programming and practices. As a part of the three-year capacity-building efforts, Clinton stakeholders decided to shift from the state-required transitional bilingual education to dual-language education to embrace the Spanish-language strengths within the school and community and nurture students' biliteracy in both Spanish and English. Over time, this language-focused work evolved into a deeper partnership within the larger TLLSC program, where Loyola teacher candidates came to Clinton to learn alongside teachers and students. Within this mutually beneficial partnership (Krueger et al., 2008), Clinton educators collaboratively prepared Loyola teacher candidates, and Loyola faculty supported Clinton stakeholders where needed, including during the efforts to shift from transitional bilingual to dual-language education.

Initial discussion on potential pipelines

In the fall of 2018, Clinton initiated the district's process to begin a dual-language program, with a team of school stakeholders coming together to analyze language programs and practices, solidify required structures and systems, and compile district application materials. Tapping into the existing partnership, Clinton leaders convened a meeting with Loyola faculty, as well as district employees at the central office, focused on recruiting teachers. To facilitate the shift from transitional bilingual to dual-language education, Clinton needed teachers licensed in the secondary content areas and endorsed to teach in Spanish bilingual classrooms. School and district officials hoped to tap into TLLSC graduates who had already spent time in classrooms and had targeted preparation to serve ELs, describing Loyola teacher candidates as eligible for early job offers in the district due to the high need for bilingual teachers. But Loyola faculty ruminated and responded that TLLSC graduates typically reflected the larger teaching force of predominantly White women, meaning few candidates had the level of Spanish proficiency needed to teach high school content (National Center for Educational Statistics, 2023).

Following this honest assessment of Loyola's inability to funnel bilingual graduates to teach in Clinton's future dual-language program, Clinton's assistant principal floated an idea: what if we recruited Clinton graduates, most of whom used languages other than English at home, to become bilingual teachers? He shared that Clinton's world language team had been deepening its implementation of the SSoBL and that this recognition could identify individuals to recruit into bilingual teacher education programs. The school, district, and university stakeholders at the meeting eagerly built on this initial idea to develop a larger GYO framework for a bilingual teacher pipeline: (a) biliterate students from Clinton and other area high schools received the SSoBL, (b) Loyola faculty used the SSoBL to recruit biliterate students into its teacher preparation program, (c) stakeholders collaboratively prepared teachers via Loyola's field-based teacher education program, and (d) TLLSC graduates returned to Clinton and other area schools as bilingual teachers. This developing idea of a bilingual teacher pipeline seemed to hold numerous benefits, particularly centered on targeting and developing heritage-language learners as bilingual teachers. This solution addressed the shortage of bilingual teachers and teachers of color by tapping into the linguistic strengths of the community while harnessing the momentum of the SSoBL initiative (Davin & Heineke, 2017).

Despite the collective support for the idea of a bilingual teacher pipeline that connected partner sites from school to university to district, stakeholders shared concerns about price and potential financial challenges for immigrant families. As a private Catholic university, Loyola certainly did not offer the most affordable route to becoming a teacher in the area. These concerns gave rise to a potential solution, which brought an additional partner into this work: Arrupe College. Founded in 2015, Arrupe College was created as a two-year degree program within Loyola University Chicago to target students with limited financial resources and help them graduate with little or no debt. Grounded in Loyola's social-justice mission, founders envisioned the college serving as a bridge between high school and college for low-income, first-generation college students, providing small class sizes and myriad supports for students to finish an associate degree in two years. In its initial years of existence, Arrupe enrolled nearly all students of color, with over half enrolling after graduation from Chicago Public Schools. Additionally, private donors funded scholarships for undocumented students who did not qualify for federal and state aid. To alleviate the cost of a four-year teaching degree, the idea emerged to involve Arrupe in the bilingual teacher pipeline. With this glimmer of hope that the pipeline could overcome the financial hurdles, stakeholders left this initial meeting with various ideas to explore and tasks to complete, which we describe in the following section.

Site-specific efforts to develop the pipeline

Following this initial meeting in which stakeholders developed an idea for a GYO bilingual teacher pipeline using the SoBL to recruit biliterate students from high school into teacher education, stakeholders set about the work to jumpstart these efforts within their own settings. Here, we discuss site-specific facets of the collaborative work to begin the pipeline, starting first with university faculty, followed by school and district leaders.

Articulating undergraduate programming: Community college and university actors

As a first step, TLLSC faculty reached out to Arrupe stakeholders to feel out the potential to develop a *two-plus-two program*, a collaborative program between a community college and university where students spend two years at each institution working on requirements for one streamlined program of study. Having recently partnered with faculty in the School of Nursing to develop a similar program, Arrupe faculty were eager and excited for the opportunity to develop another high-need professional pipeline for their students. Though the initial intent of the meeting at Clinton was to prepare secondary teachers for disciplinary dual-language classrooms, faculty quickly encountered challenges with Loyola's requirement that secondary content teachers double major in education and the focal discipline (e.g., history, biology). With the hefty number of required credits, TLLSC and Arrupe faculty struggled to craft a reasonable and meaningful program of study within the two-plus-two format. This resulted in the decision to develop the two-plus-two program in bilingual-bicultural education, an existing program of study within TLLSC that yielded elementary teaching licensure with ESL and bilingual endorsements. Although this strayed from the initial intent to route teachers to Clinton High School, stakeholders agreed that this direction facilitated the recruitment of biliterate Clinton graduates into teacher education and responded to the district's need for bilingual elementary teachers.

Having defined the goal of developing a two-plus-two program in bilingual-bicultural education, TLLSC and Arrupe faculty dove into the negotiation of programmatic requirements. Arrupe's two-year associate degrees consisted of core courses across disciplines with specialization in a select area (e.g., business, liberal arts), and TLLSC's four-year bachelor's degrees contained both university core courses and a trajectory of field-based education modules to deepen teaching expertise and practice over time. Given Arrupe faculty had used Loyola's slate of core courses when developing their two-year programs to facilitate students' transfer into the four-year institution, the overlap in core coursework emerged as low-hanging fruit to begin to merge and fine-tune the programs from six to four years. Subsequent merging and refining took additional efforts, including curricular revisions, institutional advocacy, and broader collaboration. For example, TLLSC students had traditionally met Loyola's philosophy core requirement by taking Philosophy of Education, but Arrupe faculty expressed concern regarding the difficulty of the course in its current format. Prompting collaboration among philosophers in Arrupe College and the School of Education, faculty developed a special topics section of Arrupe's philosophy course, where Arrupe faculty facilitated student learning around topics related to the philosophy of education. As reflected in this example, various Arrupe and education faculty committed time and effort to develop this program to expand options for Arrupe students and aspiring bilingual teachers.

Unfortunately, Arrupe and TLLSC faculty were not successful in all efforts to collaborate and advocate for programmatic refinement. The four-year bilingual-bicultural education major required students to take four upper-level Spanish-language courses to ensure the level of language proficiency needed to teach in bilingual classrooms. Since the proposed pipeline centered on students who had received the SSoBL, our aspiration was that this codified recognition of students' biliteracy be used to award credit and place students in higher levels of world language coursework, as has been described in previous chapters of this volume. Given the state of Illinois required state-affiliated colleges and universities to grant credit for the SSoBL, with most institutions awarding between 8 and 11 credits for the recognition, TLLSC and Arrupe faculty thought it was a no-brainer to remain competitive with other Illinois IHEs. Nonetheless, numerous efforts to collaborate and negotiate with the Modern Language Department in the College of Arts and Sciences were unsuccessful. Arrupe and TLLSC faculty were forced to begrudgingly leave the four upper-level Spanish-language courses in the two-plus-two program since providing flexibility to SSoBL recipients would require revisions to the traditional bilingual-bicultural education program prior to moving forward with the two-plus-two bilingual-bicultural education program.

Emergent from our collective frustration with the inability to use students' SSoBL recognitions for world language credit or placement, TLLSC faculty devised another plan to leverage the SSoBL. At the time, the Illinois State Board of Education (ISBE) required teachers seeking bilingual endorsements to take coursework, complete hours in bilingual classrooms, and pass the state's proficiency test in the target language. Faculty drafted a rule-change proposal for ISBE to consider the SSoBL as a measure of language proficiency for teacher licensure, thus eliminating the need for additional testing. According to the Illinois School Code, the SSoBL (awarded at the Intermediate-High level) "certifies attainment of a high level of proficiency, sufficient for meaningful use in college and a career…in one or more languages in addition to English." The Illinois SSoBL policy aimed to "provide employers with a method of identifying people with language and biliteracy skills" (Illinois School Code 105 ILCS 5/2-3.159, p. 1). By using language directly from the SSoBL's legislation, the proposal urged ISBE leaders to use the SSoBL in the way the policy was initially conceived. Two years following the submission of the rule-change proposal, ISBE passed the measure in spring 2021 to allow the Illinois SSoBL to be used in place of the proficiency test for the bilingual endorsement. ISBE later added the Global Seal of Biliteracy (GSoBL) as an additional accepted measure of teachers' linguistic competencies to further provide flexibility for individuals already proficient in the target language.

Following months of collaborative programmatic and curricular design work, TLLSC and Arrupe faculty submitted the proposal for a two-plus-two bilingual-bicultural teacher education program. After numerous layers of approval from requisite stakeholders within Arrupe College, the School of Education, and the larger university, Loyola's provost approved the program in December 2019, opening the door for a fall 2020 start. Of course, the COVID-19 pandemic had other plans, with faculty and other university stakeholders needing to pivot to other priorities in early 2020 and into the 2020–2021 academic year. In fall 2021, seven first-year Arrupe students enrolled in the two-plus-two program, followed by five in fall 2022 and three in fall 2023. Fourteen of 15 students identified as Latinx with half attending high schools within the partner district.

Strengthening high school language education pathways: School and district actors

As Loyola faculty worked to develop the two-plus-two program, Clinton educators continued to envision and develop their dual-language education program. District leaders had provided schools with a predefined proposal process to add dual-language programming, in which school stakeholders outlined their readiness to start the program and provided a detailed implementation plan that involved administrators, educators, community members, parents, and students. District leaders reviewed Clinton's application and approved their proposal to develop a dual-language program in March 2019, making them the first high school in the district permitted to offer dual-language instruction. Following district protocols, Clinton educators entered what the district called their *planning year* in 2019–2020 with an anticipated program start date for freshmen in fall 2020.

The planning year centered primarily around the collaboration of the *Dual-Language Education Leadership Team*, a strategically selected group of school stakeholders, including two administrators, one counselor, and seven teachers from various departments, including science, math, social studies, world languages, and fine arts. With each member conceptualized as an expert and leader within their respective roles and departments, the leadership team embraced the collective responsibility to plan and implement Clinton's dual-language program. In fall 2019, they began using the district's protocol to self-evaluate their existing programs and practices using the seven guiding principles for dual-language education: (a) program structure, (b) curriculum, (c) instruction, (d) assessment and accountability, (e) staff quality and professional development, (f) family and community, and (g) support and resources (Howard et al., 2018). After self-reflecting on the school's alignment with various subprinciples, the team drafted an action plan to enhance the school's foundational readiness to implement the program. Following district approval of the action plan, they began working to target focal areas of need (e.g., Spanish-language assessment systems, dual-language instructional strategies, professional learning community structures) in the winter of 2020.

As the team shifted from thinking about program design to preparing for implementation, they remained focused on their mission "for students to develop biliteracy and bilingualism, reach high levels of academic achievement, and acquire sociocultural competence so that they may succeed in an increasingly competitive global society" (Source blinded, 2023). Clinton stakeholders planned to begin implementation in the fall of 2020, though the COVID-19 pandemic and the required shift to distance learning put a damper on the initial rollout. The program began in-person implementation in the fall of 2021, with a group of freshmen who took 50% of core academic courses in Spanish and 50% in English. The program has continued to grow since its initial implementation, now enrolling 320 students spanning freshman through senior years. The shift from transitional bilingual to dual-language education has also yielded progress toward their goal of enhancing students' biliteracy. Whereas about four percent of Clinton graduates received the SSoBL in 2019, almost 10% received the recognition in 2023. This increase mirrors the larger district's SSoBL numbers, which increased by 35% from 2019 to 2022.

Current work to deepen partnerships and pipelines

Now, five years after the initial idea to use the SSoBL to create a bilingual teacher pipeline emerged at a winter meeting at Clinton High School, stakeholders have developed programs to facilitate the pipeline moving forward. Loyola faculty crafted the two-plus-two program and enrolled 15 students over the first three years. Clinton High School implemented its dual-language program to engage students in disciplinary learning in Spanish and English. The district successfully expanded its SSoBL efforts, with more schools offering language programs to develop biliteracy and more students receiving the recognition in multiple languages. These successes were paired with various challenges, including repercussions of the COVID-19 pandemic, as well as changes in personnel and leadership at all sites. Now, the work centers on building from our joint successes and merging these integral components into a holistic pipeline to recruit, support, and prepare bilingual teachers. Stakeholders have pinpointed three key areas to fortify the bilingual teacher pipeline moving forward: (a) recognizing and integrating biliteracy in teacher education, (b) advising and mentoring students from high school to college, and (c) recruiting and funding biliterate students to become teachers.

Recognizing and integrating biliteracy in teacher education

Loyola faculty remain committed to using the SSoBL as an indicator of biliteracy for college and career. Unfortunately, the Modern Languages Department still does not accept the SSoBL for credit or placement in language coursework, and departmental leaders have not responded to our attempts for collaboration. This continued frustration has incited exploration into other options to utilize students' SSoBL recognitions within the School of Education. Ideas center on using the SSoBL to indicate students' language proficiency, allowing students at an Intermediate-High level to enter the bilingual-bicultural program where faculty facilitate regular professional learning communities and upper-level methods courses in Spanish.

Students who did not receive the SSoBL in high school can seek the GSoBL to indicate proficiency. Students not yet at an Intermediate-High level upon entrance must take Spanish-language courses to build proficiency prior to taking upper-level TLLSC courses in Spanish in their junior and senior years. With this approach, bilingual-bicultural majors in two-plus-two and four-year programs can streamline programs of study with demonstrated proficiency via the SoBL while continuing to use and develop classroom-specific Spanish in university coursework.

Advising and mentoring students from high school to college

Loyola faculty have also recognized the need to strengthen infrastructure to nurture two-plus-two program students as they move from high school to college, as well as through their program of study. Arrupe College employs an ***advising-as-mentoring*** model, in which an Arrupe faculty member mentors 20 students for their two-year experience. Advising responsibilities shift at the two-year mark when students finish at Arrupe and join the School of Education, with the undergraduate advisor for the TLLSC program now meeting with students each semester to ensure they meet program requirements. But with Arrupe students starting TLLSC courses during the first year, faculty have realized the need to provide education-specific mentoring from the first day of the two-plus-two program. The School of Education (SOE) has created an *SOE-Arrupe Teacher Preparation Pipeline Liaison*, a faculty service role compensated by one course release per year, to support students in (a) understanding TLLSC structures, processes, and resources; (b) accessing university resources (e.g., wellness, writing center); (c) building professional relationships with faculty and advisors across units; and (d) fostering relationships with one another in the program. By engaging in one-on-one mentoring with students across their programs, this faculty member also provides integral data and information to TLLSC faculty and leadership, who then refine efforts to recruit and retain students.

Recruiting and funding biliterate students to become teachers

With curricular and mentoring structures in place, stakeholders can move forward with targeted recruitment of SSoBL recipients in Clinton and other area high schools. By using the original intent of the SSoBL to indicate proficiency "sufficient for meaningful use in college and a career" and for "identifying people with language and biliteracy skills" (Illinois School Code 105 ILCS 5/2-3.159, p. 1), the plan centers on providing biliterate high school graduates with attainable and financially reasonable options to use their language competencies, develop their expertise as educators, and return to area schools to nurture biliteracy with learners. Loyola faculty plan to begin recruitment at Clinton and other TLLSC partner high schools, holding informational sessions for SSoBL recipients to learn about the two-plus-two and four-year options to become bilingual teachers. The district has also recently released a request for proposals from IHEs to offer program pathways for high school graduates to become teachers in high-need areas, including bilingual education. Tapping into the already developed Arrupe-TLLSC bilingual teacher preparation program, Loyola faculty have crafted a proposal to hopefully tap into funding to jumpstart this pipeline in partnership with the larger school district. Stakeholders across sites remain committed to these efforts, recognizing the integral nature of funding to support students in participating in the pipeline.

Discussion and recommendations

As bilingual programs increase in K–12 schools across the United States, so does the detrimental shortage of bilingual teachers (Garcia, 2017; Schmitt & DeCourcy, 2022; Sutcher et al., 2016). This chapter details a partnership between school, district, and university stakeholders in the midwestern state of Illinois who have sought to respond to the growing need for bilingual teachers with a GYO pipeline centered on the SoBL (Beilstein & Withee, 2022; Davin & Heineke, 2017). Across the country, local stakeholders increasingly look to GYO programs to respond to the bilingual teacher shortage, though the literature suggests that these pipelines often center on adults working in schools (Amos, 2013; Cramer & Ryan, 2023; Garcia, 2017; Garcia et al., 2019) and living in communities (Esparza et al., 2019; Garcia & Garza, 2019; Gross, 2018). Adding to the sparse body of literature on GYO programs that target high school students (e.g., Coffey et al., 2019; Morales, 2018), this chapter puts forth a framework for a bilingual teacher preparation pipeline that utilizes the SoBL to recruit biliterate high school graduates into teacher education to ultimately return to their communities to teach in bilingual programs.

The significance of this framework centers on the integral role of the SoBL in recruiting potential bilingual teachers and integrating existing biliteracy competencies in teacher education programming. As evidenced throughout this volume, SoBL efforts continue to expand and garner attention in school, community, and university contexts across the United States. Now part of state legislation or educational code in all 50 states and DC, the SSoBLs serve as a clear indication to colleges and employers that individuals have developed high levels of proficiency in two or more languages spanning the domains of listening, speaking, reading, and writing (Davin et al., 2022). In a recent review of GYO policies and programs across all 50 states, Garcia (2020) asserts the highly localized nature of GYO programs with wide variability across state and local contexts. Given the national scope of the SSoBL movement, we see the SSoBL recognition serving as a common thread among bilingual teacher preparation pipelines targeting high school graduates. Tapping into the enthusiasm of the larger SoBL movement, stakeholders in universities, school districts, and states can use the SoBL as a key lever to recruit and prepare bilingual teachers. We detail recommendations for each stakeholder group next.

Recommendations for university stakeholders center on working collaboratively and flexibly to harness the momentum of the SoBL initiative. As evidenced in this chapter, a cross-unit collaboration facilitated the design of a bilingual teacher pipeline, whereas another unit's lack of cooperation limited stakeholders in embracing the full potential of the SoBL within university programming. We encourage faculty to engage in dialogue within and across units to consider how the SoBL can be leveraged, tapping into many of the ideas presented in this volume. In modern language departments, for example, faculty can use the SoBL for credit or placement in world language coursework, streamlining students' programs of study and avoiding unnecessary testing to place them in appropriate language coursework. In teacher education programs, faculty can use the SoBL to recruit high school graduates in partner schools, as well as consider how to recognize and integrate students' biliteracy competencies in the teacher education curriculum. Faculty in other colleges, schools, and departments might consider similarly using the SoBL to recruit bilingual nurses, social workers, counselors, and other professionals. If necessary, faculty might appeal to university administrators to bring together faculty across units with common goals to recruit students, increase enrollments, and enhance programs.

School and district leaders also make vital contributions to the design and implementation of GYO bilingual teacher pipelines centered on the SoBL. To jumpstart these important efforts and respond to bilingual teacher shortages, school and district leaders should seek out and utilize university partners to collaboratively develop GYO teacher preparation pipelines that merge and interface with local efforts to implement the SoBL. University partners, specifically those that provide SoBL recipients with tangible ways to utilize their biliteracy recognitions and competencies, can deepen SoBL implementation within schools and districts (Davin & Heineke, 2022). Tapping into the synergy around the SoBL, schools and districts can center their efforts on elevating and extending the SoBL initiative, which can subsequently bolster efforts to recruit SoBL recipients into GYO bilingual teacher pipelines. After the development and implementation of the pipeline, school and district leaders can commit to hiring employees from these SoBL teacher education pathways to facilitate local bilingual educators in returning to their communities and continuing to promote students' biliteracy development.

But GYO bilingual teacher pipelines centered on the SoBL do not need to remain localized (Garcia, 2020), which places onerous demands on school, district, and university educators with already full plates. As argued earlier, the large-scale scope of the SSoBL initiative prompts the potential for state administrators to support these pipelines with related policies, programs, and funding opportunities. According to Garcia (2020), Washington state has the only statewide program that recruits bilingual high school students into the teaching profession. Other states can follow suit, facilitating task forces to streamline bilingual pipelines and using the database of SoBL recipients to share pipeline opportunities across the state. State stakeholders can also revise existing legislation and educational codes to enhance the value of the SSoBL for professional pipelines. In all 50 states and DC, only Illinois, Minnesota, and Rhode Island require that public IHEs recognize the SSoBL for world language credit. Other states might deliberate adding this provision to their SSoBL policies, as well as contemplate using the SSoBL as an indicator of language proficiency for the certification of bilingual educators. When stakeholders across layers and contexts recognize and prioritize the SoBL, educators can enhance programs and limit barriers to developing a strong corps of bilingual teachers.

References

American Councils for International Education [ACIE]. (2017, June). *The national K-12 foreign language enrollment survey report.* https://www.americancouncils.org/sites/default/files/FLE-report-June17.pdf

American Councils Research Center. (2021). *2021 canvass of dual language and immersion (DLI) programs in US public schools.* https://www.americancouncils.org/sites/default/files/documents/pages/2021-10/Canvass%20DLI%20-%20October%202021-2_ac.pdf

Amos, Y.T. (2013). Becoming a teacher of color: Mexican bilingual paraprofessionals' journey to teach. *Teacher Education Quarterly, 40*(3), 51–73. https://www.jstor.org/stable/43684701

Beilstein, S.O., & Withee, T.P. (2022). *Chronic teacher shortages: Part 1—Content and geographic areas with high need.* Illinois Workforce and Education Research Collaborative, Discovery Partners Institute, University of Illinois and Goshen Education Consulting, Inc. https://iarss.org/wp-content/uploads/2022/04/ChonicTeacher.pdf

Classrooms Reflecting Communities Act of 2019, S. 2887, 116th Cong. (2019, November 18). https://www.govtrack.us/congress/bills/116/s2887/text

Coffey, H., Putman, S.M., Handler, L.K., & Leach, W. (2019). Growing them early: Recruiting and preparing future urban teachers through an early college collaboration between a college of education and an urban school district. *Teacher Education Quarterly, 46*(1), 35–54. https://www.jstor.org/stable/26558181

College Affordability Act, H.R. 4674, 116th Cong. (2019). https://edlabor.house.gov/imo/media/doc/REINTRO_xml.pdf

Commission on Language Learning. (2017). *America's languages: Investing in language education for the 21st century.* American Academy of Arts & Sciences. https://www.amacad.org/sites/default/files/publication/downloads/Commission-on-Language-Learning_Americas-Languages.pdf

Cramer, G.J., & Ryan, D. (2023). Responding to teacher shortages in bilingual education: A Grow-Your-Own bilingual teacher education program. *The New Educator, 19*(3), 182–196. https://doi.org/10.1080/1547688X.2023.2206454

Davin, K.J., & Heineke, A.J. (2017). The Seal of Biliteracy: Variations in policy and outcomes. *Foreign Language Annals, 50*(3), 486–499. https://doi.org/10.1111/flan.12279

Davin, K.J., & Heineke, A.J. (2022). *Promoting multilingualism in schools: A framework for implementing the Seal of Biliteracy.* ACTFL.

Davin, K.J., Heineke, A.J., & Hancock, C. (2022). The Seal of Biliteracy: A 10-year retrospective. *Foreign Language Annals, 55*(1), 10–34. https://doi.org/10.1111/flan.12596

de Jong, E., & Gao, J. (2023). Preparing teacher candidates for bilingual practices: Toward a multilingual stance in mainstream teacher education. *International Journal of Bilingual Education and Bilingualism, 26*(4), 472–482. https://doi.org/10.1080/13670050.2022.2119072

Esparza, E., Sarmiento, M., Geneser, V., & Harris, S. (2019). In support of home-grown teachers: An examination of factors that supported the success of pre-service teachers in a bilingual education program from 2012–2017. *Education Quarterly Reviews, 2*(4), 811–821. https://doi.org/10.31014/aior.1993.02.04.108

Gándara, P. (2014, October 3). *The value of bilingualism and the Seal of Biliteracy in the California labor market.* https://sealofbiliteracy.org/doc/the-value-of-bilingualism-and-the-seal-of-biliteracy.pdf

Garcia, A. (2017). *Building a bilingual teacher pipeline: Bilingual teacher fellows at Highline Public Schools.* New America. https://d1y8sb8igg2f8e.cloudfront.net/documents/FINAL_EnglishLearners_Washington.pdf

Garcia, A. (2020). *Grow your own teachers: A 50-state scan of policies and programs.* New America. https://newamerica.org/education-policy/reports/grow-your-own-teachers/

Garcia, A., & Garza, R. (2019). *Chicago's bilingual teacher residency: A partnership to strengthen the teacher pipeline.* New America. https://files.eric.ed.gov/fulltext/ED599744.pdf

Garcia, A., Manuel, A., & Buly, M.R. (2019). Washington state policy spotlight: A multifaceted approach to grow your own pathways. *Teacher Education Quarterly, 46*(1), 69–78. https://www.jstor.org/stable/26558183

Gist, C.D., Bianco, M., & Lynn, M. (2019). Examining Grow Your Own programs across the teacher development continuum: Mining research on teachers of color and nontraditional educator pipelines. *Journal of Teacher Education, 70*(1), 13–25. https://doi.org/10.1177/0022487118787504

Gross, J. (2018). *Can immigrant professionals help reduce teacher shortages in the U.S.?* World Education Services. http://files.eric.ed.gov/fulltext/ED592605.pdf

Hakuta, K., Butler, Y.G., & Witt, D. (2000). *How long does it take English learners to attain proficiency?* (Policy Report 2000-1). University of California Linguistic Minority Research Institute. https://files.eric.ed.gov/fulltext/ED443275.pdf

Heineke, A.J., & Giatsou, E. (2020). Learning from students, teachers, and schools: Field-based teacher education for emergent bilingual learners. *Journal of Teacher Education, 71*(1), 148–161. https://doi.org/10.1177/0022487119877373

Howard, E. R., Lindholm-Leary, K. J., Rogers, D., Olague, N., Medina, J., Kennedy, B., Sugarman, J., & Christian, D. (2018). *Guiding principles for dual language education.* (3rd ed.) Center for Applied Linguistics.

Institute of Education Sciences [IES]. (2022, August). *2022 School pulse panel (SPP).* Retrieved September 1, 2023, from https://ies.ed.gov/schoolsurvey/spp/

Kroll, J.F., & Dussias, P.E. (2017). The benefits of multilingualism to the personal and professional development of residents of the US. *Foreign Language Annals, 50*(2), 248–259. https://doi.org/10.1111/flan.12271

Krueger, T., Davies, A., Eckersley, B., Newell, F., & Cherednichenko, B. (2008). *Effective and sustainable university-school partnerships: Beyond determined efforts by inspired individuals.* Teaching Australia.

Looney, D., & Lusin, N. (2018, February). *Enrollments in languages other than English in United States institutions of higher education, summer 2016 and fall 2016: Preliminary report.* Modern Language Association of America. https://files.eric.ed.gov/fulltext/ED590075.pdf

Met, M., & Brandt, A.M. (2017). Foreign language learning in K-12 classrooms in the USA. In N. Van Deusen-Scholl & S. May (Eds.), *Second and foreign language education* (3rd ed., pp. 357–370). Springer International Publishing. https://doi.org/10.1007/978-3-319-02246-8_17

Morales, A.R. (2018). Within and beyond a grow-your-own-teacher program: Documenting the contextualized preparation and professional development experiences of critically conscious Latina teachers. *Teaching Education*, *29*(4), 357–369. https://doi.org/10.1080/10476210.2018.1510483

National Center for Education Statistics. (2023). *Characteristics of public school teachers.* Condition of Education. U.S. Department of Education, Institute of Education Sciences. https://nces.ed.gov/programs/coe/indicator/clr

Olsen, L. (2020). The history of the movement: Enacting the State Seal of Biliteracy in the state of California. In A.J. Heineke & K.J. Davin (Eds.), *The Seal of Biliteracy: Case studies and considerations for policy implementation* (pp. 17–34). Information Age.

Schmitt, J., & deCourcy, K. (2022). *The pandemic has exacerbated a long-standing national shortage of teachers.* Economic Policy Institute. https://eric.ed.gov/?id=ED626637

Seal of Biliteracy. (2024). *State law regarding the Seal of Biliteracy.* http://sealofbiliteracy.org

Sutcher, L., Darling-Hammond, L., & Carver-Thomas, D. (2016). *A coming crisis in teaching? Teacher supply, demand, and shortages in the U.S.* Learning Policy Institute. https://files.eric.ed.gov/fulltext/ED606666.pdf

Zhang, H., Wu, Y.J., & Thierry, G. (2020). Bilingualism and aging: A focused neuroscientific review. *Journal of Neurolinguistics*, *54*, 100890. https://doi.org/10.1016/j.jneuroling.2020.100890

PART V

Conclusions and Future Directions

11

TENDING THE GARDEN AND GROWING THE TREES OF BILINGUALISM

Opportunities, challenges, and needs in higher education

Andrew Fiegen, Kendall King, and Ayumi Stockman

Introduction

State seals of biliteracy (SSoBL) have existed in the U.S. for approximately 13 years. The seeds for these programs were planted in California alongside the anti-bilingual education Proposition 227 (passed in 1998, repealed in 2016). Seals were developed in that state as a response to this restrictive English-only legislation; advocates sought to provide support for multilingualism, and in particular, for heritage language learners and emergent multilinguals who had few opportunities or institutional incentives to maintain or develop their language skills. Over the last decade, with the support of organizations such as Californians Together and Velázquez Press, the seeds have spread, and seal legislation has dramatically accelerated across the United States (California Department of Education, 2023). With South Dakota as the final addition in January 2024, all states have now adopted a SoBL law (OELA, 2023).

To continue with the botanic metaphor, these seeds and seedlings have grown remarkably and variably over the last decade. While some states are home to saplings still extending their roots and branches in uneven or unfertilized soil, other states have cultivated new solid young trees, bearing many fruit and flowers. At the national level, U.S. Secretary of Education Miguel Cardona has provided further support for these growing seal programs through the so-called Raise the Bar initiative, which has a stated goal to "provide every student with a pathway to multilingualism" and to promote the notion that "Being Bilingual is a Superpower" (Najarro, 2023). The Office of English Language Acquisition (OELA) has identified the SoBL as one of the "key levers" for reaching this aim (OELA, November 6, 2023). National legislation has also been proposed to provide financial support for states and districts through the Biliteracy Education Seal and Teaching (BEST) Act (H.R. 1731, S.680), introduced in the House and referred to the House Committee on Education and Labor in 2021. This is a dramatic shift in U.S. educational policy and represents an unprecedented turn toward multilingualism and support for language learning in the educational practice and legal landscape. Or does it?

Alongside this maturation has been a growing and rapidly expanding field of research that has begun to address this question and to evaluate the implementation and impact of these

DOI: 10.4324/9781032667249-16

programs. For instance, although widely championed as an important step toward reframing multilingualism as an individual and societal asset, scholars and policy leaders also have pointed to glaring gaps in equity and access to these state seals (e.g., Schwedhelm & King, 2020; Subtirelu et al., 2019). This is in part because while state legislatures and education authorities establish the framework for the seals and provide broad implementation guidance, the technical, financial, and administrative burden of promoting, assessing, and tracking the seals falls to local districts. With approximately 13,800 school districts in the United States, there is wide variation in capacity to offer seals (Budke & Schmitt, 2023, Davin & Heineke, 2017). At present, only a minority of U.S. students live in districts that provide access. As an example, only 20% or fewer of schools offer the seal in Arizona, Arkansas, Connecticut, Illinois, Kansas, Louisiana, Michigan, New York, and other states (Black et al., 2020).

Another line of research has pointed to the neoliberal roots of seal legislation, arguing that these programs are framed within a neoliberal "transformation of subjectivities" (Shin & Park, 2016, p. 444) wherein individuals are encouraged to take personal responsibility for their own lives and successes, to engage in ongoing self-development, and to cultivate one's image and identity through self-branding and self-promotion. For instance, Chang-Bacon and Colomer (2022) argue that bilingual seals, like all seals, "have been used to establish and authenticate the ownership of property" (p. 6) and that through this legislation, "biliteracy can be rendered as property through laws, policies and ideologies" (p. 7). Chang-Bacon and Colomer's (2022) legal analysis finds three ways in which SSoBL laws advance biliteracy as a profit:

> (1) biliteracy is ascribed an economic value, particularly in relation to the state economy and national security; (2) biliteracy is constructed as an objectified commodity that can be attained or procured (primarily geared toward a monolingual audience); and (3) biliteracy as property is legally bound to assessment.
>
> *(p. 14)*

Pshigusa (2024) similarly documents how "globalized human capital" discourses are pervasive in Ohio's SoBL policy and promotional materials, as well as in stakeholder interviews. These texts tend to emphasize the economic marketability benefits of the SSoBLs while placing little emphasis on heritage language maintenance as intended in California's policy.

Concomitantly, a growing body of research has examined the impact of seals on students. For instance, Davin et al. (2024) analyzed the postgraduation benefits of earning a SoBL. In their interviews with 33 Minnesota SoBL earners, participants reported that the seal was linked to increased employment in the areas of education and sales; greater pride, especially among linguistically minoritized students; and improved confidence and interest in pursuing postsecondary education. The authors also noted that despite the fact that college credit is often touted as a potential benefit of the seal, few participants (only 6% in this sample) reported receiving credit for the seal, even when they enrolled in a four-year college or university. This was due to what were perceived as confusing and unclear policies and processes for requesting this credit.

An additional strand in the literature has taken up SoBL implementation. For instance, Heineke and Davin (2021) examined SoBL implementation in six high-awarding districts, finding that these districts tended to prioritize students' home and heritage languages, maintain flexible practices around assessment and funding for assessments, and involve many stakeholders both inside and outside of schools. Other studies have documented efforts at local schools or districts to implement the SoBL in a range of settings (e.g., Salavart and Szalkiewicz (2020) in New York City; Castro (2020) in an urban high school in Los Angeles, Fisk (2020) in a large suburban high school in Illinois).

While this important work has provided insights into implementation processes and on-the-ground efforts, little research to date, however, has closely examined how seals are taken up and implemented within institutions of higher education (IHE). Notable exceptions are Monto's (2022) description of an Oregon community college, which created an opportunity for students to study and receive the seal in higher education, and Eckerson and Jacobs's (2024) survey of Nebraska SoBL recipients. Eckerson and Jacobs (2024) found that SoBL recipients pursued postsecondary language study at eight times the national average rate. This Nebraska study also suggested that postsecondary language departments could use the SoBL to recruit students and point to the critical role of academic credit policies.

More research here is critical given that one of the main benefits frequently championed by SoBL advocates is increased higher education enrollment, sometimes facilitated by credit awards. Yet many questions around process, policy, and access remain unclear or unanswered in light of the limited work on how these mostly high school-level programs interface with IHEs. For instance, how can IHEs leverage seals to increase enrollment in language classes and language major matriculation? What are the impediments to closer collaboration across K–12 and IHEs? What negative or unexpected outcomes might result from awarding college credit to seal holders? To what extent (and how) might the seal recognition and uptake promote the so-called three Bs (bilingualism, biculturalism, and biliteracy) more broadly? To what extent does higher education acceptance of the seal decrease or exacerbate existing inequalities with respect to equity and access across groups? This volume begins to address some of these questions and to fill this significant research gap.

This volume takes up this challenge from an impressive breadth of perspectives and research approaches. This methodological diversity is fitting in light of the wide variation in SSoBL programs across the United States. As noted in Chapter 1, SoBL programs vary with respect to the types of recognitions offered, required language proficiency levels, funding mechanisms, English language proficiency requirements, and college credit eligibility, among many other dimensions. In parallel fashion, the present collection takes up these questions around higher education using a range of research methodologies, including, but not limited to, case studies, surveys, semi-structured interviews, and longitudinal analysis of policy over time. Many of the chapters describe innovative local partnerships between K–12 districts, on the one hand, and IHEs, on the other. These IHEs include teacher education programs, Hispanic serving institutions (HSIs), two-year colleges, and traditional four-year programs.

These chapters describe a wide range of innovations, including efforts to establish pathway programs and work to build collaborations across and within institutions (Chapter 3 by Michele Anciaux Aoki, Russell Hugo, and Bridget Yaden, Chapter 4 by Cecelia Monto), to develop a university-based seal (Chapter 5 by Cristina Alfaro and Reka Barton), to grow dual-language education at the tertiary level (Chapter 6 by Katherine Christoffersen and Dania López García), to attract language majors through initial rewards for freshman students and attractive bonuses for seniors (Chapter 7 by Grant D. Moss and James A. Gambrell), to offer credit via examination (Chapter 8 by Jesse Gleason, Sobeira Latorre, and Resha Cardone), to incentivize enrollment in world language classes via a pilot project (Chapter 9 by Janet Eckerson and Christopher Jacobs), and to build a pipeline for language teacher education

(Chapter 10 by Amy J. Heineke, Sarah L. Cohen, Eric Steinmiller, and Ji Won Lee). In addition, Chapter 2 (Nick Gossett) provides an overview of the Global Seal of Biliteracy with some reference to how that (commercially, not state-funded) award can function in higher education and adult education programs.

Taken together, these chapters suggest several themes and trends that merit consideration at this important developmental juncture. Collectively, these chapters point to opportunities for mutual enhancement of both SoBL programs and higher education, including potential increases in world language enrollments, addressing long-standing equity issues, fostering collaboration across IHEs, and positive changes in college-level language instruction, as well as addressing long-standing teacher education shortages. Concomitantly, and also highlighted in the following discussion, these opportunities are not without institutional risks, including some unintended consequences and evolving needs. We consider each of these themes in turn in the following sections.

Opportunity: Stem declining world language enrollments in IHEs

Colleges and universities across the nation are facing significant budget shortfalls; these are often coupled with declining enrollments in world language enrollments. In response, some IHEs have responded by dropping long-standing world language requirements, reducing the modern language department, or eliminating entire programs (e.g., Anderson, 2023). In a climate in which IHEs are scrambling to attract students and maintain existing programs, the SoBL provides an avenue of potential growth and opportunity. Many of the chapters here described efforts to use the seal as leverage to build, maintain, or reinvigorate world language programs in varied IHEs across the United States.

For instance, in Chapter 4, Cecelia Monto provided an example of a community college in Oregon that enrolls many Latinex or Hispanic students and showcased an example of harnessing the SSoBL. This college saw the SoBL as an opportunity to expand into higher education. Many of their students did not have access to the recognition while in high school because they were often not enrolled in Advanced Placement (AP) or International Baccalaureate Diploma Program (IBDP) courses where the SoBL was available. They successfully advocated for changes in the rule that made the SSoBL available for college students. As a part of this effort to implement the SSoBL, revision of the curriculum to align with the ACTFL proficiency guidelines and cultural relevance to the students was central. Campus leaders developed a newly titled course, *Spanish for Heritage Speakers*, to affirm students' identity by offering content that was culturally and linguistically relevant as well as aligned with proficiency-oriented teaching. The effort led to reported gains in students' pride in their heritage languages, culture, and identity as well as to boosts in enrollment. This is notable as these same courses were previously often canceled due to low enrollment.

Chapter 7 by Grant D. Moss and James A. Gambrell on a retro-credit program provided another example of increasing enrollment in a Midwestern university. The authors described how this institution started offering retroactive credit for students who came with the SoBL as part of an effort to encourage students to choose to major or minor in modern language study. Students who had earned the seal were placed into the fifth-semester-level course, and after successful completion of the course, they were granted the credit retroactively. Moss and Gambrell reported that this effort increased enrollment in the upper-level courses. While there was concern that this effort would result in lower enrollments and loss of overall credits, utilizing the students' demonstrated language skills through the SoBL, the opposite effect was observed.

Taking up similar themes, Chapter 9 by Janet Eckerson and Christopher Jacobs reported how the University of Nebraska at Kearney developed an innovative approach to recruitment. The authors described how the Modern Languages Department reached out to high school students, offering to have the testing done at the campus for the SoBL, as well as give presentations about their programs and provide a tour of campus. The chapter reported that somewhat positive results were observed. These included a relative increase in the number of students who tested for the SoBL at the campus with language courses and the overwhelmingly positive responses from participating teachers and students.

Opportunity: Expand SoBL equity and access

SoBL programming has the potential to bring equity and access for linguistically marginalized students to the forefront. Many chapters in this volume describe efforts that specifically target documented gaps in equity and access. For instance, Chapter 3 by Michele Anciaux Aoki, Russell Hugo, and Bridget Yaden illustrated how inequities can be perpetuated by existing structures and systems, such as a registrar's rudimentary intake process, to note whether a student received a SoBL. As this chapter described, efforts to revisit the policies, structures, and systems can lead to the reduction of inequities. These findings suggest the importance of these administrative processes and underline the how and why attention to these details must be an intentional and equity-oriented process.

The college in Oregon described by Cecelia Monto in Chapter 4 utilized the SoBL in their Spanish for Native Speakers Course series (later changed to Spanish for Heritage Speakers) in the Languages Department. The goal was that at the end of the course sequence, students would take the proficiency assessment for the SoBL. This effort aligned with their existing teacher education program focused on increasing the bilingual teacher workforce in the area. By doing so, they were able to provide opportunities for students who did not have access to the SoBL while in high school and thus to "interrupt the cycle of advantage for privileged students" (p. 51). In the state, the SoBL was often awarded through AP or the IBDP exams, and linguistically marginalized students, such as English Learners, were less likely to enroll in these tracks.

A similar point was made in Chapter 8 by Jesse Gleason, Sobeira Latorre, and Resha Cardone, which described how a regional public university partnered with a local public school district to award college credit based on the documented language proficiency that specifically targets the students who earned the SoBL. One of the motivators for this shift was the inequities in opportunity across students from different backgrounds. In particular, students who came with AP or IBDP scores were routinely granted college credit; students who did not have access to these programs while in high school were locked out of the same credit and placement advantage. By examining the characteristics of SoBL earners at their IHE, this effort helped provide similar opportunities for marginalized students and those attending less well-resourced schools. Chapter 9, by Janet Eckerson and Christopher Jacobs, described similar efforts. Their contribution illustrated how, by offering testing opportunities at a college campus, students whose high schools did not offer the testing for the SoBL other than through AP or IBDP exams could access the awards.

Other contributions in this volume address the aims of boosting students' linguistic and cultural identity through developing an IHE-specific recognition, such as the University Seal of Biliteracy and Cultural Competence (USBCC), which helps emphasize extended engagement with language learning well into students' experience at the postsecondary level. This was developed and implemented in a southwestern university on the border with Mexico, where many Hispanic students are served. This description by Cristina Alfaro and Reka Barton in Chapter 5, with the use of *testimonios*, offers a detailed and important account because a program like this provides space for the linguistic and cultural assets to be visible and recognized institutionally, with potentially powerful impacts downstream.

Similar themes were highlighted in Chapter 6 by Katherine Christoffersen and Dania López García. In this case, the authors described how the University of Texas Rio Grande Valley offered courses in Spanish across diverse disciplines. However, the fact that students were bilingual was not formally recognized at this IHE. To address this, they created an IHE-based program called B3 (Bilingual, Biliterate, Bicultural) Scholar Seal to recognize these students. In English-dominant contexts such as the United States, efforts like this shed a positive light on bilingualism and biliteracy and also demonstrate the institutional commitments and possibilities of valuing bilingualism and biliteracy.

Innovative efforts such as those described here also underline the need and value of ongoing language learning. It is often assumed that if one speaks a language or grew up hearing it, no further study is needed. Of course, language learning (and use) is a lifelong endeavor. And heritage language learners often do not have access to instructional support to further develop literacy skills. Incorporating the SoBL at their own IHE helps both students and instructors to become aware of the need to further develop language skills, particularly literacy. One must have both oral and literacy skills to function in a professional setting, so building on the heritage language learners' linguistic skills and helping develop refined literacy is an important step in closing the opportunity gap that is often found across traditional world language students and heritage language learners.

Opportunity: Positive changes in college-level language instruction and collaboration across IHEs

As outlined earlier and detailed in many of the chapters in this edited volume, there can be powerful positive outcomes when IHEs embrace the SoBL (or the Global Seal of Biliteracy, as Chapter 2 detailed). These IHE innovations and collaborations can promote enrollment and student engagement. An additional, less commonly noted, positive impact is the change in college-level language instruction. As Michele Anciaux Aoki, Russell Hugo, and Bridget Yaden in Chapter 3 noted, most college-level language instruction programs "still have a long way to go to become truly proficiency-based" (p. 37). Since all SoBL programs are aligned with ACTFL proficiency guidelines, and these guidelines focus on what a learner *can do* with language in real life (as opposed to knowledge *about* language), this alignment promotes proficiency-based instruction and might facilitate shifts toward it.

Students benefit from this greater alignment because they gain real-life language skills of course, but what is also notable is that these shifts can help align the instructional approaches between K–12 and colleges. This has the potential to result in a more cohesive approach to language education among all the institutions across K–16. This potential was detailed in Chapter 4 by Cecelia Monto, which focused on the SoBL at Chemeketa Community College. There, Monto notes that the SoBL "has the potential to strengthen the credential's value through improved alignment and articulation between higher education and high school" (p. 51). Likewise, Grant D. Moss and James A. Gambrell, in Chapter 7, described a college that started using the SoBL for the retroactive credit and noted that the focus on proficiency shifted the mindset for the course work being from "seat time" to a "curricular focus on Spanish proficiency" (p. 97).

These chapters also suggest another way in which proficiency-oriented instruction brought about an exciting perspective for college-level language instruction: IHEs could offer courses that are directly tied to career opportunities that use both language skills and area expertise. This example was discussed in Chapter 8 by Jesse Gleason, Sobeira Latorre, and Resha Cardone. There, the authors described how a regional public university created a degree program (BS in science, replacing the BA in Spanish) to prepare students to utilize Spanish language skills in careers such as teacher certification, translation studies, and health and human service professions. This exemplifies one of the goals of language education by making the connection between learning a language and its concrete application evident and accessible to language learners.

Opportunity: Address language teacher education shortages

A final opportunity noted here is that the SSoBL or the Global Seal within IHEs can contribute positively to resolving the serious shortage of multilingual teachers nationwide. We must tap into all of our existing human capital as we try to solve this pressing gap and fully meet the learning needs of K–12 students (Méndez & Vonderlack-Navarro, 2024; "California bill", 2023).

Several chapters in this volume take up this challenge. In Chapter 4, Cecelia Monto described efforts focused on increasing the bilingual teacher workforce and integrating the SSoBL into their teacher preparation program. Chapter 5 by Cristina Alfaro and Reka Barton detailed the USBCC utilized in the Department of Dual Language in Education, where bilingual teachers were trained. Often, these teachers go into practice without being given much opportunity to reflect on their culture and the complicated relationship between culture, language, and identity—a chance to develop cultural awareness and humility. These teachers are better prepared to work with linguistically diverse students as a result of experiencing the coursework that addresses their own complicated identity formation influenced by cultures and languages.

Chapter 10, by Amy J. Heineke, Sarah L. Cohen, Eric Steinmiller, and Ji Won Lee, described an impressive and ambitious approach to addressing bilingual teacher shortages in their local community. This effort brought three entities together—namely, a private institution, Loyola University Chicago; a local high school; and Arrupe, a two-year college. This partnership was prompted by a discussion to prepare a bilingual teacher workforce for the local high school to teach in the dual-language program. Although the effort did not address the original goal of preparing bilingual teachers to teach secondary-level content, it did illustrate what might still be possible to address bilingual teacher shortages. The idea was to recruit high school students who were heritage speakers of Spanish to be trained as bilingual teachers. Through this collaboration, they were also able to solve issues of financial burden on the students who typically did not have the financial resources to complete an entire program. With persistence and creative ideas, this example showcases an excellent program that tapped into the existing program and students' assets.

Risk: Administrative complications

Thus far, we have largely highlighted the opportunities afforded to IHE students and programs with the implementation of the SoBL. However, in line with other studies that have documented myriad challenges in implementation (e.g., Schwedhelm & King, 2020; Black et al., 2020), the chapters in this volume also speak to some risks and unintended consequences regarding the SoBL. For example, in Chapter 4, Cecelia Monto described one Oregon college's efforts to expand access to the SoBL and reported a concurrent challenge faced by its students: a general confusion with respect to the types of seals one could earn (i.e., SSoBL, Global Seal, private postsecondary certificate) and differing criteria of each of these across the 50 U.S. states. While each entity is of course responsible for their respective handling of SoBL programming, the number of options and inconsistencies across SoBL programs can undermine the value of the award—as well as generate confusion about the process for obtaining a seal—as depicted by Monto. Indeed, as described in Chapter 4, even in the "Spanish for Heritage Speakers" sequence of study, 42% of the enrolled students did not sit the exam. Monto points to this statistic as an illustration of a testing barrier, stating that the obstacle "seemed to originate from the assessment process or structure rather than mastery of language skills" (p. 51). Many of the structures critiqued in this chapter (e.g., the medium of delivery, lack of personal connections to the students, and high-stress environments) have broader applications to other contexts.

Risk: Lower enrollment in introductory-level courses

SoBL programs have been documented as successful in promoting advanced language skills and rewarding high school students for their multilingual abilities, including postgraduation opportunities (Davin et al., 2024). At the same time, language course enrollment challenges exist for some postsecondary institutions—particularly for the introductory-level courses where the potential student base might have tested out or been awarded credit with the SoBL. These concerns surfaced in Chapter 3, in which Michele Anciaux Aoki, Russell Hugo, and Bridget Yaden described various administrative concerns based on the survey respondents. These same concerns regarding decreased enrollment in language department course offerings are pointed to in Chapter 8. Jesse Gleason, Sobeira Latorre, and Resha Cardone provide insight into the process of handling these challenges between an urban university and a public school district's collaboration of awarding the SoBL.

Some of these same concerns were evident in Chapter 7 by Grant D. Moss and James A. Gambrell. This chapter discussed the issue that language programs at Pittsburg State University often conclude with the fifth-semester course, providing no further pathways for students who have earned higher-level awards like the Gold SSoBL. This limitation has the potential to discourage students from pursuing more advanced studies in the language, thus reducing the overall enrollment in upper-level language courses. The chapter also pointed out that retroactive credit for general education courses, rather than specific language courses, is currently only available for French and Spanish. This restriction further complicates efforts to attract students to other language programs and may inadvertently decrease enrollment in these less commonly taught languages (LCTLs). Furthermore, in their context, many heritage speakers stop at earning a minor or a certificate and do not pursue a major, possibly because the course content does not adequately reflect their life experience(s) and needs.

Need: Developing deep, long-term, and meaningful partnerships across K–12 and IHEs

Together, these chapters point to future needs. To fully address the challenges and take up these opportunities, this volume calls for even greater innovation, collaboration, and partnerships. An example of this is Chapter 4, by Cecelia Monto. This chapter highlighted the efforts of Chemeketa Community College in coordinating with the state department of education to develop a more robust infrastructure for academic and recordkeeping procedures. The college faculty aligned coursework with linguistic and cultural relevance and integrated testing components, which extended to disseminating information among peer IHEs. Noteworthy challenges, though, were the need for close attention to guidelines of the Family Educational Rights and Protection Act (FERPA), particularly regarding what information could be shared with external partners.

The internally coordinated efforts by the University of Texas Rio Grande Valley (UTRGV), as described in Chapter 6 by Katherine Christoffersen and Dania López García, ensured students could achieve the Bilingualism, Biculturalism, and Biliteracy (B3) Scholar Seal. The number of departments engaged in these efforts was noteworthy: University Marketing and Undergraduate Recruitment, the Office of Enrollment Systems and Analysis, Financial Aid, the Office of Strategic Analysis and Reporting (SAIR), the Office of Engaged Scholarship and Learning, and the Office of Global Affairs. This cross-departmental effort underscores the effective handling of the logistical complexity required for supporting students with programming that extends the aims of the SoBL into a local context.

Jesse Gleason, Sobeira Latorre, and Resha Cardone's Chapter 8 pointed to the potential of the SoBL for reifying existing inequalities on the basis of language (Davin & Heineke, 2022). Their chapter highlighted an effort to build a collaborative, equity-driven structure between an urban university and public school district by supporting SoBL recipients—many of whom are first-generation college students—by streamlining the number of credits awarded to students. Both this chapter and Chapter 9 shed light on an opportunity for additional SoBL administrative flexibility and creativity. The University of Nebraska at Kearney's (UNK) pilot initiative, as characterized by Janet Eckerson and Christopher Jacobs, provided considerations that may be useful for other similarly sized institutions seeking to boost enrollment and/or motivate language study. Their findings underscored that improving access to the SoBL for students (e.g., rural students and heritage language speakers) may require nimble administrative efforts. The authors highlighted examples of campus-sponsored language proficiency assessments and department program presentations as part of students' campus tours, as well as the opportunities for retroactive credit attainment. Universities across the nation may benefit from coordinated efforts such as UNK's creative use of student campus visits or UTRGV's internally coordinated efforts of supporting students and offering culturally relevant curricular offerings.

Relatedly, various administrative challenges were described throughout the volume. The case study of two institutions' development of their SoBL programs in Chapter 3 by Michele Anciaux Aoki, Russell Hugo, and Bridget Yaden highlighted this dilemma in the state of Washington. The implementation of the seals program at the University of Washington benefited from a centralized administrative process and various measures to promote the program to eligible students. Likewise, Pacific Lutheran University, a small, private institution, saw success in its faculty-led pilot project of recognizing the multilingualism of the institution's student body. Concurrently, though, the authors' findings from a survey distributed to the Pacific Northwest Council for Languages (PNCFL) region—including the states of Alaska, Idaho, Montana, Oregon, Washington, and Wyoming—shed light on challenges faced elsewhere, ranging from awareness of seals programs, access to testing, and funding. Both Chapter 3 as well as Chapter 4 served as examples of the dependency on grant-funded efforts of many SoBL initiatives.

Need: Ongoing education around the SoBL's value

The individual chapters throughout this volume provide examples of how the SoBL holds value for measures of credentialing while also providing students with credit-bearing opportunities. Yet, in certain instances, the perceived value of the SoBL remains unclear for various stakeholders. Survey respondents highlighted in Michele Anciaux Aoki, Russell Hugo, and Bridget Yaden's Chapter 3 indicated such concerns, noting that the SoBL signals minimal qualifications in addition to language skills that potential employers could not otherwise learn about regarding applicants. Additional concerns reported from the survey include the applicability of the SoBL outside the state in which a student earns the award, as well as its transferability and value at the collegiate level.

These concerns are—at least in part— addressed throughout other chapters of the volume. One example of this includes Nick Gossett's (Chapter 2) discussion of the Global Seal of Biliteracy, a recognition meant to address recipients' hard and soft skills, both of which an employer may be looking for in a future candidate. The use of the Global Seal of Biliteracy as a mechanism for credentialing students may carry a broader value that proves students' bilingual proficiency, making them more competitive in the job market. Another example is found in Chapter 6, where authors Katherine Christoffersen and Dania López García described the B3 Scholar Seal at the UTRGV. Whereas many of the courses were taught bilingually or entirely in Spanish, the transcripts did not reflect the medium of instruction. However, the B3 Scholar Seal provided students with the unique opportunity to make their linguistic repertoires visible through the credentialing associated with the B3 Scholar Seal—a credential that carries with them at the postsecondary level and one that requires skills and competencies beyond language proficiency as a standalone feature. Likewise, as Cecelia Monto indicated in Chapter 4, the SoBL provides the opportunity for value to be conceptualized outside of just language skills but in the affirmation of students' cultural and linguistic identities supported by relevant coursework in the Chemeketa College's Spanish for Heritage Speaker course. Apparent in many of these chapters is both the local value of the seal and the need for greater education and advocacy around what the SoBL means to employers, community members, and IHEs.

Conclusion

The editors of this volume set out to fill an important gap in the research literature: to document how IHEs implement seal programs to recognize students' multilingualism, boost enrollment in language departments, and grow biliteracy in their communities. The ten chapters amply and successfully take up this challenge by providing rich empirical descriptions of how IHEs can leverage states' SoBL policies by awarding college credit to recipients and advancing toward the broader goal of increasing equity and access to higher education for multilingual students. Simultaneously, the volume depicts innovative ways in which IHE stakeholders tap into students' cultural and linguistic strengths and use SSoBLs as a recruitment tool to enhance enrollment in colleges, universities, and teacher preparation programs.

The innovative, resourceful, and creative work documented in detail here provides powerful scaffolds and supports to still growing SoBL trees across the country. These chapters also underline the need for and potential benefit of greater coordination and support for both K–12 and IHEs. As noted at the outset of this chapter, SoBLs, since their beginnings, have varied widely and largely functioned as DIY (do-it-yourself) programs at the local level. This volume highlights the fact that the scaffolding that is being provided is also highly varied and done so in a home-grown, DIY manner. While these chapters demonstrate that these efforts are creative and, in many cases, effective, they also speak to the need for and value of federal-level support in the form of training, funding, and coordination.

The thoughtful, on-the-ground empirical descriptions offered here provide some solid directions in what might be needed at the federal level to help all of these different trees flourish to their full potential. For instance, more K–12-IHE collaborations would be possible with a federal funding award competition that promotes K–12-IHE collaboration, the establishment of a clearinghouse or national research center that supports such collaborations, and the establishment of an annual conference (or strand/special session at ACTFL) that brings together collaborators to showcase efforts and provide training and assistance.

At the same time, these chapters also point to the highly localized, site-specific nature of these collaborations. In all cases, institutional leaders and stakeholders were deeply knowledgeable of their local context, highly flexible to immediate and often changing needs and conditions, and fully committed to deep engagement and communication with partners. This is time-intensive and often invisibilized work. We are hopeful that federal programming might support and spotlight this work in the decades ahead but also recognize that there is not a one-size-fits-all sort of support.

We close this chapter with thanks to these authors and editors for sharing their experiences and wisdom with us and with the broader SoBL community. We admire the impressive, creative, and collaborative work that they do every day, tending the garden, watering, and supporting the SoBL trees in myriad ways and within climates that can often be hostile to multilingualism. We take this as inspiration for our work and are confident that other readers will as well.

References

Anderson, N. (2023, August 18). WVU's plan to cut foreign languages, other programs draws disbelief. *The Washington Post*. https://www.washingtonpost.com/education/2023/08/18/west-virginia-university-academic-cuts/

Black, C.R., Chou, A., & Hancock, C.R. (2020). *The 2018–19 National Seal of Biliteracy report*. www.SealofBiliteracy.org

Budke, M., & Schmitt, K.C. (2023). *Bilingual seals data dashboard: A critical lens on equity*. MCTCL Annual Conference. https://tinyurl.com/MCTLC2023

California bill to battle bilingual teacher shortage. (2023, November 11). *Language Magazine*. https://www.languagemagazine.com/2023/11/11/california-bill-to-battle-bilingual-teacher-shortage/

California Department of Education (2023). *State seal of biliteracy*. https://www.cde.ca.gov/sp/el/er/sealofbiliteracy.asp

Castro, A. (2020). Validating the linguistic strengths of English learners: Los Angeles Unified School District's implementation of the seal of biliteracy. In Heineke, A.J., & Davin, K.J. (Eds.), *The Seal of Biliteracy: Case studies and considerations for policy implementation* (pp. 123–140). Information Age.

Chang-Bacon, C.K., & Colomer, S.E. (2022). Biliteracy as property: Promises and perils of the seal of biliteracy. *Journal of Literacy Research*, *54*(2), 182–207. https://doi.org/10.1177/1086296X221096676

Davin, K.J., Cruz, K.R., & Hancock, C.R. (2024). An examination of the postgraduation benefits of earning a seal of biliteracy. *Foreign Language Annals 57*, 634–653. https://doi.org/10.1111/flan.12753

Davin, K.J., & Heineke, A.J. (2017). The Seal of Biliteracy: Variations in policy and outcomes. *Foreign Language Annals*, *50*(3), 486–499.

Davin, K.J., & Heineke, A.J. (2022). *Promoting multilingualism in schools: A framework for implementing the Seal of Biliteracy*. ACTFL Press.

Eckerson, J., & Jacobs, C. (2024). The Seal of Biliteracy as a recruitment tool in postsecondary language study. *Foreign Language Annals 57*, 654–674. https://doi.org/10.1111/flan.12769

Fisk, J.K. (2020). School-level implementation of the Seal of Biliteracy: One linguistically diverse suburban Illinois high school's journey. In Heineke, A.J., & Davin, K.J. (Eds.), *The Seal of Biliteracy: Case studies and considerations for policy implementation* (pp. 139–155). Information Age.

Heineke, A.J., & Davin, K.J. (2021). Implementing the Seal of Biliteracy: A multiple case study of six high-awarding districts. *The Modern Language Journal*, *105*(2), 395–411. https://doi.org/10.1111/modl.12708

Méndez, E., & Vonderlack-Navarro, R. (2024, April 2). How Illinois school districts can train more bilingual educators. *Chicago Sun Times*. https://chicago.suntimes.com/other-views/2024/04/01/illinois-school-districts-bilingual-teachers-shortage-english-learners-latino-policy-forum

Monto, C. (2022). Bringing the state seal of biliteracy to higher education: A case for expansion. *Foreign Language Annals*, *55*(1), 35–53.

Najarro, I. (2023, November 17). Here's why Miguel Cardona is pushing multilingual education. *Education Week*. https://www.edweek.org/teaching-learning/heres-why-miguel-cardona-is-pushing-multilingual-education/2023/11

OELA. (2023, November). *State Seal of Biliteracy. Office of English Language Acquisition*. U.S. Department of Education.

Pshigusa, E. (2024). Equity/heritage and globalized human capital discourses in Ohio's Seal of Biliteracy policy, promotional materials, and stakeholder perceptions. *Foreign Language Annals*, *57*, 593–611. https://doi.org/10.1111/flan.12771

Schwedhelm, M., & King, K.A. (2020). The neoliberal logic of state seals of biliteracy. *Foreign Language Annals*, *53*(1), 12–27. https://doi.org/10.1111/flan.12438

Salavart, R., & Szalkiewiczm, D. (2020). The seal of biliteracy, graduates with global competence, is on the rise. *NECTFL Review*, *85*(1), 29–49.

Shin, H., & Park, J.S.Y. (2016). Researching language and neoliberalism. *Journal of Multilingual and Multicultural Development*, *37*(5), 443–452. https://doi.org/10.1080/01434632.2015.1071823

Subtirelu, N.C., Borowczyk, M., Hernández, R.T., & Venezia, F. (2019). Recognizing whose bilingualism? A critical policy analysis of the Seal of Biliteracy. *The Modern Language Journal*, *103*(2), 371–390. https://doi.org/10.1111/modl.12556

INDEX

Made in the USA
Columbia, SC
12 February 2025

ef1735b2-0fa4-4900-a655-d24a30a8599cR01